TIBETAN CARAVANS

Journeys from Leh to Lhasa

Abdul Wahid Radhu

Foreword by
His Holiness The Dalai Lama

SPEAKING
TIGER

SPEAKING TIGER PUBLISHING PVT. LTD
4381/4, Ansari Road, Daryaganj,
New Delhi–110002, India

Published in India by Speaking Tiger in Paperback 2017

ISBN: 978-81-93314-19-7
eISBN: 978-93-86338-39-6

10 9 8 7 6 5 4 3 2 1

Typeset in Adobe Caslon Pro by Jojy Philip
Printed at Shree Maitrey Printech Pvt. Ltd., Noida

TIBETAN CARAVANS

Contents

LIFE IN THE BORDERLANDS

Text and Context of a Human Geography

It was the late autumn of 1942. A small caravan had just herded its pack animals into the *caravanserai* in Gilgit. It was too small to be a trade convoy and too large to be individual voyagers. The band comprised four members of the trans-Himalayan 'Khwaja'-Radhu[1] business family of Leh. They had come from Yarkand, where the clan had extended its trade links in the first decades of the nineteenth century. They were led by Abdul Hamid and included his wife Aisha, their nephew Mukarram, the latter's wife Noora Khan and two or three attendants. The plan was to winter in Gilgit before continuing to Leh via Skardu in Baltistan.

The group had travelled swiftly, without the weight of trade goods, as would have been normal. They were headed to Leh amid growing rumours that the Chinese authorities were instructing the non-Turkic people to vacate Chinese Central Asia as the civil war between the Nationalist and Communist factions intensified.

---

[1] The family is referred to only as 'Radhu' in the revenue records of Leh (See FN 2). The appellation 'Khwaja', as the family is generally known today, is probably a later development, probably because of influences from Kashmir where prosperous business families were, and are still, referred to as 'Khwaja'. This is distinct from the Central Asian usage of the term, in the form of 'Khoja', which implied teachers of some kind.

Both political blocs wanted to secure the region for China in the wake of the new world order that was emerging from the ruins of World War II. Abdul Hamid was heading home to ask his contemporaries and elders what the family should do in such circumstances. At stake was the legacy of the sizeable business house that the clan had built in less than a hundred years (Hedin, 1909, Vol. I, pp. 55–6) since establishing the base in Yarkand.

The patriarch of the Radhu clan was Muhammad Ashai Radhu (1635–1714), an eminent teacher in Kashmir. Of a scholarly and pious bent, he was also an initiate in the Chishti *silsila* (or 'order' of Sufism) in Kashmir. He laid the foundations for the order there and added the name 'Chishti' to his names. At the end of the seventeenth century, one of the patriarch's three sons, Asad Radhu, emigrated from his ancestral home in the Fateh Kadal neighbourhood of Srinagar to Ladakh and founded a trading house. Family lore has it that his son, Faruq Radhu, continued and consolidated this branch of the family's new-found profession. Thus began the Radhu family's peregrinations in Central Eurasia. Gradually, the clan established itself as a commercial success in Ladakh and expanded its linkages through commerce and kinship into Tibet, Chinese Central Asia and even mainland China.

Xinjiang, as this part of Central Asia is known today, is an oval desert dotted with several luxurious oases that acted as nodes along the Silk Road. Because of its position as a critical junction of trade routes, the province had a sizeable population of non-Han and non-Turkic residents who were being subtly discouraged or outright expelled. In part, the expulsions were motivated by events of some seven decades earlier, when the region had been at the centre of 'the Great Game' between Tsarist Russia, British India and Qing China in Central Asia and South Asia. (Meyer & Brysac, 1999; Hopkirk, 1990) The dynamics of that rivalry had also spawned a momentary regional state, Kashgaria, led by the military adventurer Yakub Khan. (Kim, 2004)

Although by 1942 the putative state of Kashgaria had long

disappeared and the Great Game had acquired an altogether new flavour, the two developments had weakened the Qing Dynasty's (1644 –1911) control over Xinjiang, a territory they had annexed to China in the mid-eighteenth century. The memory of this experience was still fresh in the minds of the Chinese ruling elite; so non-Han expatriates—traders, landed gentry, religious missionaries and others—were deemed potential spies and troublemakers during turbulent times at the behest of the British or Soviet empires. The easiest and best national security response to that likelihood was to expel all prospective mischief-makers. The trading families of the region, including the Radhus, were adjusting to these changes.

~

Let me pause here to briefly explain some geographic terms I have used and will be using, such as 'Central Asia', 'Inner Asia' 'Chinese Central Asia', 'Xinjiang', 'Russian Central Asia' and 'Central Eurasia', to denote the region that has been roamed by myriad nations and contested by several states with increasing acquisitiveness in recent centuries. The differences in nomenclature can be confusing even to specialists, so it is entirely understandable if it bewilders those who are unfamiliar with the geography and history of the region.

Specifically, the term 'Inner Asia' signifies the landmass between the Urals in the west and the Altai mountains in the east. And its north-south boundaries are demarcated by the Siberian steppe and the Himalaya respectively. In the last twenty years or so, the term 'Inner Asia' has been replaced by 'Central Eurasia' as a way of emphasising the linkages between Asia and Europe in both geography and history. Some scholars still use the two terms interchangeably and others, much less accurately, even refer to the entire landmass as 'Central Asia'.

But the latter term in fact describes two sub-regions of Central Eurasia which were referred to as 'Eastern Turkestan' and 'Western Turkestan', the Tian Shan mountain range acting as the spine of that divide. 'Turkestan' is the ethnonym derived from the region's largely Turkic-speaking people who have formed an ethnic, linguistic, historical, cultural and religious continuum over centuries. It is worth noting that a close look at a map of Eurasia illustrates that Ladakh is a part of Central Eurasia, with ancient links to Yarkand directly to the north of it in Xinjiang, which is a part of Central Asia.

The changes in nomenclature for 'Central Asia' that puzzle us today began in the early modern age. In the seventeenth and eighteenth centuries, Tsarist Russia and Qing China annexed western and eastern Turkestan, respectively, into their empires. They were referred to as 'Russian Central Asia' and 'Chinese Central Asia', with the former changing its name to 'Soviet Central Asia' after the 1917 Bolshevik revolution, while the Qing continued to refer to eastern Turkestan as Xinjiang (they had renamed it when they took over around the mid-eighteenth century) which, in its anglicised rendition, was called 'Sinkiang'. After the collapse of the Soviet Union in 1989–90, the nations of Soviet Central Asia became the independent states of Uzbekistan, Tajikistan, Turkmenistan, Kyrgyzstan, and Kazakhstan and 'Sinkiang' was firmly replaced by Xinjiang. However, it would be interesting to note that even of these republics, Kazakhstan and large swathes of Turkmenistan and Kyrgyzstan are neither culturally nor ecologically 'Central Asia'. (Cf. Beckwith, 2009, p. 385)

While this geography is cumbersome to navigate, it is not mere academic idiosyncrasy. The changes are emblematic of the consequences of the rapid changes in the world political order that were set in motion in as early as the seventeenth century. In many ways, it separated and isolated cultures that had had symbiotic pasts and, more importantly, presents that formed a continuum in ethnicity, language and culture. The rapidity of the changes in the 'world order' set in motion after the World War I made these societies vulnerable with little recourse to push-back on the divides that were being forced on them. Indeed, it is the resistances to these changes have resulted in many of the tangles that we find in large swathes of Central Eurasia and its borderlands today.

~

As the clutch of anxious caravaneers from Yarkand rolled into Gilgit, Abdul Wahid Radhu, a young member of that same family, was journeying in the opposite direction—from Leh to Lhasa—and penning the first pages of his diary, which was to form the foundation for this book. He was armed with a degree in geography from Aligarh Muslim University in British India and newly married to his cousin Ruqayyah Banu. A dreamy idealist, he had managed to persuade his father-in-law, Abdul Aziz of the Lhasa branch of the family, to allow him to accompany the long caravan journey on its tribute mission (Tib.: *lo phyag*) to the offices of the Dalai Lama in Lhasa. The Radhus had secured the right to carry this triennial tribute sometime in the first half of the nineteenth century. (Hedin, 1909, Vol. I, pp. 55–6) It was a tribute-cum-trade mission, decreed by the 1684 Treaty of Tingmosgang. It was signed following a five-year war that was fought by monarchic (Buddhist) Ladakh in alliance with Mughal (Muslim) Kashmir against an army of ecclesiastic (Buddhist) Tibet in alliance with tribal (shamanist) Mongol. (Ahmad)

The route of this caravan hugged the Changthang (Tib.: 'northern plains') of the Tibetan Plateau for more than a thousand miles to Lhasa, the capital of Tibet. If uninterrupted, it took just more than two-and-a-half months (Hedin, 1913, Vol. III, p. 34) and the average size of the caravan totalled well over two hundred and fifty pack animals. The tribute items, however, required less than ten pack animals to carry and the remaining animals carried the private trade goods of the tribute-bearers. The disproportion in the number of pack animals to tribute items was a result of the common man's contributions to the mission's expenses. Given the eventual destination of the tribute—the Dalai Lama's offices in the Potala Palace in Lhasa—it was considered a privilege and an honour for a Ladakhi to donate to the operations of the tribute mission and they contributed in kind and labour. The *lo-phyag* caravan was also exempt from paying for lodging in the villages it stopped at during the journey to Lhasa and back; and, perhaps most profitably, it flew the flag of the mission, which protected it from being attacked by brigands that frequented this trail.

All this, in effect, meant that whoever was carrying the tribute was exempt from incurring overhead costs for transport, accommodation, helpers and muleteers. It was a very lucrative privilege, in addition to being an implicit honour. Those granted the license for the *lo-phyag* used the extra animals to load them with private goods of trade. In the case of the Radhus, this included wool, gold dust, turquoise, coral, amber and other semiprecious stones, dried apricots and, in later years, consumer items, to Lhasa. They returned to Leh, usually the following year, with Chinese brick tea as the main item of trade along with wool and other items that were eagerly sought after in the outlying regions of the Tibetan-speaking world.

The objectives of the two journeys in opposite directions of Central Eurasia by members of the same family heralded uncertain futures for the region's traditional cultural links, commercial interests and trade relationships. The Radhus were simultaneously being expelled from Xinjiang by the Chinese, their prospects in Tibet were equally uncertain and the political future of Ladakh, a part of the Jammu and Kashmir State, seemed at best in limbo in the wake of the impending British withdrawal from British, Princely and the Tribal India that they had colonized and united by the time of their withdrawal. That world was on the verge of collapse.

The young Abdul Wahid intuited as much as he wrote the early pages of his diary seventy-five years ago. His college years had exposed him to the political implications of World War II, the arguments of the Indian independence movement, the accelerating discourse on the demand for Pakistan and the uncertainties of what the potential Partition meant. A romantic, he trained his ambitions on his family's interests in Lhasa as an alternative to these impending uncertainties, seeking solace in Tibet's isolation albeit unaware, in 1942, of the fate that awaited even that branch of his cultural and intellectual lexicon.

By 1948, six years later, the end of the Chinese civil war was close at hand, and, in 1949, the victory of the Communist party was confirmed. The atmosphere of suspicion that was overtaking the nascent Cold War regime further helped to expedite the expulsion of non-Turkic and non-Han expatriates from Yarkand. Mukarram and his younger brother, Abdul Hakim, had by then returned to Yarkand and, following a clan consensus, liquidated the family assets there. Their plan was to go back to Leh, this time via the more direct southern route. But as they prepared to leave, the local Han authorities refused to allow Mukarram's wife Noora Khan, a Turkic-speaking native, to leave with him. When he protested this, he was summarily imprisoned for four years after which he was expelled for good, but without Noora Khan in tow. He returned to Leh and, after living there for a few years, headed for Kashmir to live with his nephew, Abdul Wahid.

Meanwhile, the Peoples Liberation Army's occupation of Tibet in 1950 had put a damper on the family business at the Lhasa-end of Abdul Wahid's world too. For the bulk of the time after their migration to Tibet in the early nineteenth century, the Lhasa branch of the Radhus had been dependent as a base for, and a sub-trading wing of, the tribute corridor trade between Leh and Lhasa. But the opening of Tibet to British Indian and Nationalist Chinese rivalry in the first two decades of the twentieth centuries demanded modifications. Not surprisingly, this opening was provided by internal rivalries also.

Starting in the late nineteenth century, an intense debate raged within Tibet between the 'modernist' and 'traditionalist' factions of its power elite. The 'modernist' faction of this rivalry was led largely by the lay aristocracy who foresaw the dangers of isolation, advocating a gradual 'opening up' of Tibet to new ways. The other faction, the 'traditionalists', was led by the ecclesiasts of the three great monastic universities near Lhasa—Sera, Drepung and Ganden—who preferred the status quo ante. There was also the question of whether this should be done through closer ties with British India or Qing, and later, Republican China. Both groups appealed for support for their positions to the Dalai Lama, which further complicated the picture. In the event, these circumstances resulted in the opening of trade possibilities with British India to the south.

The Lhasa branch of the Radhus capitalised on these political developments, particularly after the late 1920s. They deftly adjusted to it by opening commercial contacts with points directly south of Lhasa such as Kalimpong, Calcutta and beyond. It quickly became a popular route because the tribute corridor across the Chang-thang was considerably longer (the southern trade-route took ten days to reach Kalimpong), prone to encountering violently inclement weather and vulnerable to frequent attacks by brigands, as illustrated by one such encounter in this narrative. In later years, the southern route was made even easier by modern roads and transport that penetrated deep into British India.

But after two world wars and turbulent changes in the world order in the first four decades of the twentieth century, it became clear that the 1950 Peoples Liberation Army's occupation of Tibet was destined to be of much longer duration and impact than the British and Nationalist ones of 1903 and 1913 respectively. Each of these occupations had lasted several months but, at the end of both, Tibet asserted its independent status. (Cf. Goldstein, 1989, pp. 44–366; Smith, 1996, pp. 151–263) However, the march of the People's Liberation Army into Tibet in 1950 had a radical and sweeping effect. The story of how this impacted the autochthonous population of Tibet has been recounted in many books by Tibetan exiles, starting with the autobiography of His Holiness the Fourteenth Dalai Lama. The narrative of the centuries-old indigenous settler population of Tibetan Muslims is less known.

The Central Tibetan Muslims were about a hundred and fifty families strong and lived mostly in Lhasa, Shigatse and Tsetang, just south of Lhasa. They were from the Muslim lands that surround the Tibetan plateau and had settled in Central Tibet over a span of several centuries. Many traced their origins to trading families of Kashmir. The members of the Radhu clan were among them, but distinguished by the fact that they were from Kashmir via Ladakh, which made them come to be known as Ladak-khache, or Ladakhi Muslims. So when it became clear that the Peoples Liberation Army was in Tibet to stay, the Radhus asserted their 'other' identity as citizens of Jammu and Kashmir State, despite residing in Central Tibet for more than a century and a half. As proof of belonging to this category of identity they dusted their 'State Subject Certificates'[2] and, given the status of the Jammu and Kashmir State after 1947, asked the Indian Consulate that they be permitted to return to Kashmir, their homeland. Like their settler resident relatives of Yarkand two years earlier, they were encouraged to leave and transported to the southern border in trucks. In the case of the Radhus, they were permitted to sell

---

[2] This category of identity was promulgated by Maharaja Hari Singh in 1927. It entitled and privileged 'state subject' status to the descendants of those who were born or resided within his territories 'before the commencement of the reign of His Highness the late Maharaja Gulab Singh Bahadur' in 1846, when the territorial State of Jammu and Kashmir was formed. In Ladakh such citizens are identified by a document known as the 'bandobasti', which lists all the 'original' families of its towns and villages. In Leh, for example, 307 such families were identified, of which fifty-five were Muslim and the rest Buddhist. The Khwaja-Radhu family, although identified only as 'Radhu', is listed among these fifty-five families with two branches, the 'Haji-pa' and 'Aba Chocho'. The third branch of the family that migrated to Lhasa are not listed in the 'bandobasti', which is probable evidence that they emigrated from Ladakh before 1846, therefore not entitling them to being included in the 'bandobasti' list formed after the Dogra conquest. (I am grateful to Advocate Mohammad Nasir of Leh for this information.)

their immovable assets to the Chinese army, for which they were paid in U. S. silver dollars that the Communists had confiscated from the defeated American-backed Nationalists.

The young Abdul Wahid had made the most of his introduction to the Central Eurasian landmass since 1942, crisscrossing it several times. Although challenged by insulated relatives in his in-laws, he got involved in the family business in its directly southern route through Kalimpong, befriended members of the Tibetan aristocracy and associated himself with the movement to reform Tibet. By 1947, he was living in Nanjing, the capital of Nationalist China, and had joined a group of young reformist-minded Tibetans. But the implications of the Chinese occupation of Tibet, disagreements between the young reformists and the lack of connect with his in-laws of the Lhasa branch of the family all converged to discourage this relatively worldly wise young Ladakhi from continuing to live in Tibet. By the middle of the decade, he had returned to Kashmir to establish a base there for our small nuclear family. The Ladak-khache followed soon after, in 1957.

For the Radhus, these events were literally a full circle return to Kashmir after more than two hundred and fifty years of journeying. There were many other such families in Ladakh and Lhasa, so it would be relevant to pause here to place Ladakh in the context of the Western Himalaya in general and as a part of the Dogra State of Jammu and Kashmir. It will help the reader to better understand the geographic, historic and cultural context of the narrative in Tibetan Caravans.

~

The conventional, indeed stereotypical, view of Ladakh today is that of a monolithic world of Tibetan-speaking Buddhists whose splendid isolation from the world ended in 1974 when it was thrown open to tourism. This nostalgically romantic image of Ladakh is fuelled by an abundance of ill-researched articles, fanciful travelogues and idealised books. The ground, which one must travel if one is to understand the region, is different. The autochthonous population of Ladakh is well buried in the sands of time, except in breezy political polemic. Today, and for several centuries now, it represents a mix of races and ethnicities, languages and religions. Nor can these categories be isolated territorially. Although one religion or ethnicity may be in the majority in one territorial part of it, each such part is home to 'nested' groups of the 'other'. Similarly, Ladakh's 'isolation' is a very recent phenomenon, perpetuated in the political interests of colonial rule that isolate peoples for reasons of cartographic boundary-making rather than borderland peoples' welfare.

Tibetan Caravans, I believe, should be read as an account that seeks to project the interest of the borderland dwellers, which lies in its geography, stories and cultural confluences. How did this trans-Himalayan region come to be a Tibetan-speaking region? How and when was Islam introduced here? And how did it come to be tied so closely to the political milieu of South Asia? The answers to these and other similar questions cannot be addressed in the space of this essay, for it involves a review of several intertwined histories. But, nevertheless, if not full answers, these questions merit some brief explanatory pointers.

Ladakh and Baltistan are Tibet's westernmost ethnic, linguistic and cultural extensions, an expansion that probably took place in the seventh and eighth centuries as part of the political developments in the Central Eurasian milieu. Gilgit, just west of Baltistan, though not 'Tibetan' culturally, is also part of that ambiance. And though, strictly speaking, Kashmir is set apart from the Central Eurasian milieu, it has long been the vortex, at times the crucible, and today a cauldron of linkages between Central Eurasia and South Asia. This 'connectivity' began earlier, but let us recount some events from the early medieval and early modern history of the region.

In the second half of the sixth century CE, Thonmi Sambhota, a minister of the first historical king of Tibet, was sent to Kashmir to learn more about Buddhism. (Stein, 1965; Kapstein, 2006) Then again, in 744 CE for example, Kashmir's then king, Muktapida, sent an embassy to Xian to say that he had assisted the Tang dynasty (618–907) forces with supplies in their battle against the Tibetans and to propose an alliance with the former. (Beckwith, 1987, p. 111) Similarly, ninth-century texts provide us with evidence of trade in silk (*kha-che dar*) either from Kashmir or Muslim lands further west. (Akasoy, Burnett, & Yoeli-Thalim, 2011, p. 4) These and other associations of trade, diplomacy and war drew Central Eurasia and South Asia together in the subsequent centuries. The fourteenth-century history of the Western Himalaya was defined by the establishment of a Muslim monarchy in Kashmir, catalysed by a Eurasian military adventurer known as 'Rinchena Bhota' or, in other sources, as 'Rinchen Shah'. Although he died after a brief reign of three years (1320–1323), the monarchy established by him followed, with several raids into Ladakh. This continued into the early decades of the sixteenth century. In the late seventeenth century, Ladakh and Kashmir allied themselves to fight Tibet, one of Central Eurasia's more intriguing powers, which ended in the Tingmosgang Treaty.

The cumulative result of these historical convergences was the birth of the Jammu and Kashmir State between 1834 and 1846, when the Dogra Gulab Singh joined Ladakh, Baltistan, Kashmir and Gilgit into a single state ruled by Jammu. (Singh, 1974) Not surprisingly, the four entities proved to be a 'natural fit' for the creation of an opportunistic Westphalian State at the height of the 'Great Game', the phrase famously coined by the military-explorer and spy-adventurer Arthur Conolly in 1831 (Hopkirk, 1990, p. 123) and popularised by Rudyard Kipling in his timeless novel, *Kim*, published in 1901. The stakes were high in that play between empires and, to quote Kipling's horse-trader Mahbub Ali in *Kim*, 'The Great Game (was) so large, that no one (saw) but a little at a time.' Indeed, the creation of the State of Jammu and Kashmir in 1846 may have been part of that game.

In the event, the ushering of the borderland nations of Central Eurasia into the comity of modern states may have proved to be the beginning of the end of an era of relationships between borderland peoples. It happened as deliberately demarcated boundary lines began to define states more starkly, in imitation of the experience of Europe's colonial powers at home and in other parts of the world they had colonised in the three centuries after the opening of the sea routes to their east and west.

Paradoxically, however, in the century after the creation of the Dogra Jammu and Kashmir State in 1846, the commercial and cultural relations between its diverse but linked parts grew exponentially as the traders' pony-tracks became more familiar with postal, telegraph and other governmental services, tramping the path with increasing frequency, although at a relatively moderate pace. The pace accelerated after the British withdrawal and following the war that took place between India and Pakistan in 1947–48. The war also catapulted Ladakh as a place of strategic importance as India rushed tanks to altitudes exceeding 11,500 feet above sea level to thwart Pakistan's troops rushing in from the west. It rapidly familiarised both newly born states with South Asia's Himalayan world. In 1962 when India and China were at war, the journey time between Leh and Srinagar was dramatically reduced for military reasons. By the third quarter of the twentieth century, motor vehicles carrying civilian passengers would complete the trip in two days. Today the same road journey takes just twelve hours by motor vehicle, enabling the traveller to have dinner on arrival at either end of her destination. And by air, it is a twenty-five-minute flight from Srinagar and a little over an hour in a direct flight from New Delhi.

The speed with which the changes took place, in other words, picked up considerably. It is the grappling with these changes that occupies significant space in *Tibetan Caravans*.

~

To prepare for this introduction, I tried to recall a homily or an incident that would summarise what could be called the legacy that Apalay, for that is what my siblings and I call Abdul Wahid Radhu, our father, left us. I tried to remember a conversation or an incident to anchor the introduction with, one that would encapsulate his attitude toward the world and life. He tended towards universals, away from particularities or assertions of identity, especially in the realm of politics. But it was hard to remember a concise articulation, so I scoured his early journals in search of an appropriate summary.

I did not have to go far. In an entry dated November 10, 1948, he cites Ernest Renan's definition of a nation which tended, in the liberal tradition, to distance itself from territory, bloodline and inherited power. 'Man,' the entry reads, 'is enslaved neither by his race, nor by his religion, nor by the course of rivers, nor by the direction of mountain ranges. A great aggregation of men, sane of mind and warm of heart, creates a moral consciousness which is called a nation.' Apalay then goes on in the same entry to write of his reason for maintaining a journal. 'It is too common a thing to keep a day by day diary, yet one cannot afford to forget the mental conflicts... To record the growth of our thoughts is one of the most pleasant joys to be enjoyed.'

I cite the above passages because it is difficult for us today to grasp the difficulties of a struggle that the straddling of two vastly different worlds entailed for the individuals of Apalay's generation. A concise summary of this book might be that it is the story of a young man who was practically confronting and obliquely intuiting the implications of the momentous changes that were taking place in the world order in the first half of the twentieth century.

Apalay was born in 1918. He began his diary when he was twenty-four with one foot firmly planted in the 'traditional' world. And *Tibetan Caravans* was written forty years later with the other foot tenuously lodged in the 'modern' world. While the advancements in transportation, communication and everyday living were a seductive mix that was less difficult to adjust to, the revolution in ideas and politics, much of it imported from Europe, required intellectual synthesis. The second of the entries cited above hints at that effort involved in that exercise. For Apalay it was the central theme of his life. The fifty years of journal-writing that Apalay has left as a legacy for us, his children, provides ample evidence of this leitmotif. More specifically, in the words of the Irish poet John Montague, he sought an 'unpartitioned intellect'. His peregrinations, in body and in spirit, as told in *Tibetan Caravans* narrate how a person who led an examined life attempted to synthesise for himself the causes and the consequences of the radical changes in his world.

To be sure, the story of the Radhu family's relationships of trade, kinship, cultural assimilation and political dislocation is not unusual. It will be familiar not only to families in Ladakh and Kashmir, but throughout the Jammu and Kashmir State and the Himalayan borderlands. Most, if not all, will have similar stories to tell. Stories that allude to and illustrate the symbiotic relationships developed from generations of accumulated insight by societies who have learned how to hear each other out, argue, even do battle and yet remain hospitable to each other. They are precious, intimate histories.

Tibetan Caravans shows, in microcosm, how the relationships in one part of the Central Eurasian and South Asian periphery intertwined the lives of and for their peoples. These are modest nations but with complex histories. Acquainting ourselves with them will help the grand, often grandiose, ambitions of states to understand how to achieve, to use the language of security studies, 'stability' and 'tranquillity' between large states, even if most of the time with increasing futility. For the many enclave nations of ethnicities, languages and cultures of the Himalaya—including the peoples of the erstwhile Jammu and Kashmir State, broadly grouped together as Kashmir, Baltistan, Gilgit, Ladakh and Jammu—an understanding of their histories and lifeways will determine no less than their survival, even as the status quo powers advocate grand theories of secular democracies, plural societies and globalisation; for nations, let it be said, with a priori 'globalised' social structures that were more than a millennium in the making but have been radically dismantled in the last two centuries.

There are many reasons why this far-reaching rupture took place of course, not the least of which is the politics of state-building and its polemics. (Scott, 2009) A takeaway of critical importance from reading *Tibetan Caravans* is that the loss of the memory of *organic relationships between nations* in favour of exclusive *territorial possessiveness between states* may be at the root of the problems that besiege societies that are the seams between states with 'holy wars' of a different stripe. It recalls the Robert Frost poem, 'No Holy Wars for Them':

> States strong enough to do good are but few.
> Their number would seem limited to three.
> Good is a thing that they, the great, can do,
> But puny little states can only be.
> To watch a war in nominal alliance,
> And when it's over watch the world's supply
> Get parcelled out among the winning giants.
>
> God, have You taken cognisance of this?
> And what on this is your divine position?
> That nations like the Cuban and the Swiss
> Can never hope to wage a Global Mission.
> No Holy Wars for them. The most the small
> Can ever give us is a nuisance brawl.

The present-day dispute over the Jammu and Kashmir State, which continues to confound inter-state relations in South Asia, is one such unresolved 'holy war'. Narratives like *Tibetan Caravans* illustrate that, in large part, it is an ignorance of the geography, history and lifeways of the region that divest us of the ability to contemplate imaginative explorations towards the resolution of this conundrum that has forced uncertainty onto the lives of more than twelve million citizens of the state and, arguably, well over two billion citizens of South Asia.

It is in the above context that this reprint of *Tibetan Caravans* will be celebrated by those who knew and understood Apalay, whose nomadic and universalist bent of mind allowed him an intellectual odyssey, immensely helped by his wife Ruqayyah. They also encouraged their children, grandchildren, great-grandchildren and extended family to explore new worlds, material as well as intellectual. I hope that this reprint of *Tibetan Caravans* will stimulate the publication or republication of similar pasts and practices of the Himalaya. They are the backbone of the relationship between the nations of Central Eurasia and South Asia and tell stories that are largely neglected in history, except as an addendum to the states that possess the territories of these nations today. It would not be overly dramatic to say that the continued neglect of this Himalayan 'backbone' (almost in a literal sense) threatens to sever the ties and lifeways of the Himalayan nations, which cannot but be to the detriment of 'stability and tranquillity' in South Asia.

SIDDIQ WAHID

Bibliography

Akasoy, A., Burnett, C. & Yoeli-Thalim, R. (Eds). 2011. *Islam and Tibet: Interactions along the Musk Routes*. Surrey, England: Ashgate Publishing Limited.

Beckwith, C. I. 1987. *The Tibetan Empire in Central Asia: A History of the Struggle for Great Power among Tibetans, Turks, Arabs, and Chinese during the Early Middle Ages*. Princeton, NJ: Princeton University Press.

Beckwith, C. I. 2009. *Empires of the Silk Road: A History of Central*

Eurasia from the Bronze Age to the Present. Princeton, NJ: Princeton University Press.

Goldstein, M. C. 1989. *A History of Modern Tibet, 1913 – 1951: The Demise of the Lamaist State*. Berkley: University of California Press.

Hedin, S. 1909. *Trans-Himalaya: Discoveries and Adventures in Tibet* (Vols I and II). St Martin's Street, London: MacMillan and Co., Limited.

Hedin, S. 1913. *Trans-Himalaya Discoveries and Adventures in Tibet* (Vol. III). St Martin's Street, London: MacMillan and Co., Limited.

Hopkirk, P. 2006. *The Great Game: On Secret Service in High Asia*. London: John Murray.

Kapstein, M. T. 2006. *The Tibetans*. Oxford, UK: Blackwell Publishing Ltd.

Kim, H. 2004) *Holy War in China: The Muslim Rebellion and State in Chinese Central Asia, 1864-1877*. Stanford, CA: Stanford University Press.

Meyer, K. & Brysac, S. 2000. *Tournament of Shadows: The Great Game and the Race for Empire in Central Asia*. Washington, DC: Counterpoint.

Scott, J. C. 2009. *The Art of Not Being Governed: An Anarchist History of Upland Southeast Asia*. New Haven: Yale University Press.

Shakya, T. 1999. *The Dragon in the Land of Snows: A History of Modern Tibet since 1947*. London: Pimlico.

Singh, B. S. 1974. *The Jammu Fox: A Biography of Maharaja Gulab Singh of Kashmir, 1792–1857*. Carbondale: Southern Illinois University Press.

Smith, W. W. 1997. *Tibetan Nation: A History of Tibetan Nationalism and Sino-Tibetan Relations*. New Delhi, India: HarperCollins Publishers.

Stein, R. A. 1972. *Tibetan Civilization*. (J. E. Stapleton Driver, Trans). Stanford, CA: Stanford University Press.

FOREWORD

By His Holiness The Dalai Lama

In the natural course of things, the older generation gives way to the younger generation. And yet the spirit of the one is passed on to the other. The younger generation in Tibet is just as determined to maintain their identity and to struggle for justice and freedom in their own land as those who remember life before the Chinese occupation. Similarly, our Muslim brothers and sisters retain the spirit of their forefathers in being proud to assert their identity as Tibetans, specifically as Tibetan Muslims. Their solidarity is a precious source of encouragement for us all.

I recently had the pleasure of meeting a group of Tibetan Muslims in Dharamsala who had attended the First Conference of Tibetan Muslims. Like a dream, meeting them reminded me of the days of my youth in Lhasa. When we think back on those times, an image of our Kashmiri merchants peacefully conducting their business and engaging in animated conversation in the market often comes to mind. They were an established part of Tibetan life. Similarly, our Muslim brothers and sisters from Ladakh, while observing their own religion, seemed in every other respect to be following the Tibetan way of life. This is why I have often noted that although Tibetan culture has been strongly influenced by Buddhism, Tibetan Buddhism and Tibetan culture are two different things.

This book, *Tibetan Caravans*, gives a vivid account of life in the Land of Snow from the perspective of a Tibetan Muslim. As this story shows, when we were free, we all lived together like members of the same family. We worked together, underwent hardship together and ate and drank together. Many of us, too, have since experienced the ups and downs of life as refugees together. What we all look forward to as Tibetans, whatever our religion, is living together once more in friendship and harmony in a peaceful, free Tibet.

PREFACE

The request for me to contribute some introductory comments on the present book has been the outcome of a long friendship, starting from the time when I first met the author at Kalimpong, at the Indian end of the caravan route from Lhasa, during the early months of 1947 while awaiting permission to visit independent Tibet, as it then was. With the author's family, my acquaintance dates back further still, to the year 1936 when I visited their homeland of Ladakh at the western extremity of the Tibetan world. At that time Ladakh was included in the Indian state of Kashmir. What took me there together with two companions was a wish to extend my knowledge of that Buddhist tradition I had first encountered three years earlier while taking part in a mountaineering expedition to the western Himalayas. The Sutlej valley with its high peak of Riwo Pargyul, which was climbed by us for the first time, was the native home of people who were Buddhists by religion and culture and spoke a Tibetan dialect; a detailed account of those two journeys is covered by my first book, *Peaks and Lamas*, a work which subsequently has served many readers by way of introduction to Buddhist teachings and practice as well as to the Tibetan tradition generally. That book, after passing through a number of editions, including translations into Spanish and French, went out of print some years ago but later got republished by Frank Cass, when I took the opportunity to include there a certain amount of fresh material gathered in Tibet itself during my one and only visit to that country. Some of the things described there link up with observations to be found in Abdul Wahid's reminiscences, a fact which renders the present preface all the more appropriate.

One incidental result of my visit to Ladakh was to introduce me, side by side with Buddhism, to another very different tradition, that of Islam, in the person of Abdul Wahid's maternal grandfather Haji Muhammad Siddiq, the same who figures so prominently in the early part of his grandson's story; his title of 'Haji' refers to the pilgrimage to Mecca he had accomplished. Visits to his home afforded an insight into what life lived according to the Islamic pattern might imply in terms of dignity and generosity—coupled with a spontaneous piety colouring everything a man might think, feel or do. All this was exemplified in the character of this grand old patriarch, a fact to which his grandson pays repeated tribute in the course of his narrative.

Moreover, it was while staying at Leh, capital of the ancient kingdom of Ladakh, that I first heard the sounds of the Islamic call to prayer. I still can recall the emotion I experienced when walking past the old town mosque as the magical accents of the muezzin's call suddenly struck my ears. Every Muslim man or woman is expected to obey this call five times a day throughout life, thereby imparting a rhythm to earthly existence through its constantly repeated allusion to the one thing needful; but as any sensitive soul who has listened to 'the call' can see for himself, its providential message need not stop short at the Islamic tradition alone. Logically, it concerns all men as such, regardless of the particular form of their religious affiliations. To heed it is to be kept facing in the right direction and whoever does so might fairly claim the quality of a Muslim by analogy or for that matter of a Buddhist in the sense of one who is seeking Enlightenment while profiting from whatever means his own existential situation has brought within reach. This is the message of the call to prayer, for those who have ears to hear.

If the present book offers itself primarily as an account of one man's experiences during a time of unprecedented changes, it also affords a vivid impression of the community of Muslim traders to which that man belonged by race, whose caravans kept plying their way to and fro across the broad tableland of Central Asia until the Communists closed the ancient routes. The high respect these traders' business acumen and integrity earned them in all the far-flung regions they linked together as middlemen is proved, among other things, by the fact that they were entrusted with the special task of transporting the periodic gifts which the Ladakh Buddhists were wont to send to the Dalai Lama. The first part of the present story describes the lengthy trek from Leh to Lhasa in fascinating detail and, in so doing, offers us a vivid picture of what life was like in a caravan on the move and of the human problems this could give rise to from day to day.

To hark back a little to the author's early years before he was ready to take the road in company with his elders, one is allowed to gain an insight into a question that was troubling many young people of his generation, namely, whether or not to seek the advantages, real or supposed, of a Western-style education or else to continue in the traditional ways their fathers had followed hitherto. For a Muslim at that time and place, this meant a choice between a local school where teaching was given in Urdu with a strong Islamic flavour running through the tuition offered there and one of the various educational establishments run by Christian missions where English was the official language and where a schooling along modern lines could be had at relatively small cost, leading eventually, so it was hoped, to some post or other in government service under the colonial regimen then in force. Once the wish to follow the latter road had gained a hold, both with parents and their children, it counted for little in their calculations that the missionaries themselves evinced no love, nor even an elementary respect for the religions professed by their prospective pupils and indeed, had founded these schools for the express purpose of converting them eventually to another faith. Such has been the common experience in all parts of the East in recent times.

What the author tells us is sufficient to illustrate the nature of the problem his own family had to face when making their decision concerning his future schooling. One cannot say they took the plunge without considerable hesitation because, unlike so many others similarly placed, they were people who valued their tradition and certainly did not wish to undermine it in the case of their own son. As the book shows us, the two views at issue became respectively personified in the young man's grandfather and his great-uncle Abdullah Shah, and if the latter's advice seemed to prevail at the outset, this was not the end of the story as far as the author himself was concerned. As he tells us later on, he eventually came to the conclusion that after all, it was his grandfather who had been right in principle; but at the same time he gives us to understand how irresistible the lure of a partial modernisation had seemed when first encountered. It would be both unrealistic and unfair to underrate the pressures felt in all similar cases, whatever may be the direction in which one's ultimate sympathies happen to lie.

However, as things proved, love for the ancestral tradition was too firmly rooted in Abdul Wahid's soul to succumb, as so often happens, to those profane teachings which what passes for an adequate education in the West invariably comprises, whether covered by a thin veneer of Christian ideas or otherwise. There is no doubt that veneration for his grandfather acted, for him, as a psychic lifeline in gratitude for which he gave his eldest son the name of Muhammad Siddiq as an ideal to live up to of which any man might be proud.

As one threads one's way further through the pages of this thought-provoking book, it becomes increasingly plain that another salutary influence came in later on to supplement for the author, the noble example of his grandfather. This was the influence of Tibetan Buddhism as witnessed in action during the years he spent at Lhasa, which thus came to serve as a concordant factor in favour of what his own Islamic formation had already given him. There was no question here of a systematic study of Buddhist source material; for the author it was simply a case of seeing what was visible and drawing the obvious conclusions while at the same time transposing them into the Islamic spiritual language. The idea of a conscious point-to-point parallelism did not enter in at all.

In fact, this way of assimilating knowledge is one of the salient traits which this account of the author's life reveals as it unfolds; whatever he has observed in passing he has then proceeded to relate to what he already knows without his feeling any prior necessity to analyse his own impressions, and still less to justify them argumentatively. It is, moreover, this characteristic of his which, to my mind, constitutes the peculiar value of this book as a document; whether a matter of specifically religious import under discussion or else some historical incident he has personally become involved in, the same air of impartiality remains in evidence, thus adding credibility to whatever the author has chosen to enlarge on. Had this book taken the form of a personal apologia as it easily might have done, with the inevitably tendentious selection of evidence which goes with such an intention, these reminiscences would have forfeited much of their effectiveness.

As far as his ability to bridge the gap between various traditional forms instead of resting content with what an unconditional conformity to a single form might have given him, the author was much aided, as Chapter 7 of his book explains, by his discovery of the writings of a French writer of the name of René Guénon, which he got to know through two English translations I had shown him. He also lists the names of several other writers, knowledge of whom had come to him in Guénon's wake. The fact that Guénon himself, who entered Islam in middle life, subsequently bore the name of Abdul Wahid, can hardly be dismissed as mere coincidence, as far as the author is concerned, since it corresponded, for him, with but one more pointer to an awareness towards which his own intelligence was already tending.

A country dwelling in apparent peace and contentment on the eve of an impending disaster will always present in retrospect, a tragic spectacle. Had the Tibetans but known it, the inexplicable withdrawal of the British from their former imperial possessions in India had left behind it a power-vacuum for which they themselves were sadly unprepared. The British had made it their policy to favour a sheltered and militarily weak Tibet as constituting a buffer-state between India and a possible expansion from a Russian direction. The invasion of Tibet under Colonel Younghusband in 1903 had no other purpose but this; his forces withdrew as soon as the Tibetan government had agreed to renounce all diplomatic relations in future, except with British India and China. These new arrangements, though accepted under duress, were not found altogether unacceptable by the Lhasa authorities, since these seemed to carry with them a certain implicit protection for Tibet's political independence while at the same time not constituting any threat to existing Buddhist institutions. This, however, did not prevent the Chinese in the last years of the Manchu empire from invading Tibet in their turn, only to be driven out when the Manchus fell in 1912, giving place to a republic of a supposedly Western type. A further advance eastwards by the Tibetans took place in 1918, after which the position became relatively stable until August 1947. With the emergence of the new Indian State, Tibet's security was once again put in jeopardy, with little time left for its habitually cautious and conservative rulers to face up to the problems of defence and political reorientation such as this changed situation urgently called for. The few uneasy years which followed before the Communist victory of the forces of America's protégé Chang Kai-Shek are the ones covered by the latter part of Abdul Wahid's chronicle of events. It is the fact that he knew personally so many of the leading actors on the Tibetan side that lends so much interest to all he was enabled to observe during that distressing time.

In his appreciation of personalities, our author expresses himself more charitably than has been the case with many other commentators, including some Tibetans. Blackening the old order in Tibet and those who formed its governing strata has been a practice to which what passes for educated opinion in the West has shown itself inordinately prone. The readiness with which people supposedly brought up in the habits of fair criticism have been content to accept and repeat catch-phrases culled from Communist propaganda has been worse than disappointing in the so-called liberal countries. People by now should surely know that in the Marxist jargon such expressions as 'feudal', 'theocratic' and where Africa is concerned, 'tribal', have become nothing more than dirty words devoid of any intelligible content. Thus 'feudal' no longer means a particular social system linked to land tenure (with or without the additional obligation to render military service), a system moreover, which, across the inevitable ups and downs affecting all human institutions, has prevailed over large sections of the earth during lengthy periods. It is simply treated as a synonym of brutal exploitation with landlords as its villains; according to this classification, a good landlord is a contradiction in terms regardless of context or historical circumstances. Again the word 'theocratic' is treated as if this were tantamount to organised obscurantism trading on the superstitious fears of a credulous populace for the material advantage of a small class of lamas. That the ideal animating a theoretically ordered society might be a high one, let alone beneficent in practice is, for the dabbler in Marxist thinking, including some who actually style themselves 'conservatives', a virtually unthinkable proposition, whereas accusations of wholesale exactions at the expense of the poor and the needy, backed up by brutal punishments on occasion, are swallowed without a qualm. One would have expected, from an educated public, some attempt to corroborate these dark allegations or else to disprove them by first finding out what foreign observers who had lived in Tibet had reported from time to time concerning what they found there. A good deal of literature exists on the subject, compiled by persons who do not express themselves like men lacking in the critical faculty. That they found Tibet on balance a happy country free from the dreadful material ills observable in many other places surely constitutes a criterion not easy to brush aside, to say nothing of intellectual, artistic and other cultural benefits in which the entire population shared, as these same writers have demonstrated. That the author himself, took so balanced a view of the feudal set-up, where many others have yielded to a now fashionable prejudice, is a tribute to his own discernment.

That he was not blind to the existing faults in the upper reaches of society is evident from his many critical comments to be found throughout the present book towards the end. However, he expresses the overall opinion on the strength of his long experience that the feudal form of society, as prevailing in Tibet, could claim some credit in terms of average welfare; it should also be pointed out in passing that examples of peasant proprietorship were also to be found in places, not to mention the nomadic shepherds and yak herds roaming over the vast northern prairies. In the not infrequent cases of bad landlordism one heard about, the kind of motives which commonly operated could be the wish to make good heavy losses incurred as a result of unsuccessful business ventures or else while playing *mahjong* for heavy stakes, a pastime to which Lhasa high society was inordinately addicted. One must nevertheless take due account of the existence of other landowners whose record could not be bettered; for my own brief experience I can confirm the author's view by saying that I visited a number of estates where the resident owners quite evidently cared deeply for the welfare of their tenants as well as for the land itself.

Having said this much, I must nevertheless express the opinion, as formed on the spot, that the feudal arrangements were now showing signs of immanent breakdown, chief of which was the rapidly increasing incidence of 'absenteeism' which, as history elsewhere has shown, is a defect fatal to what should remain essentially a family affair in which a landowner and his tenants together with their respective dependents will share, each in his own way. This is what a certain peasant said when invited by the Communists to denounce his old master for his alleged habit of oppression; his erstwhile tenant merely answered, not that his master had been good or bad, but that he and the peasant himself had each had a job to do and had carried it out properly, that was all that was to be expected: for this matter-of-fact reply the peasant himself was put to death. Recent years in Tibet had witnessed a marked preference on the part of members of the landowning caste to stay in the capital whence they sallied forth periodically, not in order to visit their ancestral homes, but on shopping expeditions down to Calcutta and other Indian centres where watches and cameras were easily procurable and the cinema could be enjoyed daily. Once these tendencies had gained a hold, especially among the young, the thought of a prolonged sojourn in some secluded and beautiful valley where the family seat itself was situated seemed an unutterably boring prospect. An aggravating factor in this loss of genuine values sprang from the fact that it had also become usual for the said aristocratic families to despatch their children, of both sexes and at a very early age, to seek an English-style education at one of several missionary establishments at Darjeeling or Kalimpong. A certain snob value came to affect this choice of a school just as a knowledge of the English language became a hallmark of education as such, apart from anything else that might be picked up via the linguistic medium in question.

Under the unfamiliar social pressures to which the Tibetan newcomers were thus exposed, of which an enforced competition with a majority of Indian and Anglo-Indian classmates was one of the most trying, they often developed a distressing sense of inferiority which manifested itself in all sorts of ways; a persistent preference for wearing European-style clothes was one of them. As for the claims of religion, these were virtually ignored both by the parents concerned and, astonishing to say, but the authorities at home whose motto, in regard to this vital matter, might well have been 'out of sight, out of mind'.

Quite obviously, given that certain forms of information had become a practical necessity under pressure of the times, the only solution to this new educational problem that made sense would have been to set about creating schools in Tibet itself so organised as to include in their curriculum the subjects in question. Hitherto village schools where children were taught little more than their letters were to be found in many places endowed by the local landowners, while higher education, on lines reminiscent of the 'Scholastic' centres of medieval Europe, was only to be had in the monasteries. What was now needed would have meant taking trouble coupled with not a little practice and imagination; it also would have entailed the engaging of a certain number of foreign staff, who moreover, needed to be carefully selected for reasons over and above their academic qualifications. Two short-lived attempts had in fact been made to set up schools under British auspices, in which political motivation also played a part; one of these schools was started at Lhasa and the other at Gyantse. Of the two, the latter was by far the more successful because more imaginatively run, as I learned from Abdul Wahid's friends, the Tendongs, who had attended this school in their younger days. Certainly, their feeling for tradition has not been impaired as a result, but here, doubtless, the fact that both their parents were people of intelligence as well as of great piety had counted most of all. Incidentally, both the Tendong parents (who died young) and their sons were known as model landowners whose love for their dependents and vice versa showed what the feudal bond, when mutually observed, could mean at its best.

To return to the question of the two schools aforementioned, what eventually led to their closing were the objections raised by influential members of the monastic establishment who argued that the existence in Tibet of schools of a novel type under foreign management might become a cause of psychic infection to the detriment of the Buddhist tradition. The fact that the government bowed to this pressure is far less surprising than its failure to see that sending numbers of children of leading families out of Tibet for years on end and placing them in the unsupervised charge of foreign teachers who, to say the least, cared nothing about Buddhism was ten times more dangerous than having these same children educated in the home country, admittedly on a somewhat alien line, but at least under the watchful eyes both of their parents as well as the authorities of the State. What was, above all, missing when trying to cope with such a problem was the presence in Lhasa of a few men of the intellectual and moral calibre of Haji Muhammad Siddiq and endowed with his combination of practical shrewdness and deeply spiritual insights; doubtless such men are uncommon everywhere and an emergency rarely finds them just when their presence is most required.

Since it was 'absenteeism' which provoked the present discussion in the first place, it should be pointed out that this particular evil could obviously not arise in regard to such estates as were the appanage of monasteries while following the feudal pattern in other respects. Whether abuses sometimes occurred there also, I did not have adequate opportunities for judging. At least one can say that in the case of monastic estates there could not be any interruptions in respect of personal contacts between the monastic authorities and their lay tenants, a fact which in itself provided a certain natural safeguard. This is all the more true, since members of a monastic community would be normally recruited from peasant families belonging to the adjacent districts who, besides contributing to the sustenance of their own children during their novitiate and after, had every opportunity to visit them and vice versa. This constant intercourse between monks and laity, moreover, provided an ideal means for diffusing the Buddhist spirit throughout the population: it would be difficult to imagine a better way of keeping a sacred tradition alive.

Whatever the facts about landed estates may have amounted to in the aggregate, there are good reasons for thinking that the Fourteenth Dalai Lama, left to himself, would have favoured a far-reaching land redistribution whereby the majority of his agricultural subjects would have become self-owning peasant proprietors, while the former owners of the land would have been equitably compensated for what they had to give up. Self-evidently, this would not have suited the Communists' plans for Tibet; that a popular reform should be brought about purely thanks to Tibetan initiative and under the seal of religion was the last thing they wanted. I think, however, that the author is right in supposing that the Chinese at first had hoped that the collectivisation they envisaged might be brought about through a gradual squeeze and not by violence; it was the events of 1959 which caused them to throw off the mask of moderation in favour of more brutal ways of coercion, with the nameless indignities of Mao's 'cultural revolution' to follow a few years later, under which both the Chinese and Tibetan peoples had to suffer.

There is one feature of the Tibetan Theocratic Polity which deserves special mention, if only because the author did not find occasion to refer to it specifically: this is the practice of entrusting all important offices of State, including provincial governorships, to two persons jointly, the one being a layman and the other a monk; a whole class of 'monk-officials' existed, trained for this purpose. There is no doubt that, had Tibet been possessed of a seaboard, a monk-admiral would have been appointed to exercise the naval command side by side with his lay colleague. In practice, of course, individual character would often determine which of the two partners took the real decisions. While staying at Shigatse I had occasion to do business with 'the Castle' and soon saw who was the man in charge there, namely the layman, with his amiable but otherwise inadequate clerical companion playing the part of a 'sleeping partner' whose chief interest in life seemed to lie in the breeding of charming Lhasa terriers. In other cases it might be the monk who had the upper hand, but theoretically the responsibility for decisions lay with the pair acting in common.

A slightly cynical attitude on the part of the public towards officialdom generally has been usual in many places besides old Tibet; it is but a historical truism to say that the seats of powers and patronage are where a maximum of venality and corruption are always to be found. This is true at the best of times as at the worst; where temptations are strongest the corresponding sins will be most conspicuous. One has the right to criticise the shortcomings of one's officials, but not to exaggerate them; to keep to what is fair discrimination in this respect is not always easy. It is worth pointing out in this connection that government servants in Tibet were not as a rule paid salaries in cash, as in a modern administration; they derived this main income from perquisites to them from their clients, the scale of which was determined by traditional custom and not according to a written code. Such abuses as occurred were due to the fact that some officials exacted from those who applied to them more than traditional usage warranted. Complaints on that score were heard fairly often, but the form of the corruption in question—call it accepting bribes if you will—remained relatively petty and individualistic by comparison with what can go on under cover of a sophisticated bureaucracy; both the scale and the character of official corruption will then tend to match that same sophistication and so will its results.

Fairness requires one to add that many Tibetan officials one has known personally gave evidence of a devotion to duty that left nothing to be desired, even if only a few reached the heights of excellence of a Lukhangwa (this would be rare anywhere), to whom the author pays a just tribute in his later chapters; to call him 'the Tibetan Aristide' best befits this noble patriot who was summoned to preside over the national assembly at the height of the crisis as the one man whose integrity no one would think of challenging. If His Holiness was later compelled to retire him under Chinese pressure, this was not before he had managed to stand up for his people in the face of the occupying power, with only his own moral qualities to lend him strength: this is something to be remembered with pride and gratitude by those whose rights he did his best to defend.

A brief word must be said about the monastic congregation, the Sangha, which in Tibet amounted to an unusually high proportion of the population, as compared with other countries. With such large numbers involved, a modest level of intelligence is all one could expect on average; but even so, men of saintly character were by no means uncommon, whose serenity, compassion and deep spiritual insights spoke for themselves without the need to resort to hypocritical affectation of any kind. Meeting these people in all sorts of places as if by chance was one of the rewards of finding oneself in Tibet. By no means were all of them to be found in the ranks of ordained monks; particular account has to be taken of certain contemplatives dwelling on the margin of society who are best described as 'consecrated laymen' since they often were married like Marpa, the teacher of Tibet's celebrated saint and poet, Mila Repa.[1] These were, and still remain, the torch-bearers of wisdom and method under their Tibetan Buddhist form just as, in Islam, it is the great Sufi Masters who fulfil a similar function. It does not fall within the scope of a preface like the present one to go deeply into such matters, yet they had to be mentioned, failing which the Tibetan scene would have lacked an essential dimension.

~

[1] The biography of Mila Repa as taken down from his master's life by his pupil, Rechung, is a supreme masterpiece of the spiritual life; its translation into French by Jacques Bacot is itself a work of genius. This text is now available in the Editions Fayard and includes a preface by the present writer.

The object I chiefly have had in mind when compiling this introduction to my friend's book was to afford European and American readers a certain impression of the conditions prevailing in the Tibetan world during the middle years of the present century; such subjects as have proved controversial in the past have received some added emphasis by way of restoring the balance. More than once I have called attention to the historical importance of what the author wrote; in case the reader, however, has been led thereby to expect something like a piece of meticulous scholarship on academic lines, with chapters and verse provided at every turn, let me undeceive him at once, for the present work is not like that, nor could it have been so. Except in the opening chapters describing the long trek by caravan, where he was able to refer to a rough diary he kept at the time, Abdul Wahid has had to rely almost entirely on his memory of events dating back three or four decades. Despite efforts on the part of himself and his translator to verify such details as dates, place names, and so on, certain points of doubt remain which, in all frankness, will have to be accepted; even so, one cannot but marvel at the retentiveness of the author's mind and accuracy of his reporting.

To call this book a valuable historical document as well as an enthralling personal account is to do it no more than justice, but this is not the end of the story. In *Tibetan Caravans* there is much besides historical reminiscences and personal adventures to be found by a perspicacious reader prepared to read between the lines, but this is something that he can best be left to discover for himself. To try and prompt him would be going beyond what my personal assignment as a writer properly implies.

MARCO PALLIS

CHAPTER 1

TRANS-HIMALAYAN VOCATION

It would never have occurred to me to consider myself a noteworthy person with any sort of claim to distinction and I was far from thinking that my life, vagabond and eventful, richer in setbacks than in accomplishments, was worth recounting. However, amongst the few privileges which destiny held in store for me was to have established some solid friendships with Europeans who were particularly interested in Asia. If I now undertake to relate the story of my peregrinations in Tibet and neighbouring countries, this must be acknowledged to be more the result of their insistence than a deliberate initiative on my part. Already for several years whenever the opportunity arose to meet in Delhi, each of these friends enjoyed hearing me recall some episode from my excursions beyond the Himalayas and they inevitably concluded our meeting with this remark: 'You must definitely write your memoirs.'

One day when one of my usual interlocutors, almost angry to see that I had written nothing, blamed my 'Asiatic' laziness, I finally decided to shake it off and get down to work.

My first concern then was to look through old chests for the diary which I kept fairly regularly during the time I was a caravaneer in Tibet. It didn't take me long to find the black linen-covered notebooks into which I had had ample free time to record details of the journey, thanks to the slow gait of the mules, our principal means of transport in those years. I had also expressed in these diaries the states of soul of an idealistic young man, open to the modern world, who conformed to the merchant tradition of his family as a matter of course. Fresh from the Aligarh Muslim University in India, I had kept this diary in English to give me practice in the language—something Tibet would give me practically no occasion to use.

The first notebook opened with an especially important event in the life of Ladakh, my native land: the departure of the 'Lopchak caravan'. Every two years this official expedition left Leh, our small capital, to go to Lhasa to deliver gifts to the Dalai Lama. This caravan thus contributed to maintaining good relations between Ladakh and Tibet, two countries which in reality formed one nation, even if the former was politically answerable to Kashmir and therefore, after 26 October 1947, to independent India, whereas the latter looked for ways of officialising her de facto independence. This event marked my effective entry into the family profession. With the passing of the years, I have realised that it was the beginning of a very long journey which was never to end since it would allow me an almost uninterrupted inner journey from that time on.

In the evening of this memorable day, after having gone a little more than 20 kilometres, we arrived at Matho. Having settled down for the night in one of the village houses, I inaugurated, by candlelight, my diary, the first page of which is transcribed here:

> Today, 19 September 1942, the twentieth day of my life as a married man, I left my family, my wife, aunt and sister. I left for Lhasa to learn the trade of being a merchant, supervised by my Uncle Abdul Aziz, head of the Lopchak caravan. In the seventeenth century the king of Ladakh, Delek Namgyal (1675–1705) signed a treaty with the Lama Mipham Wangpo, representative of the Dalai Lama, at the end of which it was agreed that a *Zhungtshong* (government trade) caravan would go every year from Lhasa to Leh to maintain good relations of friendship

and commerce between Ladakh and Tibet. Reciprocally, it was agreed that a *Lopchak* (biannual) caravan would be sent to Lhasa every two years by the *gyalpo* (king) of Ladakh. Both caravans would have the right to freely transport merchandise within the territories of the two countries.

The government of Kashmir had put an end to the treaty a few years previously. At the request of the Tibetan authorities, it was re-established in 1938. This is the caravan that my uncle is now directing. However, no official of the state of Kashmir could give us the least bit of information as to the real objectives of the mission. The authorities concerned seem indifferent to its political and diplomatic implications. Every time my uncle tried to question an official such as the wazir-i-wazarat (the first agent of the government) or the local tehsildar (administrator of the district), Uncle found that they preferred to avoid talking about the caravan. The authorities in Lhasa, on their part, take a keen interest in these caravans and they wish to see them continue. As for the commercial and political agents of the British government in Lhasa and Leh, they are also favourably disposed towards the caravans.

The head of the preceding Lopchak had written a detailed report of his journey to Tibet and about his contacts in Lhasa. He had sent a copy to the government of Kashmir by an intermediary of the wazir of Leh and another to the British resident in Srinagar. Whereas the latter immediately testified to the importance he gave to the Lopchak, we learnt at the beginning of the year that the other copy had not even left the wazir's office in Leh!

This morning before the departure, lively activity animated the courtyard of our house. The baggage that our servants had prepared was carried out but we lost time waiting for the *respa*s (pack animals). When they finally arrived there weren't enough of them, which forced us to leave six loads and these should reach us tomorrow here at Matho, our first stop.

Upon leaving the courtyard of our house, musicians, singers, beggars and other bearers of good wishes crowded against both sides of the doorway to greet us. Finally, we got under way. And

> there we were, embarked on a journey which is to last three to four months until we reach Lhasa...
>
> The day was very difficult. It was hot. A strong wind was blowing and all sorts of thoughts went through my mind, dominated by the pain of separation.
>
> We arrived in Matho at five o'clock in the afternoon. In spite of the excellent welcome waiting for the caravan from the *gopa* (village chief), the sadness of having left my home didn't loosen its grip on me.

Today, re-reading these notes thirty-eight years later, I again see the young man, full of contradictory feelings, who wrote them. Aware of the commercial and political importance of our expedition, I still suffered a good deal for having had to so quickly interrupt the happiness of a marriage which had been celebrated less than three weeks earlier. The profession of a caravaneer in Central Asia had certainly not made our elders sentimental, and if I wanted to follow the family vocation, I would first of all have to learn to get over many attachments. I was still far from this and my eyes were wet with tears as I put out the candle to forget my sorrow in sleep.

Matho, the terminus of the first lap of our journey, is a typical Ladakhi village with a Buddhist monastery perched like a citadel on a rocky spur with numerous *chorten*s or stupas rising in layers on the foothills of the Zangskar mountain range. This Himalayan chain closes in the high Indus valley to the south to form Ladakh, properly speaking. To the north, the peaks of the mountain chain called Ladakh rise more than 6,000 metres, passable by an ascending track up to the Khardung La pass above Leh and opening onto the valleys of Shyok and Nubra from where one can see the gigantic peaks of the Karakoram range. To the west, the valley slopes gently down towards Baltistan and Gilgit, today administered by Pakistan. To the east, the valley narrows, rising towards western Tibet where the river has its source.

Forming a slope of the 'Roof of the World', Ladakh at this time was one of the most isolated countries of the globe. Srinagar, the capital of Kashmir and the nearest city, was a twelve days' journey away on ponyback. The road, or rather the carriageable track which now allows lorries and jeeps to cover the same distance (434 kilometres) in two days, didn't exist and nobody dared land by plane in such a high and lost land (3,400 metres).

Ladakh offers only scanty resources and the inhabitants lead hard lives. At the end of that September of 1942 the scenery was austere. The barley having been harvested and the meadow grass yellowed, almost all the green had disappeared. Only the willows and poplars which grew near the streams still kept their leaves, as well as the apple and apricot trees which surrounded several farms. Snow already powdered the peaks. In two months it would cover even the bottom of the valley but with only a light layer because the climate is relatively dry behind the Himalayan barrier. At that time we would be crossing even higher and more austere lands, through frozen deserts where the mere thought of the Ladakhi homeland would conjure up the sweetness of living.

An important crossroad of the caravan tracks of Central Asia, it was due to its geographical location that Leh became the capital of Ladakh—if the title of capital can be applied to such a modest township. This, then, explains my family's vocation.

However, it was not in order to trade that our ancestor Sheikh Asad Radhu came to settle in Ladakh two centuries ago. This religious man had left the pleasant valley of Kashmir to preach Islam to the inhabitants of this high country whose climate is so harsh. Some people, it seems, were receptive to his words. In any case, his memory is not totally forgotten and a Persian inscription in the Sunni mosque in Leh mentions his name.

His father, Sheikh Muhammad Radhu, had been an eminent religious figure since he had the honour of displaying the reliquary containing a hair of our holy Prophet in the celebrated sanctuary of Hazratbal in Srinagar. This sacred relic is still there. The Radhus were descended from a Hindu-Brahmin family belonging to a sub-caste of 'Kashmiri Pandits' named Trakou, a name that still exists in India. They were converted to Islam at a time difficult to specify.

The first Radhu who settled in Ladakh, Sheikh Asad, had left brothers in Kashmir whose descendants still live in Srinagar. His son, Faruq Radhu, was the first to become a caravaneer merchant. Thanks to this long-distance commerce, our family was to acquire great fame on the tracks of Central Asia.

Faruq Radhu seems to have maintained close relations with the *gyalpo*s, the reigning princes of Ladakh. The memory of his name, which became Phorokpa (Ladakhis aren't able to pronounce 'F'), has remained attached to the village of Stok near Leh where a royal castle is located and still inhabited by the Rani, a highly respected descendant of the former dynasty. Faruq had received a piece of land there where he had a house built in pure Tibetan style.

The deep, ancient roots of our family thus permit us to affirm our adherence to the country as much as our co-patriots of the Buddhist religion. Although the Muslims remain in the minority in the high valley of the Indus, it is false to claim, as certain observers have, that they make up a foreign element in Ladakh. In fact, Muslims have been present there for centuries. An integral part of the population, they have lived in perfect harmony with the tenants of other religions and have even often realised a harmonious symbiosis of the two cultures, Buddhist and Islamic. My grandfather, Haji Muhammad Siddiq, beloved patriarch and respected by everyone, was a particularly remarkable illustration of this typical Ladakhi synthesis: his face, his clothing, his manners, the way he had furnished and decorated his home which was always welcoming and where he always appeared in garments quite similar to Tibetan dress but wearing a white turban.

I can affirm that in Ladakh I never experienced any animosity due to the difference in religions. In the villages, Buddhists as well as Muslims called us *Akhon Pa*, a Central Asian expression which originally designated mullahs, or religious teachers of Islam. The title of Khodja, or *khwaja* which we normally bear, comes from

Kashmir and is used mostly in Leh. Moreover, a fact which seems incredible in Indian society compartmentalised into castes, there even exist alliances amongst families of the two communities.

The Lopchak caravan bore witness to these excellent relations. Directed by a Muslim, it was carrying the official homage to the Dalai Lama from the Ladakhi Buddhists who recognised him as their supreme spiritual authority. In addition, amongst the servants of the caravan appeared two or three youths who were committed to becoming admitted as novices in the monasteries of Tibet.

The day after our departure was already a day of rest and inactivity since we had to wait for the six pack animals which had missed our departure the evening before in Leh. My diary also notes that Khwaja Abdul Aziz received a telegram from the wazir of Leh authorising the caravan to carry a certain quantity of grain for our use. In fact, the government of Kashmir had just decreed the prohibition of exporting cereals to Tibet, a probable consequence of the war which had turned the world upside down but which nobody thought of behind the Himalayan barrier.

21 September 1942
We took leave of the *gopa* of Matho. Climbing the length of the track to Martselang, we took a last glimpse at Leh. The weather is fine and sunny and we are travelling at a pleasant pace.

We stopped at three in the afternoon at Martselang where we were offered tea, then we left for Upshi, the end of this lap. We arrived at six and the luggage not until nine when we had already had supper. Everyone was tired. We only set up the small tents and the servants slept under the stars.

22 September 1942
I awoke after a good sleep but it was terribly cold early in the morning. After having shaved, prayed and had breakfast, I was ready. Our cook left first. With the head of the caravan, the servants and mule-drivers, we did not leave until eleven o'clock.

The day was very hot. At two o'clock we arrived at Miroo and found a warm welcome with the *gopa.* The cook had had time to prepare everything. We had tea and savoured all sorts of sweets.

An old family friend came at five o'clock with a teapot and some gifts. What a fine way to greet guests! There is something very admirable about the manners of these people towards each other.

We talked leisurely and spoke of the future. Tibet will not be able to remain a passive spectator. She must change. The old traditions of the fifteenth century, even that which is best of them, must give way to the culture of the twentieth century. I am fortunate to have grown up within the framework of an ancient and beautiful culture. But I was later re-moulded by a modern education, with its qualities and defects. At present, I feel it will be difficult to re-adapt myself to this world where nothing seems to change.

At this time, all our family lived in areas which had escaped colonial domination and the impact of modern civilisation. The two older sons of Faruq Radhu, Haider Shah and Nasr Shah, had established a flourishing commerce in Ladakh. His third son had settled in Tibet where he had married a Chinese Muslim. Relations remained very close between the cousins of Tibet and Ladakh, and intermarriages were common. My paternal grandfather, son of Haider Shah, had married a Buddhist of Tsethang, a town located several days' walk from Lhasa.

Members of the two older branches had also developed their commercial exchanges beyond Karakoram, in Sinkiang or Chinese Turkestan where some took women and acquired property. Thus did the blood of the principal races and nations of Asia mix in the Radhu veins.

Those who had gone through Western-type schools, as one of my cousins and I had done, remained very rare exceptions. The contact which the others were able to establish with the outside world was still very limited.

Residing initially at Stok, some 15 kilometres from Leh, after the family became important they built a beautiful house in the little capital very near the royal palace and on the same crag. Still called *Khangpa Nyingpa* (old house), it has remained the property of a cousin. I was born in one of the houses which was built later and located a little farther down.

In Leh, the Radhus held an eminent and envied position. They were wealthy, possessed beautiful property and large amounts of merchandise passed through their warehouses. Everyone in Ladakh knew them and their reputation spread to neighbouring countries, in particular to Tibet, where they maintained relations with the best families of the nobility and even the direct entourage of the Dalai Lama.

Several members of preceding generations attained high social positions and were even granted official distinctions. It is thus that Ghulam Muhammad, who was on the best terms with the court of the Maharaja as well as with the British resident at Srinagar, was authorised to add the title of Khan Sahib to his name. He was introduced into the leadership circles of Tibet where the English political agent had wanted to make his son, who unfortunately died prematurely, a sort of head of the Muslim community of Lhasa.

As for my great-uncle Ghulam Rasul, he had received the title of Khan Bahadur from Lord Minto, Viceroy of India, in recognition of services rendered to the Swedish explorer Sven Hedin, who often mentions our family in his work *Trans-Himalaya*. Ghulam Rasul was known for his simplicity, piety and generosity, out of loyalty to the tradition. He had refused the offer which the famous traveller had made to him to send his son to the West to give him a modern education. It was in the same spirit that my grandfather Haji Muhammad Siddiq had tried in vain to oppose my departure for Srinagar where I was to follow courses in an English-type school.

On this issue, my grandfather disagreed with his cousin

Abdullah Shah, who, on good terms with the British administration, had been named *aksakal*, which means in the Turkoman language 'the man with the white beard'. This function consisted mainly of overseeing the activities of the Turkmenian merchants of Ladakh. To carry out his duties, he depended on the official called charas officer, 'charas' meaning hashish, a grass which Chinese Turkistan cultivated in great quantities and which circulated in India. It was an officially controlled traffic and, as *aksakal*, Abdullah Shah was part of this system of control.

A supporter of modern ideas, he was of the opinion that young people should have a Western-type education and this drew the reproaches of my grandfather.

'You are going to give these young people over to the Shaitan (devil),' he told him.

Haji Muhammad Siddiq, my grandfather, was a patriarch who reigned over a household of some twenty people, members of the family and domestic help. He himself was one of the most eminent and popular persons of Leh, where he was happy enough to have been able to preserve the family traditions until his death.

His prestige and authority had won him the privilege, sometimes shared with the Buddhist family of the Srangnara, of directing the Lopchak caravan. Every time he led the caravan, he recorded a description of the journey in Urdu or Persian upon his return. These notebooks were veritable guides for Khwaja Abdul Aziz when it was his turn to direct the Lopchak. He accompanied us in 1942 and in the evenings of the journey or during the long days of inactivity which the vicissitudes of the expedition imposed upon us, I consulted these notebooks, often beneficially.

23 September 1942

It is around five in the afternoon and I am in Gya where we arrived at around one o'clock. Our watches stopped last night in Miroo probably due to the altitude. We reset them according to the projection of the shadows on the ground.

Gya is a large and beautiful village. The Lopchak is well received here according to custom. The new *gopa* belongs to a wealthy family of the area. His welcome is in conformity with the traditions, notably that of the *kalchor*.

This latter term, borrowed from Ladakhi dialect, refers to the welcoming ceremony or of leave-taking celebrated for a guest of note and includes offerings like milk, *chang* (a light beer in countries of Tibetan culture) or even cool water sometimes, dried fruit, rice or barley flour used to make *tsampa*. It was usually the children and elderly people of their grandparents' generation who brought food and drink on beautiful brass-wire trays and offered them to the travellers. The latter, in exchange, gave a few coins as symbolic payment. Moreover, the entire *kalchor* ceremony was symbolic since the guests hardly touched the offerings. But at that time I saw in all this mainly a sort of tribute due to the persons responsible for a caravan as important as ours on the part of the villagers.

24 September 1942
We left Gya with *kalchor* and other traditional greetings of the local people. This is the last village of permanent habitation before the deserts of western Tibet, the immensity of which we have now penetrated, although politically the highlands of the Rupshu, which we shall have to cross these days, are attached to the state of the Maharaja of Jammu and Kashmir.

On this twenty-fourth day of September I reflected a great deal. However, it was the hardest day since our departure from Leh. Normally the day's walk ended at Debrengma, but the Rupshopas (nomads of the region) were not able to receive us. We therefore had to continue to Zara. We are at the foot of the Taklang pass where the track goes through leading to Gartok in Tibet. I found the road terribly difficult. We were walking against a wind of sand that fustigated us. I then recalled the ideas of Rousseau on natural education. He taught that it is by instruction and experience of the natural elements that we become true men. In any case, I feel that nature has just taught me a lesson.

Pass after pass, valley after valley, all this walking has made me unbearably tired. And at such an altitude—probably approaching 5,000 metres—we are suffering from altitude sickness. Almost everyone has colic or vomiting. We can barely drink or eat.

I feel worse than last year when I easily climbed the peaks to the west of Toklang whilst taking mountain walks in that same region. Today a few steps take a great amount of effort. My health must have weakened, undoubtedly because of my prolonged stays in India. Physically, I led too easy an existence there and now I am no longer able to live normally as a Tibetan.

We arrived in Zara at about four in the afternoon. We were received according to the Lopchak traditions but the Rupshopas refused to set up our tents. We had to do it ourselves, at the same time feeling the difficult effects of the altitude.

This evening I understand how important it is to have a good tent. Outside the wind is blowing in a rage. Tomorrow is the fifteenth day of the eighth Tibetan month and the night promises us a splendid full moon. The Rupshopa *gopa* (chief of the camp) invites us to stay here in Zara tomorrow to watch a horse race. We're obliged to accept because no one will provide us with horses to continue our journey. We can already hear music and drums in the evening.

25 September 1942

The night was bad and we slept restlessly. Khwaja Abdul Aziz is suffering from a severe migraine and I myself feel dizzy. No one feels well but Uncle has experience of these regions and, knowing the cause of these discomforts, is not worried.

The *gopa* came to have a talk with us. He notified us that an officer from the mines sent by the government is in the region because the mountain chain which extends into Tibetan territory is rich in sulphur and borax. In spite of the difficulties in exploiting these minerals, there is a lively competition amongst rival companies, each one attempting to obtain the monopoly.

The music reminds me that the horse race has begun. I can't resist going. Our two servants, Lobzang and Rabgyas, accompany me.

I've returned from the festival. This magnificent spectacle gave me an impressive glimpse of the life of the Rupshu nomads. What a hard life they have! They appeared to me at once innocent, dirty and happy.

Now again it is with joy that I recall this gathering of Rupshu nomads and their horses. None of the races which I watched later in Calcutta or Darjeeling gave me as much pleasure. Here at nearly 5,000 metres of altitude in the austere background of the region near the lake, which maps generally call Tso Morari, the race represented an extraordinary performance of sport. The horsemen, young and of a mature age, were soaked in sweat as well as their intrepid little horses which, in the thin air, breathed like bellows and shared in the general excitement. The spectators, many of whom were women, clapped to the rhythm of the drums. Food and drink were served and our servant Rabgyas, who had swallowed large glassfuls of *chang*, the Tibetan beer, had difficulty returning to his tent. But the pleasure of the festival was not merely profane, because rosaries and prayer wheels were seen in many hands and the sacred mantra remained present.

26 September 1942
The morning was very cold. Uncle seems to feel better, although he slept badly. As nobody was ready, we didn't leave until noon. The lap went as usual. We stopped at Thukje where we had a splendid view of the lake formed by the accumulation of water coming from several valleys. As we approached, we noticed many ducks and other beautiful birds. We arrived at Nganor at five o'clock. The moon rose and is reflected in the lake. A pleasant, light breeze is blowing. There is no one to help us here and we have to depend upon ourselves. Lobzang, Rabgyas and Qadir have gone to collect wood so that we can heat our tents.

27 September 1942
This morning a beautiful sun shone on the lake and the surrounding snow-covered peaks. A marvellous spectacle.

Whilst riding I reflected a good deal on the life which was already behind me, on my years of college and university and on the few months I had just spent at home. As for the future, far too divided between the high aspirations of my soul and my material ambitions, I can't envisage it.

I was still absorbed in my thoughts when we arrived at Angano. It was two o'clock. I am writing these notes on a beautiful, sunny afternoon. We are waiting for our baggage to arrive to set up our tents. The Korzoqpas have welcomed us warmly but the supplies destined for our caravan are hardly satisfactory. Nevertheless *respa* ponies have come from Korzoq with yaks, so we won't have to wait for them tomorrow.

28 September 1942

Our departure was delayed because the Korzoqpas had not sent enough men for the number of animals. Our servants had to go ahead by themselves with the load assisted by several Korzoqpa who were present, so we weren't able to leave until the beginning of the afternoon. Passing through Puga, I noticed workers on nearby mountains working at sulphur mining, an abundant mineral in this region.

Today's lap was the longest since our departure and we arrived here at Langsham at seven-thirty. We were put up in the *kothi* (travellers' rest house) which is nearly acceptable. We have two rooms, one for Uncle and me, the other serving as a kitchen and dormitory for the servants. Padma Tsering, another of our servants, left Leh several weeks before us and has joined us here. He went all the way to Gartok (western Tibet) which he left seventeen days ago. He had to delay in Demchog (the first Tibetan town after the Kashmir border) waiting for news of our caravan. He also obtained some information as to the whereabouts of our merchandise expected from Tashigang (in the same region).

In effect, during the preceding Lopchak two years ago, the threat of the Hasakapa raids (a Tibetan term designating the Kazakhs) had forced Khwaja Abdul Aziz to delay considerably his journey to Lhasa and to leave most of his merchandise as well

> as a hundred horses in Tashigang. Now we had to collect them to take them to their destination. The people who were to assure our transport have made unacceptable demands and are charging double the normal price. This affair is going to oblige us to extend our stay here. While we were waiting, Rabgyas, Lobzang, Padma and Rasul charmed us by singing very beautiful traditional songs of Ladakh and Baltistan, called *zhunglu*.

After crossing the Indus at the Choklamsar bridge several kilometres from Leh, our route had gone along the left bank of the river and left the Upshi river. From there we headed south. We went further and further away from the river until we reached Tso Morari, which my journal calls Nganor Lake. In fact, in these regions, which have never been precisely documented, place names are irregular and the few maps at our disposition have considerable differences. Nevertheless, after having passed near Korzog along the bank of this lake, our caravan continued east again and approached the Indus valley as well as the frontier of Tibet, properly speaking. From then on we were entering the most hazardous phase of the expedition and were to face risks coming from men as well as nature.

First of all, there were the famous Hasakapas or Kazakhs who made the track unsafe. Muslim nomads, they had penetrated into the high plateaus of Tibet, starting from Sinkiang. Originally natives of the USSR, they had gone into Chinese territory to escape religious persecution. Small groups had also infiltrated Kashmir but the Maharaja, himself of the Hindu religion, didn't look favourably upon these newcomers who didn't fail to swell the Muslim population that was in the majority in his states. Some Muslim princes of India then agreed to receive them and it is for this reason that ever since then there have been small communities of Kazakhs in cities like Hyderabad and Bhopal.

In Tibet, the Hasakapas hadn't come with hostile intentions. They were merely in search of pasture for their herds in the vast area of Changthang (or northern plains). Nevertheless, there were some run-ins with certain Tibetan nomads of a quarrelsome nature who claimed to be the only masters of these deserts. The scuffles degenerated into raids, then into punitive expeditions, and on both sides bellicose instincts took over. The result was a general impoverishment of the population, already much decreased in western Tibet, and for caravaneers, the risk of being pillaged, if not assassinated.

As for nature in the Trans-Himalayan highlands, she could be mercilessly rigorous. Our people had already had several bitter experiences such as that of 1932, which turned into a veritable disaster.

Snow fell that year in the Tibetan Changthang desert, the likes of which had never been seen before in. living memory. Accompanied by an uncle and three cousins, my father Khwaja Abdul Karim had left for Lhasa with a caravan of mules loaded with merchandise. In the region of Kailash, they encountered a layer of snow so deep that the animals were immobilised and all perished down to the very last one. By an almost incredible feat they managed to save their own lives and reach Lhasa, but they had lost all their cargo.

I was a child at this time and the image of my grandfather overcome with worry remains in my memory. He only had two daughters, and my father, who had married one of them and for whom he had much affection, was his principal collaborator and successor assigned to head the family commerce.

In the morning and evening, it was his habit to take a walk in the streets of Leh, and the people, knowing there was no news of the caravan, shared his anxiety. Finally, a telegram arrived which announced that all the men were safe and sound. My grandfather's face brightened, tears came to his eyes, and he immediately withdrew to pray.

He returned saying, 'Let us rejoice. They are alive! And let the merchandise stay where it is!'

As for my father, his financial situation was jeopardised since his merchandise had remained under the Changthang snow. He returned to his brother-in-law, of course, who lived in Lhasa, but it wasn't to his relatives whom he turned to in order to obtain the necessary assistance for re-establishing his business. He took a lively interest in the culture and customs of Tibet where he had numerous friends, particularly amongst the Khampas whose dress he often wore. It was the Khampa merchants who lent him enough money to enable him to obtain some fifteen mules as well as servants. I still remember his return to Leh with his new caravan, himself dressed like a Khampa.

Now my father, resolved to persevere in the rectification of his situation, was above all determined to repay the Khampa merchants the money which he owed them. Against the advice of Haji Muhammad Siddiq who, aware of his poor health, would have liked to have kept him for some time in Ladakh, he left for Lhasa with his caravan soon after that. Suffering from a stomach ulcer which he had never taken care of, he was to die en route, in the middle of the desert, soon after crossing the Mayum La pass, which is located between the Indus and Brahmaputra basins.

After burying him, his servants, none of whom were Muslims, began to quarrel amongst themselves over the merchandise of the caravan. One of them, a particularly loyal and faithful Khampa, succeeded in persuading the others that the cargo should be transported intact to Lhasa where the opinion of Haji Muhammad Siddiq would be sought. At Shigatse, some of my father's cousins, knowing that his mules were carrying gifts that were destined for them, wanted to take possession of the caravan. The servants were absolutely opposed to this. They responded to the cousins' insistence by threatening to use their weapons and did not allow anyone to touch the merchandise except a representative duly sent by Haji Muhammad Siddiq. The latter, informed of the situation, asked his other son-in-law, Abdul Aziz, who was in Lhasa, to take care of the cargo.

The premature death of my father was one of the causes of the decline of the family. To replace him, Haji Muhammad Siddiq asked Abdul Aziz to leave Lhasa and come settle near him in Leh. Although he was more Tibetan than Ladakhi, my uncle accepted and thus undertook the journey accompanied by his wife and nine-year-old daughter. He had loaded his goods onto my father's mules and took a few of the same servants.

The caravan followed the usual track passing through Shigatse, Lhatse and the high Brahmaputra. Arrived in Toksum, three days' walk from Mayum La, the travellers heard that Khampa brigands infested the region and had already attacked and pillaged several nomad camps. Khwaja Abdul Aziz was not a man to be stopped by such rumours. He only took the precaution of verifying that his Mauser rifle, which he carefully cleaned, was in good order. And the caravan went on its way.

After the caravan had crossed the Mayum La, an episode occurred which has remained famous in the family annals. Abdul Aziz and his companions set up their bivouac on a deserted plateau at a high altitude. As usual, they let the mules graze around the campsite during the night. In the morning the servants had gone to collect them when my uncle noticed a group of horsemen in the distance. At first he thought it was a caravan, but when they approached, their gait seemed unusual to him and his suspicions were aroused. The strangers came up to the bivouac and whilst conversing amongst themselves, began to attach their mounts to tent pegs. Abdul Aziz noticed that each one was armed with a long flint rifle with a powder keg as well as a sword. One of the two servants who had remained in the bivouac, himself a Khampa, pointed out to them that no one had authorised them to touch the tents, to which they replied with arrogance that they had no authorisation to take anything from anyone.

So Khwaja Abdul Aziz, holding his Mauser, approached and sought to drive them away: 'You have no business here. Go away. All this is ours.'

'Who are you?' asked the bandits.

'I'm going to show you who I am,' answered Uncle in a tone expressing not the least fright but rather, growing anger.

Then the bandits began to load their rifles. Abdul Aziz, even angrier, cried out to them: 'Do you think we came into the desert without better weapons than yours? For us, your rifles are only sticks.'

At that moment, the little girl, frightened, began to howl but her mother, who was calmly eating her *tsampa*, ticked her off sharply, 'You should be ashamed to cry. Tears have never helped anything!' And, baring her chest she turned towards the marauders, 'Just kill us if it pleases you!'

Less courageous, the cook of the caravan, a Ladakhi Muslim, prostrated, terrorised, before the bandits crying, 'Kuch, Kuch! Please, please! (spare us)'.

Abdul Aziz's indignation reached its peak. He railed at his cook: 'You're as crazy as you are cowardly if you think people like this know what mercy is! You're no man!' And he spat in his face. Then, aiming his rifle at the closest bandit, he shouted to them, 'If you want to fight, I'm ready. But whatever happens, don't forget that there is law in Tibet and the government has the means of arresting criminals like you and punishing them as they deserve.'

The brigands made hesitating movements, looked at each other and exchanged a few words, which the Khampa servant understood. They wondered if they weren't in the presence of a high-ranking official and if it wouldn't be more prudent to let him remain alive. At the same time, they noticed the other servant coming back with the mules. So they withdrew, untied their horses, jumped into their saddles and galloped off.

Abdul Aziz followed them with his eyes and saw them reach a glen where some companions were waiting for them. He remained turned in their direction for a long time, his rifle in his hand, ready to fire at the first one who still dared to approach.

The little girl who was so frightened was later to become my wife. She kept all the details of the episode engraved in her memory.

Nevertheless, the caravan set off again with no further mishap. At the next lap, nomads who already knew what had happened came and prostrated in front of Khwaja Abdul Aziz. It seemed miraculous to them that he had escaped from the bandits when so many of their own people had fallen victim to them. He himself only made this brief comment about the incident.

'If those villains hadn't made me so angry, we would all be dead.'

Uncle had, in fact, a strong temperament and he wasn't lacking in pride. Perhaps he kept something of the arrogance of certain aristocratic Tibetans with whom he had been in contact for so long in Lhasa. Such a character undoubtedly made him a respected and even feared leader, but did not perfectly suit the occupation which was to be his from then on in the trading company directed by my grandfather Haji Muhammad Siddiq. With his wife and daughter, he moved into the big house in Leh over which the patriarch reigned and with whom he became the principal collaborator in place of my father. It was thus that he was assigned to lead the Lopchak first in 1940 and then in 1942 when I accompanied him.

However, certain indications already made us sense that the days of the trade caravans were approaching their end. My cousin Abdul Haqq, who didn't like the precarious existence that these long expeditions into high desert lands forced one to lead, was interested in new means of transport and in the possibility of travelling more rapidly and safely between Leh and Lhasa through India. He had taken the opportunity, which he thought was good, of selling the mules and all the caravan supplies that we still owned and the family bitterly reproached him for this. Consequently, at the time of the 1942 Lopchak, we no longer had a caravan which belonged to us. We were entirely dependent on the supplies of the Tibetan administration who put at our disposition 200 to 250 mules whereas on the Indian side, the government of Kashmir advanced us the modest sum of 10,000 rupees.

At the end of that September of 1942 when we went down towards the Indus after having crossed the Rupshu, also called Ladakhi Changthang, and when we approached the border of Tibet, Khwaja Abdul Aziz at least had the satisfaction of telling himself that he was going to cross it as an official. As for myself, I was not easily consolable, having had to be separated from my young wife. All sorts of confused thoughts rushed into my mind. My diary is a witness to this. I also express in it the confused hope of finding light at the end of the way and I wrote:

'Lhasa, perhaps, will give a direction to my life.'

CHAPTER 2

TRADITION AND PRESTIGE

The insecurity caused by the Hasakapa incursions and the steps taken to recover the merchandise left in the region two years before forced us to stay in Langsham until 3 October, not far from the Indus valley and the Tibetan border. Of this prolonged stop my diary especially recalls the hot bath I was able to take in the *kothi* which lodged us, a particularly welcome event as it was the first since our departure from Leh.

Finally, our caravan set off again. It stopped before sunset in a vale whence we could already see the river.

> Surrounded by glaciers, rocky crests and arid slopes, I delight in looking at the grassy valley, yellow now, and the pure, blue Indus which flows southward. What a beautiful evening. The sky is clear. A pleasant breeze is blowing. Uncle is busy writing his journal and Rasul preparing the evening meal. Rabgayas and Padma have gone to collect dry brush to make a fire.
>
> I am thinking of the heavy responsibilities my uncle has, of the life which we must lead together and the work of the servants. Certainly, their task is hard...

The next day, 4 October 1942, as we were walking in the direction of a horizon lightly powdered with snow, an unpleasant thought came to my mind: the war. However, behind our Asian mountains, the terrible events which were turning the world upside down seemed of little concern to us.

> In this desert where everything is so peaceful and harmonious, what should one think of the civilised world? What do all these battles, this destruction, this human loss, this diplomatic manoeuvring mean for civilisation? Where are these confrontations going to lead us? In any case we must prepare ourselves for a world overturned by convolutions and revolutions. One has to adapt oneself to it. Even Tibet herself may be affected.

On 6 October we arrived in Demchog, the first location on the Tibetan side of the border, which used to belong to Ladakh. In the seventeenth century, the *gyalpo* of Ladakh, Delek Namgyal, unwisely intervened on the side of Bhutan in a war opposing Tibet. The government of the Dalai Lama retorted by sending an army consisting mainly of Mongols against the *gyalpo*. The Mongols, after having fought the Ladakhis, were stopped by Kashmiri troops who had come to the rescue. A peace treaty was then negotiated between Lhasa and Leh, and Ladakh had to give up the high Indus valley as far as Demchog with the exception of the enclave of Mansar where we were to stop several days later.

It is this same treaty which instituted the Lopchak, and, inversely, the Zhungtsong. The status of the two caravans included great advantages because in Tibetan territory they were authorised to levy any requisition which they might need and call for the work of the serfs for their transport. In the state of Kashmir the system was obviously different and the government paid subsidies to cover their costs.

After being guests of the village leader who extended genuine cordiality to us, we set off again the next day for Tashigang. The welcome there was much less keen and we had to set up our tents ourselves. We had to stay there two nights because Rasul, our Muslim cook, had fallen ill.

I now wonder whether this health failure was not linked to the profligate life which he led. At almost every village where we stopped for the night, Rasul succeeded in winning the favours of a girl. These successful attempts, to tell the truth, did not testify to a particular ability to seduce, taking into account the loose morals widespread amongst many peoples of the Mongol race. The fact is that he suffered from an unrespectable ailment from which he was never to completely recover. During this journey, when he found himself incapable of fulfilling his function as a cook, he was replaced by his assistant Lobzang, a young Buddhist of sixteen years who had left his village of Sabu, near Leh, to enter the monastery of Tashilungpo as a novice in Shigatse and we couldn't complain about him.

Despite the inconvenience of the time lost in our uncomfortable camp of Tashigang, I was seized by the powerful charm of this high country. And I noted in my diary:

> This Tibetan land blessed with such magnificent natural landscape but so sparsely inhabited is at once light and darkness. I feel more and more at home in Tibet, with its immensity, the men I meet here, with its birds, climate, its light and dark visions, with its past, its present and its future... My mirror reflects the image of my face bearing the mark of sunburn and frost bites. I am happy to feel that I am physically adapting to the country.

It was a young man of twenty years and with a romantic temperament who wrote these lines. Re-reading them now, I am inclined to smile but I also see in them an expression of this fascination with Tibet that I had felt from my first stay in Lhasa two years earlier. During the entire Lopchak, the thought that I would soon be in Lhasa stimulated me and dissipated the melancholy which sometimes overtook me.

On the morning of 9 October, Rasul's condition was well enough to permit us to lift camp and set off again. After losing our way in the scrubland of Gar, we made our entrance into Gargonsa, or Gar Dzong, one of the two 'capitals' of the province of Ngasikorsum, the other being Gartok or Garyarsa, two days' walk to the east. The place consisted of nomad tents and a few houses, as well as hovels. Our caravan was warmly welcomed here.

We were lodged in the 'residence' of one of the two governors (in the Tibetan administration, all posts of any importance had two officers, one civil and the other religious) where we were to spend three nights.

In Gargonsa we had difficult accounts to settle with the cattle breeders and shepherds of the region. For several generations our family had been owners here of a fairly large quantity of cattle, especially yaks and goats, and our renewable property rights were transferred to the herds. The breeders profited from this but they owed us dues which they paid mainly in the form of butter. This produced accounts which were even more complicated by the fact that the lists attached to them were written in Tibetan characters which we could only decipher with difficulty. Moreover, the poverty of these people prevented us from exacting the entire payment from them. I even came to ask myself if this system was morally justified and if it were permissible to levy taxes from cattle which our ancestors had acquired so long ago.

Confronted with these inherited customs of the past and, in a general way, in contact with these peoples who still escape all modern influences, I often reacted in conformity to what I had learnt during my studies. Assuredly, I remained attached to the traditions the value of which I discerned; I respected and admired a man like Haji Muhammad Siddiq, my grandfather, who personified them. But the modern mentality had penetrated me through my teachers and the books they had made me read. I had become in a way one of those many Orientals who with a Western education, were caught between two cultures and had lost the homogeneity of their personality.

In Ladakh, we remained relatively distant from modern influences. The life of the people had hardly changed during the preceding centuries. The wheel was not used and electricity was totally unknown. However, one suspected that beyond the peaks a world of unheard of possibilities and irresistible seduction opened up. Already as schoolchildren in the primary classes in

Leh, we admired our elders who had crossed the passes leading to Kashmir to experience this modernism whose marvels haunted our imagination.

My first school was a traditional Qur'anic *maktab*. It was run by an old beloved and respected master whom we called Memey Lassa. Amongst the students, I believed myself to be particularly important since I was the only male descendant of Memey Siddiq Mal, as my grandfather was usually called, and who held considerable prestige. With my classmates, boys and girls, we sat on the ground around Memey Lassa, who often fell asleep in the middle of the lesson, and who unfortunately, died shortly afterwards.

I was then sent to Memey Ghulam Muhammad, the *muezzin* of the mosque, whom we called 'Akhon' (preacher). Thanks to him, I made good progress in Urdu and Arabic.

Then I was made to enter the secondary school of Leh. A high level of instruction was assured by Kashmiri Pandits who were certainly better than teachers nowadays. Their methods were undoubtedly less modern but they were more efficacious in any case. High-caste Brahmins, they strictly observed the rules of their community and regularly attended the Hindu temple of Leh with their wives. This did not at all prevent them from being very close to their students of a different religion whom they sometimes invited into their homes and, similarly, we received them into our homes. One felt that they belonged to the same traditional world into which we were all integrated.

The first language we learnt was not our native language, Ladakhi, a Tibetan dialect, but Urdu. Moreover, the Muslim students had to follow courses in Persian as a second language, so we did not even have the opportunity to learn the Tibetan alphabet. In practice, the Tibetan lessons were reserved for the Buddhists and I always regretted not having been able to attend them.

On the whole, I wasn't a brilliant student, but average, and I passed my examinations without too much difficulty, despite a weakness in mathematics. The programme obligatorily included gymnastics and sport, in particular, field hockey, which I didn't like at all.

Outside of school the young men had a preference for football. They played it mainly in the winter because the layer of snow was never too deep. Although less popular than in Gilgit, polo was sometimes played on our little Ladakhi ponies and I remember the surprise caused one day by the arrival of polo players mounted on Kashmiri horses which seemed gigantic to us.

Whenever a representative of the Maharaja or of the British administration arrived from Srinagar, all the schoolchildren of Leh were mobilised to welcome him. Under the supervision of the physical education master, we lined up along the high street to greet the important person, which we did willingly because his visit gave us a day off.

According to the English system, the final year was the eighth. When I left school, a decisive episode occurred in my life. I was fourteen years old. Most of the students who had reached this level learnt a trade or went to work in some family business. My grandfather strongly desired that I also begin an apprenticeship in the trade which he managed. He had already envisaged entrusting me to one of his nephews who knew the trade well and who had experience with the caravans.

However, I had a strong desire to go see the outside world of which so many amazing things were said. This desire was aroused by the proposals that my great-uncle Abdullah Shah, the *aksakal,* had passed on to me. According to him, only a modern type of education would turn me into an important person and worthy of the social position of the family. I allowed myself to be all the more easily convinced that, in fact, the rare 'educated' men whom we had known in our valley seemed to carry an aura of all the prestige of civilisation. Certainly, the English who sometimes visited Ladakh seemed strange and disconcerting to us, but being adolescents, we would have been ready to imitate them in everything, for example, to give up the *gos*, the Ladakhi dress, which we always wore and wear trousers like they did.

Although during most of the year no English people stayed in Leh, there was a delegation of the British administration which was much more prestigious than the office of the *wazir* representing the government of the Maharaja. The least important of its pen-pushers was already a person of rank. However, the British administration did not get involved in local affairs and occupied itself exclusively with what was called the 'Treaty Route', that is, the caravan track which, starting from Srinagar, crossed Ladakh and by way of the Karakoram led to Sinkiang. The treaty in question was the one which the government of India had signed following the military campaign led by Lord Durand in 1891 in the northernmost part of the state of Kashmir in order to assure the liberty and security of the commerce along the tracks leading into Chinese territory.

In actual fact, this British post wasn't very important. It was rather a pole of attraction and a reminder of the supreme power which ruled over the empire of India. Its presence inspired ambitious Ladakhis with the desire to learn the language of these lords and educate themselves in the same way as they were. The *aksakal*, in particular, enjoyed great respect because he maintained close relations with the British. He even received the British commissioner into his home when the latter came to Leh for his annual stay where he owned a beautiful summer residence. The *aksakal* spoke English and had adopted certain modern habits and, in particular, had European-type chairs in his house.

My grandfather strongly opposed these tendencies as well as all foreign influences which penetrated Ladakh little by little and damaged our traditional customs. For example, those who drank their tea in the English style irritated him.

'Why are you so intent on putting sugar in your tea, much more expensive, whereas in Ladakh we have always put salt, which, in reality, you prefer since you have drunk it like this since your childhood. By drinking English tea, you imitate even the gestures of the English and make fools of yourselves.'

We, the younger generation, were more and more inclined to view him as 'backward' and 'old hat'. I often told myself that I would have to shake off the weight of his tutelage if I wanted to 'progress'. With the passage of time and given the present state of the world, it seems evident to me that in the final analysis it was he who was right.

In fact, Haji Muhammad Siddiq realised to some extent at least the necessity of adapting oneself to the modern world. For example, understanding that a merchant should know English, he had sent me to take lessons at the Moravian mission of Leh whose headquarters were next to our house.

Ever since the last century, these Protestant missionaries who were still widespread in other regions of Central Asia, mainly in Sinkiang, had played a special role in the history of Ladakh, whence they established the first relations with the Western world. The two most noteworthy were A.H. Francke and J.A. Jaschke, authors, one of respectable studies on the history and culture of our country and the other of a Tibetan–English dictionary which is still useful.

The titular of the mission in the days of my childhood was Reverend Peter with whom my two grandfathers had maintained very close friendly relations, although marked by different nuances. Haji Abdul Ghaffur, my paternal grandfather, admired and sought to imitate the lifestyle represented by the modern West, whereas Haji Muhammad Siddiq was absolutely against it. However, this did not at all prevent him from getting along very well with Reverend and Mrs Peter and even carrying out some business transactions with them. It was thanks to this intermediary that he was able to import from Germany various quantities of amber and coral, which he then resold in Lhasa where these articles were in high demand.

Reverend Peter was succeeded by Reverend Driver who was my first English master. What fascinated me more than his teaching was the pipe he smoked whilst settled in his armchair as he made me repeat the rudiments of his language. Its perfumed tobacco had a smell which I much preferred to that of my grandfather's *hookah* even though he always put flower petals in the water which made the smoke gurgle. My visits to the mission also familiarised me with the customs of the West which contrasted so sharply with our traditional life. In fact, at home we didn't even sleep in beds but on mattresses which we spread out in the main room as in early times. The Reverend, who knew Ladakhi quite well, also spoke to me of life in the West, of London, where he was from and his words stirred my curiosity. In any case, thanks to his lessons, I made tangible progress in English, which contrary to the wish of Haji Muhammad Siddiq, increased my desire to leave Ladakh and go acquire this prestigious education, the key to power and success.

In the opinion of my grandfather, Western education was mainly suitable for administrative careers. Now, he had almost no respect for such careers which, to his mind, partly included servitude which an independent merchant was exempt from.

'Your veritable education,' he said, 'you will better get by experience and the example of your elders than by spending years on the benches of those colleges and universities.'

When I finished school in Leh, then, the big question being debated in the family circle was to decide whether I should be allowed to go to Srinagar to complete the ninth and tenth classes. One of my cousins, Ataullah, was already there and his academic results were very encouraging. This precedent was a strong argument in favour of my departure. But the patriarch, who had the last word, was not yet ready to cede.

My mother realised that she played an important role here. She was a modest, self-effacing and innocent woman. Illiterate, she was incapable of counting beyond twenty. Yet she was generous, as the beggars who came and presented themselves at the door of our house well knew, and she wanted happiness for everyone, especially for her son. Seeing how much I wanted to go to Kashmir, she began to plead my case with her father. My younger sister was also on my side. Finally, Haji Muhammad Siddiq, whose health was already deteriorating, had to resign himself to this.

However, he believed he had found an intermediary solution which, whilst responding to my desire to discover the world beyond the peaks, would perhaps prevent my final entrance into the modern academic system. He thus decided that I would leave for Srinagar under the direction of Khwaja Abdul Aziz, his son-in-law, giving him instructions to show me Kashmir whilst drawing my attention to the negative aspects of life in this region where I would inevitably feel isolated and homesick. He also advised him to carry on the journey to the Indian plain and to show me Lahore, perhaps even Peshawar, in order to satisfy my curiosity. And then he had added:

'Try to persuade him to return of his own will. Try to make him give up this idea of college and modern education!'

Uncle did exactly the opposite. As I realised later, he himself was under the influence of Abdullah Shah, the *aksakal* whom he greatly admired. Thus, when we were in Srinagar, he did not make the slightest attempt to make me give up the idea of college.

'The best thing you can do is to acquire a modern education. Your grandfather doesn't see things as they are. He really doesn't know what the modern world is and doesn't understand that new weapons are necessary to confront it.'

When he had to let me leave, Haji Muhammad Siddiq was determined to organise my journey in such a way as to already interest me in the traditional commercial activity of the family. He entrusted to his son-in-law, who was assigned to escort me, an entire cargo of merchandise to be sold in Srinagar or perhaps even in Lahore. It included mainly rugs and other products of Tibetan handicraft. The load also included silks and brocades of Chinese origin as well as bricks of black Tibetan tea which would easily find a buyer in Kashmir. This tea came from Szechuan and in this compressed and agglomerated form, it was sent to Lhasa where the Tibetans were great consumers of it. Some quantities were loaded onto caravans destined for Leh whence they were sent to Sinkiang and sometimes also Kashmir. This trade was one of my grandfather's specialities.

Thus, my first departure from Leh was with a small caravan. This was our only means of communication with the outside world. During the preceding days, Haji Muhammad Siddiq had personally supervised the preparations, inspecting the equipment and baggage, designating the servants and the cook who were to accompany us. Then he organised a big farewell dinner.

On the morning of the departure, according to custom, a string to which was tied a small packet containing several verses of the Qur'an was put around my neck which I was to wear on the right side. When everything was ready, men, horses and ponies left the courtyard of the house and after 200 metres, stopped on the Srangnara Square. All the travellers, masters and servants alike, lined up to pray, imploring divine protection all along their route. My grandfather, mother, sister, a good number of uncles and cousins, friends and servants were there to wish us well. After the prayer we embraced each other, then Haji Muhammad Siddiq advised me to write to him often and gave me some advice which has remained engraved in my memory.

'Always be happy, never reveal a bad mood to anyone, smile at everyone. If lassitude overcomes you, don't hesitate to come back. You will always be welcome here and will always find affection with us and something to occupy yourself with.'

Our little troop then set off along the track which descended to the bottom of the valley and then followed the course of the Indus in a southwest direction. At last I was going to traverse the mountain barrier which separated us from Kashmir and the rest of the world. The thought of the discoveries which awaited me filled me with excitement and pride.

Our laps averaged 25 kilometres. Towards the end of the journey we were slowed down by floods and it took us twenty days to cover the 434 kilometres separating us from Srinagar. We would set off at dawn, fasting, then stop around ten or eleven in the morning. Then we took a snack followed by a meal which permitted us to avoid walking during the hottest hours of the day, whilst the horses and ponies looked for grasses to graze on, often without success. Then we set off again and stopped before sunset. The tracks were most often deserted and the only people we sometimes met were shepherds. In the villages, the inhabitants almost always knew who we were because the names of my grandfather and my uncles were known in these regions, and they welcomed us warmly.

At this time the British had set up a network of lap shelters called *dak* bungalows for their employees on tour. They still exist all over India where they continue to serve the administration and even foreign tourists very usefully. The reputation of the family gave us the possibility of using these bungalows and this contributed to the pleasantness and comfort of the journey.

When there weren't any bungalows we were lodged with the local inhabitants. This was the case at Khalatse, a two days' walk from Fotu La, a pass at an altitude of 4,100 metres which marks the culminating point of the route. We were to be put up in the house of a former servant of the family, a Tibetan retired in Ladakh where he was spending a peaceful old age. I was happy to get there because the girls of Khalatse had a flattering reputation. However, I have a detestable memory of the night spent in the house of our old friend where the fleas were so aggressive that we had to fight them off until the morning, unable to get a wink of sleep. This annoying experience remained unique and didn't even repeat itself at Kargil on the other side of the pass, a place described by some travellers as the 'flea capital of the world'.

During the twenty days of the journey, my relations with Khwaja Abdul Aziz were not always very cordial and sometimes a little strained even. An intrepid and experienced caravaneer, he had a difficult character and it didn't take much to make him angry. He was born in Lhasa where he had spent his childhood and youth. He had a little wispy beard like Himalayan and Chinese Muslims. He was not entirely acclimatised to Ladakh where he had settled only after the death of his father. Through his grandmother he had Chinese blood and his manner reflected his close contact with the Tibetan nobility. He often seemed arrogant to me, especially with his inferiors whom he willingly treated as if they were Tibetan serfs, whereas Ladakhis considered themselves free men and expected to be treated as such. I often wonder whether the influence of Islam had not contributed to making human relations less hierarchical with us. However it was, as head of the caravan, Uncle behaved as if 'these people', be they officers or bungalow servants, owed him everything.

At the end of the lap when we settled down to eat, the villagers often came and sat near us and engaged in conversation. However, this irritated Uncle because he did not like to be watched whilst he was eating, and he made them feel this. They, of course, felt disappointed and offended and wondered who this strange *khwaja* was who was so ungracious.

We usually had the use of relay horses and ponies, which, upon payment, were arranged for us at each lap. As a general rule, the guests of the *dak* bungalows were in this respect better and more rapidly served than ordinary travellers. But the haughty moods of Uncle often had the effect of cooling the goodwill of the suppliers who then would only provide us with animals of mediocre quality.

After passing through Kargil, halfway between Leh and Srinagar, and ascending again for three days through the cold valley of Drass, our caravan arrived at Zoji La (3,800 metres) which appeared to me as a door into another world. The southern side of the pass, covered with green vegetation, offered an entirely new spectacle for me and the warmer air gave me a feeling of lightness, whilst walking alongside our mounts. We followed the track carved into the rock which descended towards Kashmir.

Our next lap was Sonamarg, now a holiday resort, where Khwaja Abdul Aziz granted us a little rest. From there, two days would normally have sufficed to reach Srinagar. But we needed four because the river had flooded and had rendered the tracks impassable which immobilised us in Kulan. Having taken refuge in a village house, we were confined to one scanty room from which we watched the rain fall, more abundantly than I had ever seen before. The few Kashmiris that I noticed seemed real strangers to me, as much from their facial features as from their dress. Uncle, unhappy about this forced rest, was grumpier than ever. I began to think of the words of 'Memeylay', my grandfather, warning me that the journey would not always be a pleasure and I would have many an occasion to miss the family home of Leh...

Most certainly, the life of a modern college student which I had obstinately wanted to lead held in store for me much suffering and many difficulties in a milieu where I would inevitably feel isolated. But on the other hand, weren't our elders who were faithful to the family traditions often exhausted and suffering during their wanderings across the highlands of Asia?

Having experienced both types of existence, I wonder if they can be compared. It seems to me in any case that the companions of my childhood and of my Tibetan caravans were more at peace with themselves than the modern men with whom my studies more or less assimilated me. When I already had my university degree and followed Khwaja Abdul Aziz who led the Lopchak caravan, I was struck by the company of the people I found myself with, who were more homogeneous, less complicated and more accepting of their destiny than all my former classmates and professors. Uncle himself, despite his irritable character, was a balanced man and perfectly integrated into the austere environment which surrounded him. As for the nomads and shepherds whom we met along the way, they were poor, dirty and tattered, but their looks and the expression on their faces told me that at the same time they were happy.

On 13 October 1942, after we had worked out the accounts that we had with the people of Gargonsa and had taken the delivery of their butter, the Lopchak caravan set off again towards the east in the direction of the sources of the Indus. Two days later it arrived in Garyarsa or Gartok, the centre of caravan trade and 'summer capital' of western Tibet. In this large village where nomad tents were more numerous than 'solid' houses, we were extended an excellent welcome:

> We were greeted by the representatives of the two *urku*s (governors) who draped the traditional *khadag*s (ceremonial scarf) around our necks. Our arrival produced a procession which people watched from the terrace of their homes or from in front of their tents. Then the servants of the *urku*s and the two officers in Zhungtsong presented us their gifts in the traditional style. A very beautiful spectacle! The manner in which these servants welcomed us testifies to a refined culture. I'd like to be able to adapt myself to it but I still have a lot to learn, and in particular I should perfect my knowledge of the Tibetan language.

During our stay in Gartok we heard quite alarming rumours concerning incursions of the Hasakapas in the regions which we had to cross to go to Lhasa. That is why it was a relief for us to see the arrival of the *atung*, the delegate specifically sent by the Tibetan government to escort us all the way to the capital.

This person who had come from Lhasa in twenty days, a hitherto unheard of feat, had importance and power. Depending on his mission, an *atung* disposed of more or less extensive authority. When it was a question of escorting a caravan coming from beyond the frontiers and having an official status as in our case, he had the authority to demand what he deemed opportune from the population. He took advantage of this to such an extent that his arrival was considered a calamity. If the fresh supplies or the number of animals which he demanded were not delivered rapidly enough, he had the villains flogged. It was said that his requisitions sometimes extended to the girls he wanted at the lap. When news came that the *atung* was near and it was believed that the bells of his horse could be heard, fear spread and spines began to shiver.

However, before setting off again on the route to the east in good company, Khwaja Abdul Aziz had to settle a series of business deals in the region. I accompanied him to Gar Sharshan, a few hours from Gartok, a bazaar where the family caravans never failed to stop. Merchandise from various places was exchanged, mainly from India. I took an active part in the transactions and my diary dated 17 October notes:

> We completed several negotiations. Uncle sold his horse, in exchange for which he acquired some foreign cloth, mostly Indian. It was today that I truly made my entrance into the business profession. It is of course old, traditional and primitive business. This is what my starting point should be if I want to become a modern businessman.

The next day we returned to Gartok where we had to stay several days doing nothing whilst waiting for our merchandise from Tashigang. This loss of time worried us, for the season was getting on and our caravan was the last one that was headed for central Tibet before winter. It is true that the weather had been fine until then, but we feared snowfalls, thinking of the disaster that my father went through ten years earlier in these regions. Upon the advice of the *atung* and the *urku*s, we decided then, on 26 October, to set off again.

After Gartok, we got father away from the course of the Indus which has its source in the northern mountains. We had to cross the Sherko pass, approximately 5,000 metres in altitude, and come down again in the high Sutlej valley, a branch of the Indus which rejoins it 1,000 kilometres from there in present-day Pakistan.

These were very hard laps. It was very difficult for us to obtain the mounts and pack animals which we needed and without the intervention of the authorities and of the *atung* we would have been immobilised. As it was, we didn't have enough animals and our servant Kadir had to be content with riding a yak.

Mansar, sometimes spelled Mense or Missar on the maps, where our caravan arrived on 29 October, had a very special status. The place and the neighbouring territory constituted a small enclave over which treaties had maintained the sovereignty of Kashmir so as to facilitate the pilgrimage of Ladakhi Buddhists to the very sacred places of the region, Mount Kailash and Lake Mansarovar. Thanks to the revenues of this far-off possession, the *gyalpo* of Ladakh was said to have fuelled lamps with butter in order to illuminate the sacred mountain.

When we arrived, there was no Kashmiri officer there. The government of Srinagar must have made its authority felt, however, since the inhabitants complained of having to submit to double tax payments by paying taxes to the Tibetan administration as well as to the representative of the Maharaja. In any case, discontent reigned, which did not facilitate the transactions which Uncle had to settle.

The site was very beautiful. Unfortunately, our lodging conditions hardly corresponded to the pleasantness of the landscape:

> We occupy a dark, dirty room almost constantly filled with a pungent smoke which penetrates the lungs. Filth and rubbish surround the house, the dust of which seems to filter into the inside and mix with the smoke.

We very soon had had enough of the charms of the local cuisine.

> This morning, 1 November, we were fortunately served a little milk. Otherwise the diet is as follows: meat in the morning, meat at noon, meat in the evening. However, I was able to obtain a little rice and bread as well as some *tsampa* for Uncle's breakfast.

At least some good news reached us: thanks to the interventions of the *atung* our servant Padma Tsering had been able to leave Tashigang with our merchandise and was hurrying to join us. Everyone was relieved.

We were then able to prepare to leave again. We still had to wait because there were further delays in supplying animals. If the people of Mansar did not put their goodwill into it, the insecurity caused by the Hasakapas gave them an excuse. Finally, we had to resort to loading yaks with baggage, merchandise as well as servants. Only the two *khwaja*s were on horseback.

The laps which followed were veritable trials. The altitude made every movement heavy and the northern wind lashed at us. The horses advanced at a slow and tired pace. We ourselves were close to exhaustion. On his mount, somewhat less foundered than mine, Khwaja Abdul Aziz had taken the lead and I dragged far behind, asking myself how to interpret such a striking contrast between the majestic grandeur of the surrounding nature and the insignificance of the small beings, exhausted and suffering as we were.

Through sheer effort, we nevertheless advanced. The mountains which surrounded us seemed as if they no longer belonged to the earth. We were approaching some of the most sacred places of upper Asia.

CHAPTER 3

THE BEGINNING OF DECLINE

When I arrived in the valley of Kashmir for the first time with Khwaja Abdul Aziz, a pleasant surprise awaited us: a group of college students, all natives of Ladakh, came to meet us to welcome us and bring us fruit. There was another surprise, even more unexpected than the first: my cousin Ataullah, who was part of the group, had a contraption with wheels, the likes of which I had never seen before: a bicycle. He got on it, started up, whizzed off like an arrow, disappeared round a bend, reappeared riding backwards, always going at an amazing speed until he had rejoined us. His demonstration left me flabbergasted.

With electricity, telephones, radios, cinemas and all the motor vehicles, Srinagar held many and even more thrilling discoveries in store for me. I soon realised that even the most extraordinary technical novelties didn't fascinate me for long and after several days I got used to them. It is only interior discoveries that one does not tire from.

Ataullah had followed classes in the missionary college of Srinagar for two years. His presence contributed considerably to facilitating my entrance into this new life. Thanks to him, I didn't feel too distressed and isolated. I, therefore, took lodgings in the boarding house where a good number of other students from the school lived. Finally, I was presented to the director, Reverend Biscoe.

This missionary had founded the first modern college in Srinagar. He had obviously done it with the intention of proselytising Christianity, but in this state where Muslims were in the majority, its successes had remained meagre and the missionary had only succeeded, it seems, in converting one or two families of Hindu Pandits. The school gave special solicitude to the sons of several Christian families of Leh who attended the school, arranging to obtain good jobs for them in the administration. In any case, he welcomed me with much kindness and I could only congratulate myself for the education I received in his institution.

At the beginning of my stay, Khwaja Abdul Aziz shared the same lodgings, until he had settled his business matters in Srinagar. Friends of the family came to see us and I, above all, remember a former servant who had worked for us in Leh and then worked in the house of an important person holding an official position. Having learnt of our arrival, he brought us a magnificent cake which he had baked in his employer's kitchen. When I wanted to try some of it, my uncle objected claiming that it should be saved for a better occasion. This occasion presented itself a few days later in the person of another visitor but when my uncle told me to take the cake out of the cupboard where it was waiting, there was no longer any question of eating it because it was black with ants.

Although I often suffered from homesickness, even severely sometimes, I was keen to prove my strength of character and I managed to overcome it even after the departure of Ataullah who didn't delay leaving Srinagar to enter the Aligarh Muslim University, southeast of Delhi. I soon became accustomed to my new life as a college student which lasted two years.

Every morning I left the boarding house, which was near the 'first bridge' on the Jhelum in the new town where most of the English lived, with my classmates then at a hurried pace we covered the three kilometres which separated this bridge from the school which was located near the 'seventh bridge' in an area mostly inhabited by high-caste Hindus. Although Muslims, Hindus and Buddhists made up the vast majority of students, as soon as they arrived at school they had to attend a short Christian religious service with prayers and hymns.

The headmaster was a Brahman who was nearly an octogenarian and much respected, Pandit Shankar Kaul, who also taught us Persian language and literature. Most classes were given in Urdu but great emphasis was placed on teaching English. The academic programme was Western-style and the history courses were centred on England and the British empire. In a way, everything was organised so as to make us good servants of the British.

The discipline weighed heavily upon me, particularly during the physical education classes. We also had to learn to swim—a strange and not very attractive sport for a Ladakhi! I didn't like the fire-drill exercises, which took place regularly in military style, any better. But nothing was more detestable to me than the obligatory boxing lessons. Reverend Biscoe himself excelled in the supposedly 'noble art' which the end of his nose bore witness to. For my part, I found it humiliating to be a party to these exchanges of punches, and this removed the little that was left of my feeling of importance.

In fact in Srinagar, to be the grandson of Haji Muhammad Siddiq was no longer sufficient to confer glory upon me. There was an abundance of important people. Amongst my classmates were several descendants of aristocratic families, like Shawqat, the son of the prince (*mir*) of Nagar, a small state neighbouring Hunza in the Karakoram chain. Living in the same boarding house as me, he was treated like an ordinary student, but had his own servants. A twenty-year-old Shia Muslim, he was especially strict in observing his religious duties.

In general, I didn't easily form close relationships with Kashmiris, properly speaking, and most of my friends were like myself, natives of the high frontier regions of Gilgit, Hunza,

Ashtor, Punyal. There was a great solidarity amongst the representatives of these mountain countries so different from the rest of India. However, my closest friend was a Ladakhi Buddhist named Stobdan. After the departure of my cousin, I found most comfort with him when homesickness overtook me.

Amongst the happy memories of these times were the two Christmases which the Reverend and our Christian classmates celebrated with us in accordance with European customs featuring a Christmas tree, candles, songs and delicacies. The school also organised excursions. In this respect, Kashmir has always offered marvellous and countless walks and hikes in her mountains and valleys. It was the time when winter sports were beginning to be popular and there was a dramatic accident which upset the whole region deeply. Seven young English skiers setting off from Gulmarg, the famous station to the west of Srinagar, were lost in the mountains and perished in the snow.

We all came under a very strong attraction to the modern West at this time. We were keen to dress like Europeans and the highest ambition of many of us was to one day be able to enter the British administration. In the meantime, there was no greater dream, no privilege more sought after than to be included amongst the few chosen each year to go to London, thanks to scholarships granted by the government of the Maharaja. For England was in the centre of our thoughts. I entered the missionary college in 1936, the year marked by the death of George V and by the abdication of Edward VIII. We followed these events with great interest.

Such was the mentality I myself had adopted after a few months. I was keen to be an independent and open young man. My ambition went far beyond the Biscoe College and I wished to continue my studies in a university in India like my cousin Ataullah or like another Ladakhi whom I especially admired, Sonam Norbu. He had an engineering diploma and soon after went on a training course in London, making certain fellow students ill with jealousy. This eminent Ladakhi was to become a minister in the government of Jammu and Kashmir and remained a minister until his death in 1980.

After completing the tenth year, I wanted to prepare for my entrance into the University of Aligarh. However, news from Leh had informed me that my grandfather was ill and his life seemed to be approaching its end. I could not shirk my duty of going to his side.

Since my departure from the family home, he had written to me himself almost every week, whereas I had only sent him my news by letter or by telegram once a month or sometimes at even longer intervals. I learnt later that he often expressed concern when I remained silent for too long. In truth, I didn't have a very good conscience when I set off for home.

The journey was surprisingly rapid, thanks to the facilities granted by the father of one of my classmates who worked in the postal administration. I was able to join a small caravan which took seven days to get to Leh, thanks to some excellent relay horses. This was equal to the speed of official couriers.

When I arrived, I painfully realised that Haji Muhammad Siddiq's state was very serious. When I entered the courtyard of the house on horseback, he came down with great difficulty from the first floor which he normally didn't leave anymore. In spite of the joy which he expressed embracing me, I felt how weak he was. This however did not prevent him from organising a feast to celebrate my return and all the guests congratulated him on having found his grandson again. I then realised to what extent my absence had made him suffer.

I was his only male descendant. He pinned all his hopes on me with the idea that I would be able to take over the family patrimony. With the passage of time, I have understood the entire meaning and greatness of this tradition, which I wasn't able to maintain as he had hoped I would, and I feel a deep sadness when I think that I didn't know how to live up to his expectations and foresee the decline of the family which began after his passing away. At present there are several of us amongst the relatives who miss the patriarchal existence that we led in Leh at that time. But when Haji Muhammad Siddiq was living, we weren't aware of the priceless values which he personified. We didn't listen to his advice and we deliberately went against his ideas and principles because we were all more or less seduced by Western modernism. This tendency was most pronounced in the other branch of the family whose members began to wear European clothes, furnished their homes in Western style and took their meals in the English fashion.

My grandfather, for his part however, had always refused to bring anything into his home which wasn't an obvious necessity or didn't conform to the customs of the country. Nothing decorated his walls except the official diploma conferring the title of Khan Bahadur on his eldest brother Ghulam Rasul. He only had Ladakhi or Tibetan objects in his house and everything was homogeneous. For heat in the winter he remained faithful to an old brazier that was miserly in giving off heat, saying that his ancestors had been content with it and he had no need of a better heater. Even in the coldest weather, he slept with his window open.

Even now I regret having been ignorant of the values he defended. Remorse seizes me when I think back on those weeks spent near him in Leh, after my first two years of college in Srinagar, when he was suffering from a disease from which he would never recover. I had all sorts of suggestions which went against his dearest ideas. Certainly, it wasn't intentional. On the contrary, I even thought I made him happy by talking of my plans for the future, of my intention to go to the university, to become an important person holding a well-paid post and driving a car. None of these ideas seemed to him to conform to the profound vocation of men like ourselves, caravaneers of the highlands of Asia, and he suspected the dangers which a modernised life influenced by the West could have for our faith as believing Muslims and on the religious practice which structured our lives.

Two or three weeks after my return to Leh, one day whilst we were having our midday meal in the company of a few cousins, a telegram arrived for me. It was news that I had passed my tenth year school-leaving examinations. I naturally felt much joy and pride but I immediately saw from my grandfather's look that he didn't feel any happiness. Undoubtedly, he felt that a failure would have been better for me and for the family because then I would have remained in Ladakh and would have succeeded him as head of our trading firm. If there were assuredly other candidates for this succession, in particular his brother-in-law Abdul Aziz, he did not find in them the qualities required and he had the most affection for me.

Realising the seriousness of his illness, Haji Muhammad Siddiq called for an *amchi*, a traditional Tibetan doctor, but with little success. He himself was versed in *hikma*, the traditional Muslim medicine. He possessed several books which dealt with the subject and his knowledge in this domain was vast. He also had at his disposition all the supplies of a *hakim*, as the Muslims called doctors, with numerous medicines and drugs, which were derived from plants and minerals as well as certain Tibetan remedies which he had brought from Lhasa. People frequently came to him to consult him about illnesses of various degrees of seriousness and he relieved a good number of them.

My grandfather knew very well that the condition which he was suffering from, a cardiac disorder, was going to take him away. He told those around him forthrightly so, recalling that his father, Nasr Shah, had died of the same affliction. This did not prevent him from organising the celebration of the *Mauloud*—the anniversary of the birth of our holy Prophet, as had been done every year for generations. It was the occasion for a big reception offered to crowds of guests, rich and poor, who came to feast well and benefit from his generosity.

This year it was also a pretext for difficult discussions amongst our relatives and family because certain Muslims of a puritan and fundamentalist tendency disputed the legitimacy of this feast, feeling that its commemoration was *bida'*, *an* innovation foreign to the pure Islamic tradition. However, once again, my grandfather meant to remain faithful to the traditional customs which had always been observed in the house.

And the feast took place. Haji Muhammad Siddiq was incapable of coming down from the first floor to greet all the guests who crowded into the tent which was set up in the garden. A tray with a few dishes was brought to him and served to him with assistance. He didn't touch any of it and was content to sniff their aromas.

The next day he passed away. It was 28 May 1937, the anniversary of the death of his father.

He remained conscious up to the last moment. Speaking in a clear voice, he asked pardon for the wrong he might have caused to others, then added that he was grateful and satisfied for everything that life had brought him. He still made the canonical prayer to which he added invocations imploring divine mercy. To his daughter who had spent the night at his bedside, he spoke in a tone of great serenity.

'Do not weep for my departure,' he said. 'The hour has come for me. All is well this way. I have nothing to complain about. Help me to turn my face towards the *qibla*' (the direction of Mecca). Then, with perfect lucidity, he added, 'Now my sight is extinguished. My sense of smell is disappearing. The final moment is approaching.'

He still called for me. Frightened by this proximity of death, I refused to go to his side. I will never blame myself enough for this attitude of an adolescent which I then was.

I often wondered if Haji Muhammad Siddiq hadn't wanted to pass on to me a tradition, perhaps of an initiatic nature, for he was attached to the Chisti *tariqa*, the great Indian Sufi brotherhood. Perhaps it was also his intention to make me recite a special *du'a* (prayer) like those of the *Uddat ul-liqa'* (Preparation for the Meeting), a collection of litanies composed by our ancestor, Sheikh Muhammad Radhu.

Twenty years ago I found a copy of this little book by accident in a pile of papers that were to be burnt. Since then I have recited passages from it every day trying to make up for the mistake made by not answering the patriarch's last call.

The death of Haji Muhammad Siddiq marked the beginning of a decline of the family which no one was aware of at first but whose effects were manifested little by little. Disputes and divergences of interest broke up our solidarity and sometimes even set us against each other. At the same time, Western influences crept into our lives and our customs and destroyed their homogeneity.

It is true that the golden age of Leh was also approaching its end and that in the years preceding the war, the importance of the little Ladakhi capital had already seriously diminished as a warehouse of the caravan trade between Kashmir, Tibet and Sinkiang. When Khwaja Abdul Aziz took charge of the Lopchak caravan in 1940, it no longer played the role of guaranteeing good relations between Leh and Lhasa. When I participated in it in 1942, many indications led me to understand that it no longer had the same *raison d'être* and had, in a way, outlived itself. Two years later, the caravan crossed the tracks of the Trans-Himalayas for the last time.

~

On 7 November 1942, we arrived in Parka. The sun of the high altitudes had been so unrelenting and my horse had shown so many signs of fatigue that, taking pity on him, I had preferred to walk part of the lap. The surrounding landscape was of a grandiose and recollected beauty corresponding to the reputation of the sanctity of these regions. Numerous *chorten*s, or stupas as they are called in India, marked the track. They were often linked by *mani* *ringmos*, prayer walls covered with stones, on each of which was engraved the mantra, *Om mani padme hum.* Out of respect for Buddhist customs, we took care to walk in such a way as to always have these monuments on our right side.

Parka, a small trading centre and meeting point for caravan tracks leading to Gartok, Rudok and Purang, was mainly inhabited by nomads who had covered the plain with *rebo*s, their tents of black yak hair. A house with fairly clean rooms was put at our disposal but the courtyard was full of rubbish and mud, which irritated Khwaja Abdul Aziz. He gathered the *shagno*s or nomad chiefs together and admonished them in a sharp tone for not receiving us in a manner conforming to traditional customs, and with the consideration that was due to us. His haranguing got him a few apologies and the promise of a better welcome the next time.

Our stay at this place was extended to an entire week, for we were awaiting news of our baggage coming from Tashigang and Mansar, the *atung* having accepted to take care of it. I didn't complain too much about this long, forced stop, as the house which we were staying in offered the possibility of taking hot baths.

Parka also seemed to be a lap of the Buddhist and Hindu pilgrimages to Mount Kailash. My journal doesn't mention any pilgrim, however, and I don't remember having met any. Perhaps there again a certain decline could be felt.

The Kailash, which the Tibetans called Tisay or Kangrimpotchay, has been sacred since time immemorial because it is also venerated by the faithful of Bon, the religion of Tibet prior to Buddhism, still practised in a few places. For the Hindus, its summit is the inaccessible abode of the god Shiva. For Buddhists, it represents the greatest and holiest of all the *chorten*s of Tibet, a privileged place where contact between heaven and earth is established.

Several lakes lie at the bottom of the valleys to the southeast of the Kailash. Reflecting the almost always blue sky, they have often been compared to turquoises inlaid in their settings of cloudy peaks. They are all sacred, but it is the Mapham—the celebrated Mansarovar of the Hindus—that my journal calls Mawang, which is the most sacred. It was said that no one ever dared to commit the sacrilege of bathing there or navigating its waters. However, it is difficult to point out its location precisely, because considerable differences exist amongst the various maps of Tibet. Even the most recent, especially those of the Changthang still contain white spots labelled 'unexplored'.

Until recent years, the pilgrimages to Kailash represented phenomenal feats of strength. The Hindus, who in the manner of sadhus most often had but two pieces of cloth and a pair of sandals for all their supplies, reached Kailash after having crossed some of the highest passes in the Himalayas west of Nepal. Amongst Tibetans, some had made the vow to go from Lhasa to Kailash and return by making a prostration at each step and this pilgrimage could take several years.

Once they reached the foot of the sacred dome, white and majestic, the pilgrims went round it, which required two or three days. For this there was a circular path marked out by temples offering shelter for the night. When tradition was still fully alive, butter lamps burnt permanently in these sanctuaries. The *gyalpo* of Ladakh was supposed to contribute to this illumination, thanks to the revenue of Mansar. I admit that in spite of clear weather, we never noticed the slightest glimmer in the direction of the Kailash.

Finally, it was possible for us to leave Parka. We continued on our route towards the east. Again I confided to my journal my admiration for the snowy peaks and glaciers. Wild asses galloped about in the valleys and on the plateaus and splendid birds circled above the lakes.

> After having travelled in such a setting with ease, we were in good spirits when we arrived here in Laikia, the place planned for the bivouac. To our great surprise, we could find no sign of our cook

> who had gone on ahead of us in order to arrive two hours earlier. There we were, quite at a loss without fire, hot water or food except for some dried apricots and hard bread. Fortunately, the yaks carrying our tent and sleeping bags arrived before nightfall. Fortunately also, a stranger driving two yaks agreed to lend us some utensils and even helped us to set up the tent and light a fire in the foot-warmer. We, therefore, had to content ourselves with tea, without salt or sugar, and *kolsha*, a dry Tibetan biscuit.

Because of Rasul's, our cook's, extended disappearance, our breakfast the next morning was reduced to the simplest fare. On an empty stomach but consoled by the rising sun which provided a magnificent background and the mountainous scenery surrounding us, our caravan set off in the direction of Tokshan, a small crossroads of tracks and nomad camps where several houses were also located. Upon our arrival in the afternoon, we found Rasul, who, having lost his way in the mountains the previous evening, had wandered for a long time, lost along diverging paths and was finally lucky enough to find the right track. After doing the honours to the dishes which he had prepared whilst waiting for us, we went out of the little house where we had taken our quarters to marvel at the spectacle, at a beauty which defied any description, offered by the dome of the Kailash in the distance, the turquoise of the Mansarovar lake and farther south, a grandiose glacier illuminated by the setting sun.

The baggage problems, which the *atung* who had stayed behind had attempted to solve, forced us to extend our stop in Tokshan for five days. Due to the uncertainties caused by the incursions of the Hasakapas, difficulties developed, resulting in a lack of available caravan animals. This stop thus allowed me spare time to recall perhaps the most disastrous episode in the family caravan annals and to contemplate the scene, because it was in this region of Tokshan where, ten years before, my father, his brother Abdul Hakim, and three of their cousins, surprised by the snow, nearly lost their lives.

> As usual, they had left Leh for Lhasa with their servants and some sixty mules. It was not too late in the season when they set out. Now the weather was unusually bad and snow began to fall in quantities over and above anything that had ever been seen in living memory. The weather deteriorated completely between Parka and Tokshan. Struggling through deep snow, the caravaneers arrived here with great effort but there was no question of going any farther. The unfaithful servants abandoned their masters and each one went off to save himself. My father, his brother and his cousins managed to save themselves by reaching Purang, on the southern track, where they could go into Indian territory, but I don't know exactly at what point they passed through.
>
> Though they came out of it alive, the event caused them enormous losses. They had left all the merchandise in Tokshan in the very house where I am writing these lines at this moment, but it disappeared in the course of the winter and nothing was ever recovered from it. As for the mules, they all perished. And it was thanks to the Mercy of God, who by his *Taqdir* (divine decree), saved my father and his companions.

The succeeding laps took us through beautiful regions of valleys, lakes and plateaus where we sometimes spotted black tents of nomads. On 22 November, we set up our bivouac in a place called Lhulung, at the foot of the great Mayum La, the pass separating the Indus basin from that of the Brahmaputra. There was no house there to protect us from the icy wind. As I wrote in my journal, 'the true life of Changthang (literally, "plain" or "northern prairie") had begun for us.'

Again, we had to undergo long days of waiting in this uncomfortable encampment. These days were not pleasant. Clouds began to dance above our heads and the first snow fell, fortunately, in small quantities. The cold was bitter and the brazier in our tent demonstrated its inefficiency, the altitude giving us sensations of dizziness and great fatigue.

Uncle was really suffering. Complaining of headaches, he was struck with vomiting. This altitude sickness was aggravated by the worry caused by our position. Never had the caravan ventured into this difficult region at a time so late in the season. Fearing death along this route like my father, Uncle even considered interrupting the expedition and, instead of continuing in the direction of Lhasa, he considered crossing the nearest pass leading to the south of the Himalaya to reach Nepal and India. However, he managed to pull himself together, thus avoiding making a decision which would have had all the aspects of quite a humiliating failure.

For my part, I tried to occupy myself by observing the nomads. I noted:

> Living in a tent and drawing their sustenance from their cattle, of which goats are the most important animal, they stay in places which are richest in pasture, generally close to lakes and streams. They lead an innocent existence, typical of nomads.
>
> Filthy, they are not at all worried about being dirty. Almost all of them wear clothes of sheepskin. They live on meat, tea with butter and sometimes *tsampa*. Bread seems to be unknown to them. They are marvellous shepherds, capable of climbing the highest peaks. In this region the vegetation consists mainly of thorny brush as in the Himalayas at the same altitude. Could they lead any other life? Maybe they would be the best soldiers in the world if they could be inculcated with some discipline.
>
> One or two families live in tents very close to our camp, in a state of perfect simplicity. Whilst I was watching them, a few boys and little girls, the picture of innocence, were playing with some pebbles around big rocks, unconcerned about the outside world, except for the cold wind which lashed them. How could they know that a war had broken out elsewhere, in countries which are said to be civilised?

Khwaja Abdul Aziz's health did not improve any more than the weather, which presented us with a few ominous snowfalls. Nevertheless, we set off again on 1 December. It had been two months and twelve days since we had left home.

We arrived in the beautiful valley of Gyantse Sumtsok after crossing the pass of the great Mayum La. A biting wind was blowing there and it was snowing. There had been cloud cover all day and we had to fight against a penetrating cold. Uncle began vomiting again, but now is complaining of something else. This beginning of December has been especially difficult for him. He felt very uncomfortable on his horse and we had to exchange saddles in order to try to give him some relief. Now I'm using an old saddle which belonged to my dear father.

Nothing had been planned here to receive the caravan. The people who had accompanied us from Lhulung had to do everything themselves. We had to leave part of the merchandise at the west of the pass with the promise that it would reach us the day after tomorrow in Tamtsang. And now the stove is lighted, the candles are flickering, Uncle has fallen asleep, the servants are chatting in their tent, and I am finishing these notes whilst waiting for supper.

Finally, on 3 December, we left the valley of Gyantse Sumtsok to accomplish a long lap which included crossing new passes and very difficult passages through narrow gorges. We had fairly good horses, but this did not prevent my unhappy uncle from suffering a lot. In Tamtsang, where a small house was made available to us, he felt worse and had to rest for three days. The servants and I did our best to relieve him, but without great success.

I always think about these few days spent in Tamtsang emotionally because we were near the place where, eight years earlier, my father had breathed his last whilst on the way to Lhasa. The stomach ulcer which he had suffered from for a long time had suddenly been aggravated and he started to vomit blood. After a few hours he had ceased living.

I was told without hesitation that his tomb was located in a place called Larung Dabo, near Tamtsang. I went there several times, deeply moved, crying a lot and asking myself why his life had to end prematurely in such a deserted place. I said prayers, recited passages from the Qur'an, believing that my father had met his destiny as a true Muslim, faithful to the virtues of *iman* (faith) and *amal* (hope). At that place, at that instant, I understood better what his end must have been. Surrounded by mountains and glaciers, my father was in an environment of natural beauty and purity when he left this life.

When Uncle had regained enough strength and it was possible to leave Tamtsang on 7 December, I found it difficult, as if I had separated myself once again from my father. Whilst riding, memories of my childhood came back to me. I remembered his kindness, his simplicity, cheerfulness and humour. And I reflected as I have done so many times since then, upon the disastrous consequences which his premature disappearance had for the family in general and for me in particular.

For there is no doubt that Khwaja Abdul Karim, my father, would have been more qualified than his cousin and brother-in-law Abdul Aziz to head the family business in Leh. The mortal remains of Haji Muhammad Siddiq had barely been buried when disputes erupted over his succession. Of all the goods which he left, one part of them was to go to his nephew Abdul Haqq rather than to his direct descendants, by virtue of previously made arrangements. There was confusion as to the definition of this one part.

Though I was still an adolescent of less than sixteen years, I held a central position in all of this affair since, as the only male descendant of Haji Muhammad Siddiq, I was the principal heir, and moreover, I was going to take possession of the patrimony of my father, which the patriarch had managed in my name. Having become the legatee of this double inheritance, I took on much importance in the eyes of all the relatives. And as I was not spared any flattery, I began to consider myself an important person, which was certainly detrimental to the development of my character.

Two clans were formed, one supporting Abdul Aziz, the other Abdul Haqq. An arbitrator became necessary and, according to custom, this role had to be entrusted to a senior member of the family. This was none other than Abdullah Shah, the *aksakal*. Everyone went to him and recriminated and submitted to him plans of dividing up the goods and other more or less ingenious schemes.

These discussions provided an opportunity to examine every aspect of the family's financial situation. In particular, it was recognised that Ladakh seemed to be declining in importance as a business centre, and the future didn't look very bright. Was it not appropriate to consider from then on a definite change in the family business in order to adapt to new conditions?

This opinion prevailed. Instead of proceeding with a complicated division of what was due to each person, the principle of a common agreement was decided upon whereby all the goods belonging to the close relatives, including those of Khwaja Abdul Aziz in Lhasa, would be consolidated in order to be managed in a more efficient way.

At the same time, a decision was made which had extremely serious consequences for us. Since Ladakh showed signs of economic decline, the centre of our business enterprise would be transferred from Leh to Lhasa where most of us would go and settle. It was certain that business would be easier and more lucrative from the Tibetan capital, such a large city compared to our Ladakhi township, and which offered so many more possibilities.

It could have been argued that the members of our family already established in Lhasa were not in a particularly flourishing financial situation, and lacking the financial basis which was at our disposal in Ladakh, they were often in debt. But this consideration hardly played any part in the decision and my uncles had high hopes that, thanks to the agreement concluded under the auspices of the *aksakal*, the family trade would expand in leaps and bounds.

The least satisfied was undoubtedly Khwaja Abdul Haqq. It didn't please him at all to become the co-owner of the property of his cousin Abdul Aziz in Lhasa, where he wasn't keen to go and live. It is true that his opinion didn't carry much weight because it was known that he wasn't very good at business. But his wife, who was from Lhasa and said to be very clever, could make up for his incompetence. However it was, they insisted on living in Leh where, in the end, they got themselves out of trouble relatively easily than many of their cousins.

Even though outwardly the family gave the impression of being united, it was, in fact, divided. The arrangement which was made amongst the uncles presented problems which needed much time to be resolved. Decided upon in principle, the transfer from Leh to Lhasa was a procedure which was to last several years.

For my part, although I understood nothing about business, I had been involved in the dealings and I strongly approved of the decision to go and settle in Tibet. But prior to this I was keen to continue my studies in order to acquire this 'education' which seemed to bestow so much prestige.

Since the death of Haji Muhammad Siddiq, no other member of the family objected to the opportunity of modern studies and that was why the decision was taken, approved of by all, to send me to Aligarh Muslim University in the north of India. My cousin Ataullah, who had already been there for two years, had come to Leh that very summer to spend his holidays accompanied by a friend. Everything I heard from them reinforced my desire to go to Aligarh.

Unfortunately, the negotiations involving my grandfather's succession had lasted so long that I had missed the deadline for registering at the university. I found myself obliged to wait until the following year. What to do in the meantime? There was another college in Srinagar where I could have enrolled until my departure for Aligarh. But I felt that the institutions in Kashmir were not at a high enough level and I wanted to follow courses at a better college which had a greater reputation.

Some friends in Peshawar then tried to get me admitted into the Islamiya school of that city but there again the deadlines were past. A Christian college in Lahore was suggested to me by some Ladakhis, themselves Christian, and they gave me a letter of introduction to the director. This could have been a good temporary solution and so I left for the great metropolis of the Punjab.

From Srinagar to the Indian plain I hired a place in a car, which, for the first time in my life, allowed me to cross the frontiers of the world locked behind the Himalayan chains. At Rawalpindi, also for the first time, I saw a railway. The station, with its commotion, pushing and shoving and hubbub, stunned me. I couldn't understand why so many people were in such a hurry and were running in every direction. Without the help of an obliging passenger, I would never have been able to find my way through the mob, which seemed to belong to a universe completely foreign to the one which I had hitherto belonged. I was at once excited and bewildered when I got onto the train and took my place.

The next morning I arrived in Lahore. I was warmly welcomed by the Christian friends of my Ladakhi friends. They invited me to their lodgings, which were far more comfortable than anything I could have imagined. My stay there was very pleasant. Unfortunately, in spite of my letter of introduction, I very soon had to yield to the facts: the institution was full and there was no question of accepting anymore enrolments.

Disappointed at this failure, but at the same time happy and proud to have caught a glimpse of something of the vast world, there was nothing left for me to do but to return to Srinagar. Upon arriving, I set out on the route to my former school and went to seek the advice of Reverend Biscoe. He received me with much kindness and soon found me a job in his institution where I became a supervisor and assistant in the primary classes. I thus resumed my former routine in the capital of Kashmir. And my year of waiting went by uneventfully.

CHAPTER 4

ZAHIR AND *BATIN*

In the course of his long life, my grandfather, Haji Muhammad Siddiq, had undoubtedly attained a remarkable degree of wisdom. He had understood that any human existence not centred on the remembrance (*dhikr*) of God was in vain and he himself practised this remembrance in the form of invocations and daily litanies. His home was thus a sort of sanctuary where the presence of the sacred was felt. In the position of material ease and authority which destiny had placed him in, he maintained an attitude of detachment which permitted him to leave this terrestrial world without regret and in total serenity.

In his concern for putting me on my guard against the traps of pride and egoism, a short time before his death, he had given me a traditional teaching based on the symbolism of letters. In Urdu, he told me, the word *main*, which means 'I', begins with the letter *mim*, which is equal to a naught and which is also the beginning of the word *maut*, death. Likewise, he referred to the letters of the Tibetan alphabet which are all written with straight lines with the exception of the letter *nga*, which is crooked and is, in fact, used to write 'I'.

I must have been penetrated, almost in spite of myself, by this wisdom which my grandfather explained so simply during the conversations he liked to have with me in the evenings. At the time, overcome as I was with the desire for action, I did not grasp their true value. However, I believe that enough of them remained in my subconscious to help me when the time came to understand more profoundly the significance of our Islamic tradition.

However, such wisdom was less and less a part of the family framework. My grandfather disagreed with some of his nephews who, as I had noticed, permitted themselves to criticise the way in which he celebrated the feast of the *Mauloud* (the Prophet's birthday). Such was the effect of the reformist and puritan ideas which had become widespread in Indian Islam and had penetrated our Himalayan valleys. It was inevitable that I myself should undergo these influences, which tended towards a more formal and exclusivist interpretation of Islam. And my years at Aligarh University were to distance me even more from the spiritual tradition represented by the patriarch who had left us.

Not yet realising it, I was thus exposed to these two fundamental tendencies which Islam had given expression to throughout its history, the *zahir* (outer) and the *batin* (inner), notions which in a way correspond to what Occidentals call exoterism and esoterism. For centuries, the Muslim presence in India had testified to this duality. The conquerors and sovereigns established the reign of Islam and its temporal power by force, but it was the holy people, mystics and Sufis, who by their spiritual radiance attracted the most converts to Islam and planted the roots of Islam into these people, who were thirsty for the Divine and the Absolute.

The piety of Haji Muhammad Siddiq certainly derived from the *batin*, for it was a piety of a spiritual quality which went beyond forms and allowed him to sense that a tradition like the Buddhist one was not the popular *kufr* (paganism) as was believed by the narrow Muslims of the *zahir*. The world of our time is, however, marked by the predominance of all that is exterior and quantitative and people of the *batin* are more and more foreign to it.

Normally, *zahir* and *batin* should be complementary so that the religion meets the requirements of terrestrial and social life as well as the spiritual aspirations of the faithful. Now *zahir*, which should suit the mentality of the greatest number of people, is limited by definition and cannot resolve all the problems presented by the confrontation of Islam with other religions.

~

There have been periods in the history of India when *zahir* and *batin* have been in happy equilibrium, as under the Mughal emperors from the time of Akbar. At that time, denominational peace reigned for nearly a century between Hindus and Muslims. And the tolerance shown by Islam was neither a sign of weakness nor of lukewarmness. On the contrary, this was its age of greatness, of radiating spirituality and of brilliant civilisation as numerous monuments admirably bear witness to.

In the seventeenth century Shah Jahan, the illustrious builder of the Taj Mahal of Agra, was the last Mughal sovereign to practise with success this policy of mutual understanding. With Aurangzeb, his son and successor, the equilibrium was broken at the expense of the *batin* (the gain of the *zahir*) and from then on a spirit of intolerance and puritanism took over. Signifying this evolution was the conflict of Aurangzeb, who was a remarkable person in many other respects, against his eldest brother Dara Shikoh, who should have ruled in his place. The latter was a man of the *batin*. Of a mystical tendency, he saw expressions of the truth in other sacred traditions, particularly in Hindu metaphysics and he affirmed that the *Advaita Vedanta* (non-dualist) and *Tawhid* (the Islamic doctrine of unity) as the Sufis interpreted it, were essentially equivalent in spite of a few differences in terminology. He himself translated the Upanishads into Persian and thought that these fundamental texts of the Vedas expressed truths that were implied in the Qur'an.

In his battle against his brother, Dara Shikoh lost and Aurangzeb, who kidnapped him, had him executed for heresy and blasphemy. The accusation was undoubtedly unjust. It was a pretext for the murder of Dara Shikoh, a murder which was in fact the murder of an ideal—an ideal which had guaranteed peace and promoted understanding between Muslims and non-Muslims for a century.

In any case, since that time the *zahir* had predominated more and more in the Muslim communities of India where Sufism, which normally derives from the *batin*, weakened whilst the *zahir* was strengthened. The reformist movements which appeared from the eighteenth century onwards were generally typical expressions of the *zahir*. As was Wahhabism, imported from Arabia, which had claimed to lead the *jihad*, the 'holy war', at once against the British as well as against the Hindus, inciting bloody insurrections. Its puritan influence has marked vast areas extending as far as Kashmir and has left its mark on our Himalayan communities.

Other reformist tendencies, more concerned with the confrontation of Islam with Western civilisation, which was then in full expansion, manifested themselves throughout the nineteenth century. They opened the doors wide to modernising influences. The Aligarh Muslim University was a typical expression of this trend.

According to the concept of its founder, Sir Sayyid Ahmad Khan, the main function of the institution, which opened in 1875, was to promote the political and social progress of Indian Muslims, whose position had suffered more than that of the Hindus with the great revolt of the sepoys in 1857 and all that followed. Thinking that the English were in India to stay, and that this was a fact to be accepted, he called on the Muslim community to have enough strength of character to make its weight felt and to counterbalance the influence of Hindus or other non-Muslims, such as the Parsis, who were often more 'advanced' and closer to the British. The best way to achieve this, from his point of view, was to donate to the Muslims an establishment offering a modern type of higher education. Aligarh was, in fact, organised on the model of an English college.

Sir Sayyid admired the West and envied its power. He thus attempted to highlight the common points of Islam and modern thought, particularly on the scientific and philosophical plane. This could not fail to attract sharp criticism from other Muslim circles who blamed him for being a friend of the English and serving their interests. But he reacted by claiming that Christianity, as opposed to Hinduism which was plainly polytheist and kafir, was closer to Islam and that Muslims would not deny their faith by collaborating with Christians, 'people of the Book' (*ahl al-kitab*), according to the Qur'an.

In any case, Aligarh became one of the main centres where Western thought penetrated Indian Islam. This influence was combined with religious beliefs which were considered tolerant towards Christianity and modern ideas, but in reality remained superficial and incapable of assuring the continuity of our cultural identity in the face of the intellectual seduction coming from the West. In order to truly resist this seduction, a deepening of the religion would have been necessary, that is, recourse to the *batin*. The predominant mentality was very far from this.

However, at the beginning of my studies, I didn't yet see things so clearly. I had arrived at Aligarh full of goodwill and resolved to expend all my efforts to acquire a prestigious 'education'.

My cousin Ataullah, who had studied there for two years, travelled with me to this university city located some 90 kilometres from Delhi. He facilitated my entry into this new environment and guided my first steps. As he was an old student, his protection was precious to me and spared me excessive fresher ragging. Most of all, his presence provided me with the opportunity for personal contact with students and some of the most eminent professors of the university.

I shared a room with him where these knowledgeable persons sometimes came to talk with him. I listened with respect to their conversations, which opened up so many new perspectives to me and made me believe that I was at the summit of human thought.

In reality, these meetings were mainly a witness to the Western influence which reigned in Muslim intellectual circles at a time when the civilisation represented by the British empire held all its prestige. Implicitly believing in evolution and progress, our professors had an apologetic attitude towards Islam as if it were a matter of integrating it into the modern world at any price.

A similar attitude was found in the history and philosophy professors whom I frequently met. Their main preoccupation seemed to be summed up in this question: How can the position of Islam and Muslims be strengthened in India and the world?

Characteristic of this thinking was the continual use of Western thought as a reference point offering the best criteria with which to judge the validity of all knowledge, even of that knowledge which was related most typically to the East and to Islam. One professor, in particular, at every turn, liked to establish parallels between the traditional teachings of Islam and the theories of Rousseau.

Of all the authors I was to discover then, Rousseau particularly drew my attention the most and reading his *Émile* won my total support for him. Along with Rousseau, we had to study the most important Western philosophers from the Renaissance to the twentieth century. And we inevitably ended up with Marxism which was undoubtedly too much opposed to all religion to be able to convince us, but whose dynamism exerted a certain attraction for us.

As for Islam, we were made to study it much in the same way, that is, from the outside and without realising how foreign it was to all the profane thinking which they cluttered our minds with since Islam derived from the domain of the sacred. Moreover, in such an environment no one seemed aware of the possibility of envisaging Islam from any other angle. In fact, we thought we made up an elite amongst Muslims, understanding and practising Islam in a more authentic and 'progressive' way, and we hardly suspected that we were all already more or less contaminated by

Western ideologies, which were in reality foreign, if not opposed, to our religion. Neither did we realise the existence in Islam of an inner way, that of *batin*, which would have offered us a deeper and more solid foundation from which to confront the challenge of the West, a challenge of which, under the effect of the optimism flowing from the idea of progress, we could not even discern the real and far-reaching impact.

Many Indian Muslims during these years, especially in intellectual and university circles, were under the strong influence of a remarkable and famous person, Muhammad Iqbal, who represented one of the most important elements of Islamic reformation of this century. He was already dead but remained present at Aligarh through his ideas and writings.

A well-known poet, philosopher and author admired all over the East, Iqbal has often been called the spiritual father of Pakistan. Although some Indian intellectuals want to deny his moral responsibility in the drama of the 'partition' and the creation of the Islamic state, it seems certain that he favoured a form of political activism amongst Muslims, contributing to popularising the idea that they constituted a nation different from other communities living on the soil of the subcontinent. In any case, his prestige was considerable amongst the students of my generation, many of whom were to declare themselves nationals of Pakistan from 1947, and leave their native regions of India to establish their careers there.

Iqbal, whom we considered the most 'advanced' thinker of Islam, had in many of his works emphasised the necessity for Muslims to shake off what he called their 'torpor' and to act decisively in the world, to be inspired with the dynamism of Westerners. Claiming to 'reshape Islamic religious thought', as one of his most widespread works is entitled, he gave traditional Muslim doctrines interpretations which were heavily tinged with modern philosophy. For example, he turned Al-Ghazali into a precursor of Descartes or sympathetically commented on the theories of Nietzsche, whom he qualified somewhere as a 'modern prophet', and the same applied to Bergson and even Freud. The entire university was in admiration before the erudition of this great man who spoke with as much ease as authority on the masters of modern thought. Not a professor was to be found who could discern the ambiguity of his stance and denounce the formidable confusion.

Over the years, I have understood the harmful nature of this philosophy of the modern West, thanks to friends versed in the sciences of *batin*. In spite of all the appeasing things that Iqbal believed could be said of it, this philosophy denies traditional wisdom, accelerates the process of secularisation, and ends up in the intellectual chaos that the world is presently plunged in. And when the opportunity arises, I am not afraid of reacting against the influence of this philosophy on our Oriental minds.

It was thus that much later, when I was working in organisations helping Tibetan refugees, I found myself in Dharamsala in India, the residence of the Dalai Lama. When I was told that he was studying such Western philosophers as Kant, Nietzsche and Bergson, I was astounded and as I didn't have the opportunity to meet him for some time, I sent him a message through someone close to him saying something like this:

'These so-called philosophers are the devil's henchmen. For the love of Heaven, may your Holiness realise at what a low level they are situated in relationship to the intemporal wisdom represented by His Holiness himself.'

It seems that the Dalai Lama was not totally indifferent to this warning which bluntly severed the servility of so many Orientals before the official intellectuality of the West. In any case, he didn't hold it against me because since then he has even called upon me to consult me on various questions. And I should point out in passing that he himself suggested that I record my memoirs, which greatly encouraged me.

During my years at Aligarh, I was still quite far from such a critical stance towards Iqbal. If his poetry, endowed with such great charm, remained generally faithful to the traditions which make up our cultural identity, no one at the university seemed to realise that his philosophical thought actually bore very serious harm.

Typical of this was his point of view regarding Western music, which he said he preferred to the music of the East. In the various types of modern music, even in jazz, he found more dynamism, tension and life. For him, Western music inspired man with a more positive attitude in face of the world. As for Oriental music, Indian in particular, he reproached it for being pessimistic, negative and for distancing itself from action. The misunderstanding which the great writer had evinced in this respect became clear to me later, after I had rediscovered the invaluable treasure which Indian music represents and of which so many Muslims have been and still remain marvellous interpreters. I have understood since then that this traditional art, so unknown by modern people, is at once cosmic and platonic, since it fundamentally tends towards universal harmony, it is in conformity with the great rhythms of the created world and at the same time brings man back into his inner self. As for specifically modern music, I don't deny that it is more 'dynamic', but judging from several of its expressions like 'pop' and other derivations of jazz which reach us in the East, it seems to me that it flows rather in the direction of disintegration and dissolution.

The spirit of *zahir* reigning at Aligarh prevented us from understanding the true values of our traditional civilisation. On the contrary, giving automatic priority to the outward aspects of Islam, a tendency towards modernism, the key to temporal power, inevitably developed. The teaching of all the masters of Muslim reformism is proof of this.

Of these masters, there was one who began to be widely talked about: Maulana Abul Ala Maudoodi, who at the time was at the beginning of a career which was to confer upon him fame and influence which went far beyond the university environment.

Although he had not yet published very much, the mainstream of his thought was already coming out very clearly.

Compared to Iqbal, Maudoodi was more narrowly religious, a formalist and literalist. He represented a more fundamentalist current of little intellectual consequence, but his works were and still are fairly widespread for they are accessible to readers with an average level of education. Calling for a return to the original purity of Islam as so many others before him, his ideas were not unrelated to Wahhabism which, ever since the last century had left its imprint on the mentality of so many Indian Muslims.

One of his favourite themes was the establishment of Islamic power, which would permit one to apply to the letter the precepts and ideals of the religion which are proclaimed by the Revelation and codified in the traditional law (*shari'a*). And he exhorted Muslims to concentrate their efforts on the realisation of this supreme goal: the establishment of government according to the orders of God (*hukumat-e ilahiya*).

With its seeming clarity and rigorous logic, Maudoodi's thinking seduced a good number of our classmates who believed they had found suitable arguments with which to strengthen their Islam and defend it against the Western invasion. In reality, his thinking did not offer us any effective weapon with which to resist the challenge of the modern world, with its secular tendencies and negative ideologies of the intemporal and transcendent Truth which is the essence of Islam. Intellectual, spiritual and metaphysical resources, which in our religion are only accessible through the *batin*, would have been necessary. Now Maudoodi was a typical representative of the *zahir*; he neither knew nor understood Sufism, the main depository of the *batin*, and was suspicious of those who followed the Sufi path.

Amongst students, our conversations continually revolved around the political and cultural problems of the Muslims in India. It is true that my cousin and I perhaps did not share as great an interest in this subject as most of our classmates did. By the fact of our Himalayan origins, we were conscious of a certain special status and this feeling brought us closer to students from other Asian countries like Malaysia, Burma, Insulind (which was not yet called Indonesia) and Ceylon.

Nevertheless, I had excellent friends amongst the Indians 'in majority'. They often represented an elite of the population and many later went on to brilliant careers, mainly in Pakistan. Some came from princely families such as a cousin of the *nawab* of Bhopal, another was the son of the minister of finance of Hyderabad where the reigning *nizam* was reputed to be the richest man in the world. There were also the sons of former 'Aligarians', several of whom held important posts in the British administration. One of my best friends, Azizur Rahman, came from Assam where his father was a tea farmer.

~

In 1940, my first university holidays gave me the opportunity of an unforgettable experience which was to strongly influence the direction of my life. Khwaja Abdul Aziz, my uncle, had invited me to spend the summer in Lhasa where he had been staying for a short time with the Lopchak caravan, which he was directing for the first time.

After changing trains in Calcutta I arrived in Siliguri at the foot of the Himalayas which I reached by the Kalimpong route, an obligatory passage for any journey between India and the Tibetan capital. A servant of my uncle's waited for me with two sturdy mules which permitted us to make good time.

It was the first time I had followed this famous caravan route—the main line of communication for Lhasa with the outside world, now transformed by the Chinese into a paved road. Several Oriental and Western travellers have given picturesque descriptions of this journey, emphasising the total impression of foreignness that this route gave them. For me as a Ladakhi, I had the feeling of coming back to a familiar environment despite the difference in the abundance of the vegetation and the beauty of the flowers, especially rhododendrons in Sikkim and, after crossing the Tibetan border, in the Chumbi valley.

Soon the scenery became as dry as in Ladakh and the altitude did not cease to become higher until we reached Phari-Dzong at more than 4,000 metres. According to some authors, this place is one of the dirtiest in the world. I admit that it is not clean, but the striking beauty of the background of immense mountains and the purity of the continually dry air which one breathes in spite of the heaps of rubbish and refuse makes it a very tolerable lap. At this first stop I was surprised at seeing people, both men and women, who answered the call of nature in public without the slightest embarrassment. This habit certainly did not contribute to the cleanliness of the place, but one would be wrong to be too offended by it because Tibetans, who have a free and spontaneous character, are completely ignorant of modesty.

The houses in Phari are not as poor as it is said and that of the Khanshar family, where I was welcomed, was really comfortable. The mistress of the house, in her early thirties, left a deep impression on me. She had a captivating beauty which often characterises Tibetans and which Lhasa was to offer even more opportunities to admire.

The more I penetrated the interior of Tibet, the more sensitive I was to its fascination. I thought of the special charm my grandfather's home in Leh always had for me, the Tibetan objects, and I recalled his descriptions of this country with which he had so many affinities. In a way it seemed that I had always belonged here and it was here that I had rediscovered my true homeland.

It must be recognised that I travelled in especially comfortable conditions. Thanks to the arrangements made by Khwaja Abdul Aziz, at almost every lap I was able to use a bungalow which was reserved for official travellers.

However, I don't think that these material facilities particularly contributed to stimulating me to love Tibet and Tibetans. Later, when I had to be content to sleep in village houses or under a tent, I felt closer to the people and my attachment to their country was reinforced.

Gyantse is the first town worthy of this name on the route to Lhasa. Built along a wide, well-cultivated valley, it is dominated by rocky foothills, on one of which rises an ancient fortress. Behind its ramparts, the largest and most beautifully decorated buildings housed at that time a population made up entirely of monks. The whole offered a spectacle of beauty no traveller could be insensitive to. In an outer quarter named Changlo was a British post fortified by a political agent of His Majesty, a detachment of the army of India and a medical dispensary. Over the latter, Dr Bo Tsering, a Sikkimese aristocrat, presided with devotion and distinction.

Some eight days later, I arrived within view of Lhasa.

Since my earliest childhood, I had heard this town spoken of in such admiring and superlative terms that I imagined it to be a city of dreams. I was not at all disappointed. On the contrary, the reality went beyond my expectations.

I feel incapable of describing the beauty of Lhasa. It goes far beyond physical, natural and architectural forms that are possible to describe. The area is surrounded by mountains and all the buildings, be they the houses of paupers or a palace like the Potola, then corresponded to a principle of unity. The vegetation of the numerous parks and gardens also contributed to the harmony of the whole. At 3,600 metres of altitude, the air was thin. It often seemed to me that it was animated by subtle vibrations, which contributed to the happiness of feeling oneself breathe in such a place. This impression was probably related to the sacred function of Lhasa, a holy city of Buddhism, as well as to the prayers and mantras which monks by tens of thousands constantly sent towards heaven.

However, I also found other more profane pleasures in the Tibetan capital which contributed to causing me to love it.

Summer was not the great season of business for the merchant class which my relatives belonged to but rather that of vacation and society life. One of the favourite amusements of the inhabitants of Lhasa was to organise picnics outside the city. I was often invited to these and every time I went it was like attending a party, for I met young and charming cousins who were subject to less strict social rules than those in Ladakh and in countries of Muslim influence. I was particularly interested in one of them, but my uncles observed me, fearing that my leanings did not coincide with the matrimonial plans they had already drawn up for me.

In any case, those summer holidays of 1940 left a marvellous memory and I had a real infatuation for Lhasa. I then felt certain that the decision taken by my uncles to set up the main centre of our business in Lhasa rather than Leh had been the best. And I could find only advantages in the project of transferring from Ladakh to Tibet.

After two months of this relaxed and worry-free existence, much to my regret, I had to leave Lhasa and make the journey which I had undertaken at the beginning of the summer again, but in the opposite direction.

~

As soon as the train from Calcutta let me off in Aligarh, I immediately went to bed. My cousin Ataullah, who was still my roommate at the university campus, arrived at night. Opening the door, he was surprised to hear my voice in the darkness. It was me, already asleep, dreaming aloud of Lhasa.

During the following semester, my thoughts often returned to Lhasa. In our conversations amongst students, however, I didn't dare say how much I felt at ease there, for Tibet was considered a particularly 'backward' country. Moreover, I still had not found anything firm with which to cement my instinctive resistance to the aggression of Western thinking which impregnated most of the university people of Aligarh, as it did most of the intellectuals of my generation.

At the beginning of the autumn of 1940, Ataullah left the university equipped with an MA in history. He went to Srinagar soon afterwards where, thanks to the good contacts of our great-uncle, the *aksakal*, he obtained a position of a junior officer in the office of the British resident. His salary at the beginning was 75 rupees per month which in those days already represented a comfortable income.

A new roommate was assigned to me. This was In'am, the son of an important figure in the service of the *nizam* of Hyderabad. We became good friends, followed the same courses and had to pass the same examinations together.

When the summer of 1941 came around, I decided to go spend my holidays in Ladakh with my mother. These were happy weeks. The family members were in good spirits and they considered all the problems presented by the succession of Haji Muhammad Siddiq to be solved. And thanks to our Tibetan projects, I was sure that a brilliant future lay ahead of us.

As in every year in July, the festival of the monastery of Hemis took place. I attended the celebration with my cousin Abdul Haqq whose custom it was to set up a small shop where he sold turquoises from China, brocades and tea in bricks. While he was busy with his mainly female clientele, I allowed myself to be captivated by the spectacle of the ritual dances which at that time remained perfectly faithful to tradition.

In that summer of 1941, the most important reincarnated lama of Hemis had been dead for some time. The search for his new reincarnation was going on in Tibet whence he had always been found. In fact, he was to be discovered a few years later amongst nomads of the Digung region far into the northeast where a famous *kagyupa* (red-hat sect) monastery is found. He came to Hemis where he was received with great pomp but, much against his own will, he soon found himself mixed up in a very complicated intrigue led by Kushok Bakula, a lama of the neighbouring monastery of Spituk who was at the same time, a great amateur politician. It was, therefore, arranged that the lama would return to Tibet on the pretext of studying there. However, he returned to Indian territory but Bakula, who must have considered him a potential rival, took action to send him back to Lhasa which in the end the Chinese would not permit him to leave again. Much unhappiness was to result from this in Ladakh.

As I was weary of the road from Leh to Srinagar via Kargil which I had already travelled so often, I decided to organise my return journey by a different itinerary, an opportunity offered to me by two Arghons, Ladakhi Muslims trading in pashmina wool. They were going to Dozam on the high Rupshu plateau where a fair was held and attracted a good number of Gya-Khampas, Indians of Tibetan origin living mainly in the Kulu valley, every year.

At first, our route took us through the same regions which we crossed the following year with the Lopchak, then it led us farther south to Dozam. I had the surprise of meeting a European prince, Peter of Greece, who had a passion for Himalayan and Tibetan culture and whom I was to get to know later.

After three days spent at this fair at probably more than 4,000 metres of altitude, one of the highest in the world, we had to confront the Paralatse pass. Its southern slope was so steep that we had to unload the animals and carry the loads on our own backs. The track came out in Lahul, a region of a completely different nature, because the monsoon causes abundant vegetation to grow there. I met a former classmate from Srinagar there, Thakur, a descendant of a noble Buddhist family who offered me hospitality in his parents' castle. Then, via Kulu, Ambala and Delhi I soon made my way back to Aligarh and the university.

At the end of the winter semester of 1941–42 I passed my examinations for the BA degree. Then, without really knowing what I was going to do, I went to Srinagar to my cousin. I had not been there long when the painful news of my mother's death reached me. I thus hastened to return to Leh.

~

On the way I thought about my mother, this woman of an innocence, integrity, and simplicity which no longer exists today. She was certainly not 'cultured' since she couldn't read, but her great piety and practice of frequent invocations had given her a radiance to which many were sensitive. A total stranger to the modern world, she was not familiar with any of its inventions. When life in Srinagar was described to her, she didn't believe what was told to her and, for example, could not imagine that in rich houses water came directly into the kitchen through taps. For at home in Leh, carriers would go and collect water at a nearby torrent and pour it into cisterns serving as water tanks. As for electricity, there was no need to think of explaining to her what this consisted of.

In Leh, only my sister remained of my immediate family, and she was several years younger. I did not feel at ease anymore with the other relatives. They seemed no longer to maintain relationships which were as harmonious as they were during my last stay.

The ambience in the house was no longer like it was in the time of Haji Muhammad Siddiq, and under the puritan reformist influence of which Maudoodi was one of the spokesmen, religious practice tended to take a more literalist direction. My uncles and cousins thus decided to eliminate the orisons and invocations which had been the rule on our great feast days. Amongst the texts which they stopped reciting was the *Awrad al-Fatiha* of Mir Sayyid Hamadani, who in Kashmir is called the 'Second Ali' and whose litanies were very popular in the Himalayan regions. The Muslims of Tibet also recited them and great importance was attached to them in Ladakh.

My uncle Khwaja Abdul Aziz was in Leh at that time. In that summer of 1942 he was once again getting ready to direct the Lopchak caravan and counted on taking me with him.

Although I wished to continue my university studies, I had to give them up because members of the family had had bad deals and my uncles gave me no choice:

'There is no more money in the family funds,' they said. 'If you are to return to the university, we'll have to dip into capital. We can't permit this.'

Besides my participation in the Lopchak, they also had other projects for me. Since my visit to Lhasa, marriage plans for me had materialised.

These projects did not displease me at all and on the contrary, made me happy. I obviously knew the young girl destined for me since she was my cousin. Undoubtedly, it was a matter of an arranged marriage as demanded by the customs in our circles, but we liked each other and it wouldn't be exaggerated to say that it was also a marriage of love.

In Ladakh at that time practically all the marriages, Buddhist as well as Muslim, were arranged by the relatives of the two spouses. There was no question of a young man and woman marrying simply because they had fallen in love, as has often been the case since the beginning of the penetration of Western practices into our society. However, when traditional customs prevailed, this did not prevent the young couple from almost always falling in love by virtue of the arrangements made by the families. This resulted in solid unions capable of facing the trials of life. And the happiness of the young people filled the hearts of the older generation with joy.

For the two years I had known the girl who was to become my wife, I felt more than well disposed towards her. We had met on occasions of religious feasts and family gatherings which were always an opportunity for the elders to outline engagement plans. These plans took into account the leanings observed amongst the young people, who did not have the feeling that their liberty was being threatened. In reality, this traditional framework, which kept the sacred nature of marriage intact, spared them many crises and worries which poison the lives of many couples, married or not, in modern secular society.

Customs don't vary much from one community to another, even though the Muslims generally have applied traditional rules more rigorously. The Buddhists still commonly practised 'carrying off of the bride', a custom rarely imitated by Muslims. It could happen that the fiancé himself was the object of a kidnapping organised by the parents of an only daughter. In all cases, nothing like this ever took place without previous confirmation of the two parties concerned.

It was decided to organise our marriage at the same time as that of a cousin, Abdul Latif, the son of Abdullah Shah who married a sister of Abdul Haqq. This double wedding party had to be worthy of the social rank of the family and, in conformity with the custom passed on from Haji Muhammad Siddiq, who under similar circumstances had invited nearly the whole town, it was decided to do things in a big way.

The ceremonies were carried out in accordance with the traditions of Kashmir. They began with the *sermosi* or 'staining of fingers', which consisted of putting the couples' hands in henna. The next day the feast itself took place in the presence of a crowd of guests.

Unfortunately, the preparations were interrupted by thorny domestic problems. We had an old cook, Memey Amir, who had worked in our house for many years and was, so to speak, a member of the family. From the time of my grandfather, he had already entertained numerous guests invited to participate in similar festivities and he had been looking forward to preparing the dishes and sweets for the 500 to 600 people expected at our home on the day of the great feast. He had already started to bake succulent cakes in the earth ovens and in copper cauldrons, whose reflection illuminated the kitchen. Everything seemed to go marvellously until Memey Amir had some nasty run-ins with my uncles from Lhasa.

The latter, as we have seen, didn't always conduct themselves in a way adapted to the Ladakhi mentality. In their relations with their inferiors, they sometimes used the haughtiness of Tibetan aristocrats. In addition, they had some fixed ideas in the domain of cookery which they attempted to impose on the old servant. On his part, Memey Amir didn't have an easy character and did not intend to let himself be pestered by these gentlemen. They all raised their voices and the cook declared he would quit carrying on with the wedding preparations if he were treated in such a way. And in effect, he interrupted his work and left the ovens and pots there, plunging the household into a real fix. No one at that time had enough authority to get the incident under control as the deceased patriarch would have done without difficulty.

Another even more regrettable event complicated the situation: a nephew of my grandfather, who had been sick for some time, died a week before the day set for the wedding. He himself, who felt his end approaching, had advised me not to change any of our plans because of him and not to postpone the feast.

However, this sad circumstance, added to the difficulties in the kitchen, made us delay the marriage a fortnight and all the cakes and sweets already prepared by Memey Amir were lost.

The wedding finally took place and the festivities were carried out according to the traditional arrangement and customs. Alas, following the defection of the cook, the fare did not measure up to the level of the event. The rice, in particular, reduced by the chef's substitute to a glutinous thick mass, was far from being regal.

For the next fortnight after that, the wedding feast fuelled conversations in the homes and streets of Leh. For the inhabitants of this town, where nothing much exciting happened and where the terrible war which turned the world upside down was almost unknown, the episodes for which our kitchen had become a theatre, took on the dimensions of major events.

~

My life as a married man lasted three weeks, during which time I was very busy preparing for my departure with the Lopchak caravan on 19 November 1942. I wasn't to see my wife again for a year and a half.

To the pain of this separation was added the intellectual confusion that my university studies had plunged me into. For I was more and more pulled between two contradictory tendencies: on the one hand, the seduction of the modern culture the doors of which Aligarh had opened for me, and on the other, the irresistible attraction of Tibet.

Was it possible that a country so manifestly imprinted with spirituality and whose inhabitants were so fervently pious could be the domain of a false religion? Did not the true and deep nature of Islam demand the recognition of the truth in all forms?

The slowness of the caravan allowed me much leisure to ponder these questions. I felt an affinity with the inhabitants, almost always Buddhists, of the highlands which we crossed, finding in them beautiful human attitudes corresponding to the ideals of Islam. Their souls seemed to be in peace, they lived in harmony with the austere natural surroundings, and their serenity bore witness to a perfect acceptance of their destiny.

After a long ride, when we arrived tired in a nomad camp, there was always at least one who was turning his prayer wheel. With these simple, illiterate men, recollectedness seemed to be a normal state and their piety gave an impression of inwardness. In comparison, the religion of the intellectuals whom I had frequented at Aligarh seemed to me formalist. All these thoughts only fuelled my perplexity.

CHAPTER 5

MISSION ACCOMPLISHED

8 December 1942
After leaving Nahshaq, our route took us through a landscape of grandiose beauty. Unfortunately, Khwaja Abdul Aziz continued to suffer throughout the lap. But a true caravaneer of the desert should know how to accept such trials and learn to put up with them.

We are camping along the Lio Tsangpo (a branch of the Brahmaputra) where the nomads have prepared us an excellent welcome.

The sky is beginning to cloud over. Khwaja Abdul Aziz feels a little better.

9 December 1942
Early this morning I admired the magnificent view presented by the Lio Tsangpo. The sky was clear and a bright sun was rising just above the horizon. As Uncle's condition continued to improve, we were able to set off early enough to arrive in Toksum Tasam at noon. We took up our quarters in a house without a roof but covered with a *rebo* (tent canvas) of yak hair.

As the season was very late, most of the nomads had already gone to their homes at lower altitudes so that on the following days we were going through regions which were almost completely deserted. However, near Kasho (or Ganju) we noticed a *gompa* (monastery) on a rise where it was perfectly integrated into a landscape at once austere and harmonious.

On 13 December we arrived at Tadum Tasam, a real village made up of some twenty houses and a *gompa*. The presence of the inhabitants gave us the feeling of regaining contact with the world. Our caravan spent three nights there. It wasn't so cold and Uncle felt better.

Tadum (or Tradum) is a small trading centre, a day's walk away from the Nepalese border. Various articles imported from Lo (Mustang, in Nepal) like rice, wheat, wood and low-quality coral could be found here. This was an opportunity for us to sell some merchandise and buy things that we needed. With our Buddhist servants I went to visit the monastery dominating the site and was able to admire numerous works of art of great value.

The following laps were difficult. We had to cross passes where freezing winds were blowing. I caught cold, suffered from a sore throat and felt like I had the flu. And I noted pitifully in my diary:

> All these physical trials have made me understand that this journey is not so much a commercial apprenticeship but rather an expedition destined to make me think about the meaning of life and about the weight of the responsibilities that the human condition carries with it. These thoughts helped me a little to endure the fatigue and long distances.
>
> We are now in a smoky, dirty, dusty room. However, in a region like this, such a lodging is already a privilege...

On 19 December, noticing that I had left Leh and had been separated from my wife for exactly three months, I confided to my diary some melancholy thoughts about the brevity of my life as a married man. On that day we were at a place called Ngugue Tasam where a roof sheltered us but on the following lap we had to camp under the tent, which was hardly a means of getting over my cold.

After crossing rivers which were completely iced over and using as roads streams which were completely frozen in spite of the brightness of the sun, on 21 December we arrived in Saka

Dzong, a village from where we could see the majestic silhouette of a monastery several kilometres away. Our stay there was delayed until 24 December, a day on which we had to cross several high and sloping passes before going down to Ukshut at the bottom of a narrow valley. Several cultivated fields stretched around the five or six houses making up this village, proof of a lower altitude. These were the first that we noticed since our departure from Gya in Ladakh, three months earlier.

However, on the following days we had to climb and scale passes again. On 27 December we were in Ragha on a vast plateau exposed to all the winds, at the same level as the great glaciers which glimmered in the distance. The cold and altitude sickness forced us to spend a very bad night, then, during the next lap, riding bad horses, we had to confront three passes windswept by sandstorms. However, these were the end of our hardships because, although the road to Lhasa was still long, the worst difficulties of the trip were behind us.

In Gyado (or Gyaltro) on 30 December, a relatively comfortable house was waiting for us. This small township, located on a windy and barren plateau, had nothing charming about it but we were happy to give ourselves a day of rest here.

That day of 1 January 1943 marked our renewal of contact with sedentary peoples. The house which received us on the Lahgnia lap was not merely a nomad shelter again but a veritable dwelling and, however modest, it seemed almost luxurious and assured us an excellent rest.

At Sangsang at the end of the following lap where Uncle decided to spend two days in order to finalise several business transactions, we were even better lodged and, thanks to the lower altitude and less rigorous temperatures, we all felt cheered up and in good spirits. The countryside, which we crossed during the lap of 4 January, seemed to me full of seductions and I was joyful to see, instead of barren, windswept mountains which had been our usual scenery for so many weeks, hills and valleys covered with grass and coppice. My enthusiasm was such that, in my diary, I compared this scenery to the tropics!

In fact, the temperature remained below zero and crossing the largest currents became difficult because the ice made fording impractical. In order to cross the Lhatse river we, therefore, had to make a whole detour to a place where the ice was thick enough to bear the weight of our pack animals.

Our arrival in the market town of Lhatsay on 10 January where we were to stay two days and carry out several good trading deals, made us really happy. After taking a nice warm bath and walking through the bazaar in the evening, I noted: 'For us, who have just spent more than three months in wild, almost uninhabited regions, the sight of these houses and streets has something grandiose about it.'

However, a final trial was still in store for us during the next lap. In freezing cold, the worst sandstorm that we had to undergo during the entire expedition broke out. But in the evening at Phuntsokling (or Pindzoling), the lamas of the local monastery extended us much respect and kindness.

After all these unforeseen events we had accumulated a considerable delay with regard to the original schedule of the Lopchak caravan and we had to cover the distance which still separated us from Shigatse—the fief of Panchen Lama and, in a way, the second capital of Tibet—in three days instead of four. At the entrance of Naytang, a day's walk from the city, our cousins Atiullah and Inayatullah, coming to meet us, caught up with us. The following evening, amidst much merriment, was the opportunity for endless conversations about the family and the world from which we had been separated for so long.

The following day, mounted upon mules brought by our cousins, we accomplished the easiest and happiest lap of the entire journey since our departure from Ladakh. Along the way, the lamas of a neighbouring monastery came out especially to greet us. The peasants of the surrounding area were lined up along the road to see us pass by, sticking out their tongues as a sign of respect.

The closer we got to Shigatse, the more people there were who came to welcome us. And when the caravan entered the city it turned into an important procession which was joined by other lamas, children, as well as almost the entire local Muslim community, and of course, our relatives. The cheering of the inhabitants and the warmth of the welcome made our joy perfect. The notes I took on the evening of this memorable day are barely legible. I must have been too tired or too excited, probably both at once, to write correctly. In any case, it is with this episode that my diary of the Lopchak caravan closes.

~

When one of our family members stopped in Shigatse with an ordinary caravan, he was received into the homes belonging to the family. But the Lopchak conferred upon us a special status and we were the guests of the government who put at our disposal an apartment in the hotel reserved for official people.

In this pleasant lodging we were not far from the famous monastery of Tashilungpo where there was a building for monks and novices coming from Ladakh. There were several dozen of them at that time and all of them were keen on coming to cheer our entrance into the city. Many came to visit us in our apartment. On our part, we went to the monastery and were able to find out something about the monastic life. None of the monks had any complaints and they all professed themselves happy with their lot. In effect, they seemed perfectly integrated into the greater community and maintained the most fraternal relations with local Tibetans.

This visit was also the occasion to take leave of the young Lobzang who had joined us to enter as a novice in Tashilungpo and all along the way had served us with so much devotion and kindness.

Traditionally, Shigatse was under the autonomous administration of the Panchen Lama who had his residence in Tashilungpo. But at this time, following political circumstances which I shall come back to, the government of Lhasa administered the town and its region directly where it had delegated a *Shi-Dzong* (governor general) representing the *Kashag* (council of ministers) and the regent who exercised his power whilst the Dalai Lama was still a minor.

As head of the Lopchak, Khwaja Abdul Aziz had to make an official visit to the *Shi-Dzong* and I accompanied him. It seemed he knew this prominent figure of the upper nobility of Lhasa quite well.

In the bazaar, the Muslims constituted the majority of the local merchants. We met the most important of them as our cousins invited them to a great dinner organised in our honour.

All Ladakhis, like Kashmiris and other Indians, were as a general rule considered British subjects and they counted on the British resident in Shigatse to stand up for them in any disputes that they might have with the Tibetan authorities. In this respect, an important merchant in our family was disappointed in an affair which put him in opposition to the local administration. The appeal he made to the representative of the empire had not been followed up effectively. As Khwaja Abdul Aziz then played the part of a person of rank introduced into the highest circles, he took on the task of intervening for this merchant with the *Kashag*. Unfortunately, I think he was also unsuccessful.

A grim future lay ahead for this active and industrious merchant community. At the time of the revolutionary upheavals provoked by the Chinese at the end of the 1950s, the members of this community were no more protected than other Tibetans against the extortions of the occupying power and their flight to India was a sombre tragedy. Some like Atiullah were able to make a living again by sheer work, but many continued to vegetate as poor refugees.

After a week spent in Shigatse our caravan regrouped itself. A young cousin, the future wife of Atiullah who was to go to Lhasa, joined us. All our uncles and cousins escorted us a good distance from the city as well as the Ladakhis of Tashilungpo who followed us, praying for our safety and success.

To get from Shigatse to Lhasa we had a choice of two itineraries. The shortest, through Rong and the Tsangpo (Brahmaputra) valley took nine days. We preferred the other route however, two days longer but easier and more trod upon, passing through Gyantse. After the deserts of the Trans-Himalayas, we were joyful to walk in regions covered with vegetation. There were many villages and everywhere the inhabitants welcomed us eagerly and kindly. The lives of the people had not yet been touched at all by the modern world and the Buddhist tradition which penetrated these lives seemed to have maintained all its vigour.

Passing through Ralung, the pass of Karo La and Zara, the track gave on to a plateau at a high altitude, went round the huge Yamdok Tso lake, crossed another pass, the Kamba La, then went down into the deep valley of the Tsangpo. The scenery was beautiful and our pace became lighter as we walked alongside our mounts as every respectable caravaneer should do when descending a steep slope. In a pleasant region with rich agricultural resources, a wooden ferry took us across the river with loads and animals whilst other travellers gave themselves over to goatskin boats. We were not far from the Lhasa valley.

The next locality was Chushul, an important district seat. An unforeseen complication kept us there for eight days.

The incident happened at the government rest house where we were lodged. The chief of the district had delegated one of his subordinates to welcome us who was in charge of giving us shawls of honour (*khatak*) as well as some gifts. But Uncle did not consider this reception worthy of the rank and importance which he attributed to himself and began to recriminate them vigorously.

His protests were supported by his brother, Muhammad Asghar Tsakur, who came to meet him from Lhasa, richly dressed and taking on the airs of a person of rank.

The conflict grew more intense but the Tibetans never raised their voices. Expressing themselves courteously, the officials did not give in to the demands of the head of the caravan but deliberately created difficulties for him. They politely let him know that the mules necessary for continuing our journey were not available. Unable to convince them with words, Khwaja Abdul Aziz, whose anger continued to increase, hit them with his cane, which made them even more recalcitrant.

For my part, I disapproved of my uncle's attitude. I preferred to keep my distance, and since the temperature was mild, I went to the banks of the river. I found a group of young people there, boys and girls, all completely undressed and stretched out on the bank sunbathing. In the end I didn't have too bad a memory of this unexpected stay.

Many years later I met the district chief who had irritated my uncle so much in Dharamsala in India, where he was a refugee. We spoke of this episode and laughed cordially about it.

~

Two days' walk remained to Lhasa and I was anxious to see this town again which I had dreamed of so much since my first visit two-and-a-half years earlier. After spending a night in Nethang in a beautiful agricultural region, our caravan embarked upon the final lap of the Lopchak. Stepping up our pace, we soon arrived in sight of Drepung, the famous monastery which, in its many buildings, then sheltered thousands of monks, exactly 7,777 as the Tibetans liked to specify at that time.

There also, all the monks of Ladakhi origin waited for us along the road to welcome us. They cheered us and the older ones who years ago had welcomed Haji Muhammad Siddiq in a similar way came to express their joy at seeing the continuation of the tradition of this caravan. Uncle was so happy about this that he forgot about the difficult interlude of Chushul.

In the first row of the crowd who came to welcome us were, naturally, a large number of Radhus, our relatives, and other members of the Muslim community of Lhasa. Three hours were spent listening to their good wishes and congratulations.

A whole crowd escorted us after our caravan was on its way again. But soon, after arriving in Kyanda Gang, we stopped again. There was a park there which, it seems, had been previously occupied by the Jesuits before becoming a sort of Muslim enclave with a mosque, a cemetery and terrace which I knew well, having picnicked there several times during my first stay in Lhasa. We were given another reception with tea and pastries and we exchanged wishes and congratulations.

Finally, after four months of journeying, the long awaited moment of our entry into Lhasa had arrived. Leaving Norbulinka on the right and Potala on the left, our happy procession, expanded with numerous Muslims, Ladakhis and other fellow travellers, paraded through the streets to the cheers of the inhabitants and passed in front of the Kunphela house, which was called Chensay Phodang, because the Dalai Lama had paid a visit there. The procession stopped in front of the door of the Tsakur residence as the main house of the Radhu descendants was called.

It was in this large building, which constituted one whole block with the seat of the Nepalese diplomatic mission, where we decided to stay in preference to the government hotel that we had the right to stay in. There was a specific reason for this: by lodging the head of the Lopchak in the Tsakur house, the uncles sought to have themselves recognised with a status of extraterritoriality that would help them to avoid paying taxes. But to obtain this, they would have needed the support of the British resident, which they could never get.

~

After our arrival in Lhasa, a series of obligations was still incumbent upon us as representatives of the Lopchak. The most important was our participation in the great durbar of the *Monlam*, the Tibetan new year, regularly organised in Potala in the same season. During this solemn audience the members of the various government bodies and representatives of the communities and social classes, including Muslims and foreign residents, came to pay homage to the Dalai Lama. For us, this was to be the occasion for presenting the tribute and gifts on behalf of the Ladakhi Buddhists which they sent to His Holiness and, according to traditional custom, was made up of a small quantity of gold, saffron, shawls from Kashmir, various textiles from Sinkiang, as well as a product native to their country, dried apricots.

~

Unfortunately, a large part of our baggage was still missing and remained somewhere on the road under the supervision of the *atung* who nevertheless did his best to get them to us on time. As soon as they arrived in the capital, Khwaja Abdul Aziz did everything possible to try to speed up the transport of the missing cases and packs so that they would reach us in time. But when the day of the big ceremony came we still hadn't received them. The entourage of the Dalai Lama did not hold it against us, for it was known in official circles that all communications along the western tracks were delayed because of the Hasakapa incursions.

In any case the Tibetan authorities had no intention of creating difficulties for the Lopchak and its representatives. On the contrary, they showed much goodwill and consideration towards us and made every effort to make our stay in Lhasa enjoyable.

This positive attitude, which moreover reflected the feelings discreetly expressed to the *Kashag* by the British resident was in fact in conformity with the interests of the Tibetan government because the Lopchak provided an argument pushing the government's claim for independence from the Chinese. In effect, it was the custom of the Chinese also, under the imperial regime, to periodically send a tribute to the Dalai Lama whom they then considered a sort of high priest having a sacred function concerning all of China. In Lhasa this historical fact was seen as proof that Tibet owed no allegiance to China and could claim complete sovereignty for herself. It is true that in Peking the reverse conclusion was drawn.

Not wanting to give an exaggerated political significance to the modest mission which we accomplished in the name of a tiny people who made up a part of a great empire, it was obvious that our arrival in Lhasa gave Tibetans a welcome opportunity to re-affirm their friendship for the Ladakhis whom they did not regard as foreigners but as brothers sharing a common cultural heritage. We received much evidence of this, in particular from the prime minister, Phondong Shoba, and from several high-ranking dignitaries.

The participation in the durbar demanded clothing which strictly conformed to traditions of protocol. As Ladakhi Muslims, we wore white turbans and Khwaja Abdul Aziz, the head of the Lopchak, wore a richly embroidered shawl over his coat (*gos* or *shuba*). Upon arrival at the palace, the harness of his horse was shown off by two red pompoms, one above the withers (neck) and the other on the breast, which indicated a relatively high position because, according to the protocol, the Lopchak gave the right to the fourth rank. I followed as an assistant to the head of the caravan and we had an escort of Buddhists wearing the *mahmal*, a high velvet hat typical of Ladakh.

At the entrance of the Potala, the monk guards of the Dalai Lama, impressive with their iron cudgels and their whips, prevented pushing and shoving amongst the guests, each of whom was going to occupy a seat in the audience room that was assigned to him according to the regulations. I saw with my own eyes guards intervene and roughly hit important people, regardless of their rank, who had only moved one step.

The customs which had to be respected remained present in the minds of the dignitaries because, inside the palace, frescoes reproduced the different phases of the durbar. It was in a way an illustrated treatise of the protocol.

After everyone had found his seat and everything was ready for the ceremony, the spectacle of the great hall was gripping. A total and solemn silence was established, the likes of which I have never seen anywhere.

On his throne, dominating the presence, the Dalai Lama was seated cross-legged. He was then a child of less than eight years but his innocent face already seemed imprinted with dignity and authority. Behind him, the highest dignitaries, the regent at their head, didn't take their eyes off him, as if he were their prisoner, whilst at the same time watching over the members of his family, especially his father whom certain people accused of abusing the situation.

A magnificently dressed chamberlain stood on each side of the throne. Then, all in formal attire, came the ministers, clerks and laymen wearing golden headdresses followed by descendants of the families of the preceding Dalai Lamas in hierarchical order and other members of the nobility. The least important of all those present kept their eyes fixed on the child sovereign.

On the left side of the throne, the English and Nepalese residents had taken their place but I don't remember anymore if there was also a Chinese representative. As for us, members of the Lopchak, we were amongst the foreigners and Tibetan subjects, a position which we shared with the Bhutanese of the Dugpa Lopchak which had come to Lhasa at the head of a mission very similar to ours. The other Muslims formed a group amongst the representatives of the various Tibetan communities and the crowd of monks. The ceremony began in an air thick with incense smoke.

~

Adhering to hierarchical order, the audience filed slowly one by one before the throne, prostrating in front of the Dalai Lama. But there were exceptions. Neither the British agent nor the Muslims prostrated. In virtue of the custom which had always been respected by the Thirteenth Dalai Lama and which his successor had to confirm as soon as he became of age, the latter greeted him in the Islamic fashion with salams, or greetings of peace. This peculiarity was significant of the status of the Tibetan Muslims and the good relations they continuously maintained with the highest authorities of the Buddhist theocracy which constituted Tibet.

The small meal following the homage ceremony gave way to indescribable pushing and shoving. Then everyone rushed for the pastries and biscuits served by the Dalai Lama and placed in the centre of the room. It was not at all a question of gluttony but desire on the part of the Buddhists to derive as much as possible from a food considered to bear beneficial spiritual influence emanating from the sacred personality of the religious head. As soon as he had withdrawn, free passage was given to disorder. And the audience in the room could be heard as their exclamations and protests resounded: 'Don't push! Stay in line! Don't you know how to conduct yourselves? On your guard!'

The excitement increased, the din became louder, and politeness was forgotten. Even the hierarchic order didn't seem to count much anymore.

For the next few days in Lhasa only the durbar and what had happened there was talked about. I then heard about an episode which took place several years earlier. The British resident, who had been admitted to take part in the ceremony only a short time before, wanted to bestow a relatively high status upon the clerks in his office in Lhasa so that they would be given a warm welcome. He had several of them given the title of 'Rai Bahadur' attempting to have it admitted that this was the equivalent of the fourth rank. Now one of them, wearing the clothes and insignia of the fourth rank, made a blunder which was immediately interpreted as an ignorance of protocol. He was strongly apostrophised by the assistants: 'How dare you come here with such insignia if you are not even aware of the most elementary of our customs!' And the guards began to flog the poor man.

On the occasion of the *Monlam*, the New Year, the holders of temporal power entrusted the administration of the country to the monks. Then for a month the lamas of the 'Three Monasteries', Drepung, Ganden and Sera, assumed the responsibilities of the government, which certainly did not contribute to its efficiency.

~

As for us, the participation in the great durbar did not end our official obligations. It was still incumbent upon the members of the Lopchak to accomplish the visits of protocol at several monasteries and places of pilgrimage in central Tibet.

This tour took us to Samye, Tsethang, Thangtu, Digong and Digongthi. For the Tibetan Buddhists, the most important of these holy places was the monastery of Samye. A famous sanctuary called Ukang was located there where monks of Ladakhi origin showed us around. Meaning 'residence of the dead', Ukang was an obligatory sojourn for souls who had left human bodies that had just died. We were assured that it was possible to hear them, but I was unable to verify this.

In Tsethang, a town of some importance, the small local Muslim community grouped around an attractive mosque and cemetery, detained us for several days. We were the guests of a family who were related to the Radhus. One of the family members was to make himself famous from 1959 on in the revolt of the Khampas against the Chinese Communists. We took part in the Friday prayer and, before setting off again, we recognised that these Muslims forming such an isolated island in a Buddhist land remained perfectly faithful to their traditional customs and to the practice of their religion. Apart from a few exceptions, they seemed to have all gone into exile following the upheavals in 1959 provoked by the occupying power.

Thangtu was the seat of a monastery harbouring a celebrated statue of Dolma, a divinity of compassion very popular in Tibetan Buddhism, who corresponds to the Tara of the Hindus. In the forehead of the idol a sapphire, the size of a walnut, was inserted. The sanctuary where the idol was located was strictly guarded and a door reinforced by a heavy chain forbade access to it.

In the proximity there appeared a series of tantric sculptures of an erotic nature, veritable artistic masterpieces. For the average Muslim, the sight of these images was horribly shocking and my uncle visibly turned away from them. At the time, I also found them at least surprising but, all the same, I finally understood that they could have a profound symbolism of true spiritual significance. In any case, I was able to ascertain from this time on that the Tibetans themselves approached these sculptures with much respect and recollectedness. Hundreds of faithful men, women and children filed past them, their hands clasped together, reciting mantras in an attitude of adoration, obviously very far from any profane or impure thought.

Visiting such a sanctuary in the company of Buddhist friends who had accompanied us all along our route, I certainly wouldn't have thought of lewd jokes because it was much too obvious that we were in the presence of the sacred. With them, I visited many other holy Buddhist places, each time making an effort to assume a respectful attitude. Khwaja Abdul Aziz let me do as I wished but I saw that he was inclined to consider Buddhism as a form of paganism and its practice as idolatry in the same way as Muslims of the *zahir* who were influenced by modern reformers. He even appeared to have a bad conscience when he was obliged to visit temples in exercising his functions.

These Ladakhi Buddhists had given themselves to the service of the Lopchak with the sole intention of performing a pilgrimage, and the tour which we made in central Tibet filled them with happiness. They encountered a good number of their compatriots in the monasteries included in our itinerary, in particular at Digong and Digongthi.

Upon returning to the capital, they pressed me to accompany them on their visits to holy places such as the various temples and chapels of the Potala. They even took me to Jokhang, the central temple, and in a way the 'cathedral' of Lhasa. As a general rule, non-Buddhists were not admitted inside, with the exception of the Bonpos who practised the ancient religion of Tibet. The Newars and other Nepalese Buddhists had access to it but not the Hindu Gurkhas. Taken in by my friends, I was perhaps the only Muslim to enter it and I even made several visits. However, I avoided prostrating myself each time as the other visitors did, even though I felt tempted to. In any case, I took care to conduct myself discreetly and not to make my abstention shocking to the faithful of this holy place.

We had brought the Lopchak to its end and I felt happy to be in Lhasa. I didn't know what turn my life was going to take. When I thought of our modest township of Leh, the Tibetan capital appeared to me to offer resources which could help our enterprise develop. I was thus eager to transfer the centre of gravity of the business inherited from Haji Muhammad Siddiq to Lhasa and to have my wife come there. And to prepare myself for the busy time which I foresaw, I began to study Tibetan, which I still spoke quite poorly.

CHAPTER 6

MUSLIMS, ARISTOCRATS AND PLOTTERS

My closest relatives in Lhasa were Khwaja Abdul Aziz and his two brothers, Muhammad Asghar and Sirajuddin. They were generally called the 'Tsakur brothers' after the name of the house they lived, in one of the best sections of the town centre and where I also settled. Descendants of Omar Shah and the 'Chinese' branch of the Radhus, they were moreover, related by their mother to the Ladakhi branch of Haider Shah to which I belonged through my father.

Born and educated in Tibet, they had the Tibetan mentality and mannerisms which clearly differed from ours. At the beginning of my stay, I often felt like a stranger with them. But I told myself that the best thing I could do would be to adapt myself to their customs and co-operate openly with them in order to contribute as best I could to the success of our common business.

However, the uncles themselves were not in as prosperous a financial situation as I had presumed. They had heavy debts, mainly to high government officials, and often found it difficult to pay the interest on them because the income from their commercial dealings was irregular. In such conditions, the prospect of being able to have access to capital coming from the inheritance of Haji Muhammad Siddiq was a godsend they were determined not to pass up.

From the time of the Thirteenth Dalai Lama (who died in 1933), my uncles Muhammad Asghar and Sirajuddin had travelled extensively for their business in various regions of Tibet, especially in the Kham country in the east where they sold—or traded because money circulated little amongst these peoples where bartering was commonly practised—various articles, in particular coral, which was much appreciated amongst the Khampas. They were patronised by a great aristocrat, Doring, whom they often followed in his movements. He was always followed by a pack of dogs—it was moreover, said that he had more consideration for his dogs than he had for his people.

Wherever they stopped for their trading, the Tsakurs exploited a source of supplementary income. Thanks to a device of lighting projections which they set up in front of a screen, they showed slides and other fixed images to a fascinated public. The electrical power, still totally unknown in these regions, came from a magneto which they worked by pedalling. This activity gave them special fame amongst the Khampas and they returned from these expeditions loaded down with gifts.

The profits made from this allowed them to import a real cinema projector from India which they proposed to use in Lhasa. But they needed a special authorisation from the Dalai Lama in order to use it. Now the person who was in the best position to obtain it for them was Shensay Kunphela who enjoyed the favour of the sovereign and whose power then went beyond all the ministers put together.

This Kunphela had a certain interest in modern civilisation. It was he who, thinking his master would be pleased, had brought in parts from India the first automobile to be seen in the streets of Lhasa. He was interested in the two brothers' idea and called them to Potala for a demonstration. Fascinated and impressed, the Tsakurs came and installed their gadget in a room of the palace on the same day.

For this first cinema performance, Kunphela had assembled

numerous guests, mostly members of the upper nobility. They were so curious to see this marvel that it was announced to them that if they pushed and shoved where the projector was set up, they would risk breaking it. The head of the palace became angry and grabbed a battery-run torch and, even though he himself was a commoner, he hit the most undisciplined of the aristocrats regardless of their rank and threw several of them out. The show was finally able to begin. It was an undisputed success and my uncles obtained the necessary licence authorising them to exploit the extraordinary invention.

However, their brother Abdul Aziz, who was under the influence of reformist and puritanical Islam, regarded this activity with suspicion. Were the profits earned from projecting animated images legal from the point of view of Islamic law? He wasn't able to clarify this point of law and decided to keep silent, leaving his brothers to exploit this first cinema in Lhasa which, over the years, would bring them considerable revenue. Much later, after the Chinese revolution forced the Tsakurs to close their cinema hall, Khwaja Abdul Aziz declared that, all things taken into account, he considered the cinema contrary to Islamic law.

My uncles also had a shop in Lhasa which brought them significant revenue. They would have liked me to be associated with it but I did not feel much attraction for this type of business. I did not like the workplace, which was dark and stuffy, and I looked down on businesses where most of one's time was wasted.

I would have preferred bulk trade and the life my grandfather led to this small-time business and the life of a small shopkeeper. And, moreover, because I didn't feel attached to my uncles by any strong affinity and as they were aware of this, our relations were sometimes a bit strained. But they treated me considerately because I represented the link with the family of Ladakh, holders of the capital which they were anxious to see transferred to Tibet.

To get away from these often grumpy uncles, I willingly went to other family members, with a preference for my three cousins—the sons of Khan Sahib Faizullah. The latter, a particularly influential person and well integrated into the circles close to the court, had a plan to regroup all the Muslims in Lhasa and place them under the authority of the British resident with whom he maintained close relations. He saw this as an efficient means of strengthening the position of the Islamic community. The resident had proposed that he be the officially recognised head of this community, but Faizullah died prematurely and the plan was discarded.

Intelligent and educated, my cousins attended the British mission school during the short period of its existence, and then the Chinese mission school of the Kuomingtang. They learnt Chinese perfectly there which later got them important posts as translators and Central Asian affairs experts in the Pakistani administration. Within the family framework they had also acquired real Muslim education, reading the Qur'an perfectly and possession of Urdu and Persian, the two other languages of Islam.

Another relative whom I had the pleasure of meeting was Habibullah. He lived in Shigatse but often came into Lhasa for his business. Belonging more to my uncle's generation, he had married a girl from the Tibetan nobility who converted to Islam and gave him two sons, Atiullah and Hedayatuallah.

A peculiar destiny was in store for the latter. Although he was a fervent Muslim, he was claimed to be a *Rimpoche* or reincarnated lama by a Buddhist monastery. In spite of his persistent and lively denials of this, the monks never wanted to give in to him. Far from becoming a lama, he himself in his turn was to marry a Buddhist who followed him in Islam. He died in 1959 at the time of the great revolt of Lhasa against the Chinese, struck by a stray bullet.

~

The Islamic community of Lhasa, whose total population could never have gone beyond a thousand, were divided into two groups which did not mingle much with each other. The Chinese

Muslims or Hobalingpas, as they were called because of the Hobaling section where they lived and had their mosque, were often butchers and meat suppliers to the court of the Dalai Lama and the aristocracy, a job which orthodox Buddhists looked down upon. Others, who had plots of land were market gardeners and sold their vegetables in the bazaar. In general they were well integrated into the local life, and the Tibetans did not look upon them as foreigners as they did the other Chinese.

Preferring to live on the west side of the capital, the Muslims of the other group were descendants of immigrants who, over the recent centuries, had come from Kashmir and other provinces of northern India like Bihar as well as Nepal. They were almost all merchants and had often managed to build up prosperous and envied positions for themselves. They were all called 'Khache', a term derived from 'Khachul' meaning Kashmir in Tibetan.

Their trade, which depended on the Indian market, was based on the communication axis between Calcutta and Tibet via Darjeeling and Kalimpong. Specialising in textiles and cosmetics, they supplied themselves in India and then sold half their merchandise wholesale and the other half retail in their own shops. At this time, their business was going fairly well and they led a relatively easy and prosperous life. Some of them, particularly amongst my relatives, had gained the confidence of the upper reaches of the aristocracy in whose service they had the occasion to make business trips to south of the Himalayas.

Summer in Lhasa was not a great season for business. This time of year was spent enjoying life, and picnics continued to be organised in the countryside surrounding the capital. In the winter months, however, a lively trade went on in the markets of Lhasa where many people from the provinces congregated: Changpas from the north, Khampas and Amdos from the east, Pembos and Kongpos from the south, and other people from the west. They came in for trade or simply to celebrate the New Year in the holy city. This was the time when our uncles and cousins did the best business. Later in the season, fairs were held like those of Shera and Shambaling in central Tibet which numerous Muslims always took part in.

Because of their Indian and Kashmiri origins, the members of the Islamic community sometimes thought that it was in their interest to pass for British subjects. This was especially the case for those of Ladakhi origin, but most of them did not recognise any authority but that of the Dalai Lama. At the beginning of the occupation, they were still considered exclusively Tibetan and were considered as such by the Chinese. However, as things degenerated, they ended up going to the general consulate of India to register there as Indian citizens. Several notables, however, were arrested by the occupying forces and taken to detention areas and were never seen again. Thanks to the help of the Indian representative, most of them managed to escape to their countries of origin where they had difficulty re-adjusting and did not live much better than the masses of Tibetan refugees. In the end some of them remained in Lhasa and collaborated more or less closely with the Chinese.

In general, this small Muslim minority in Lhasa lived harmoniously with the Buddhist population as well as with the authorities who never objected to the privileged relations which they sometimes had with the British resident. On the contrary, the commercial activity of the Muslims gave them somewhat the function of acting as intermediaries with the outside world. In certain cases, they acted as exchange agents for highly placed officials and even for monasteries.

All those who knew this community are in agreement that these Muslims, completely isolated within the universe of Tibetan Buddhism, remained remarkably faithful to the spirit of the letter of traditional Islamic law which they observed according to the Hanafi rite. Although they were naturally adapted to the customs and mentality of the environment in which they had lived for centuries, they had kept their religious identity intact. They certainly benefited from Buddhist tolerance but, on their side, they also knew how to maintain the attitude of respect, which was called for in the face of the existing sacred tradition, without considering themselves as inevitably better—since they were Muslims. In the climate of lamaist spirituality, this position often encouraged a fervent practice of Islam, with a tendency towards the *batin*, the inward. It is true that some reformist influences which came from India and Kashmir encouraged some members of our minority to view the Buddhists with a more critical eye.

These same reformist circles of the *zahir* often reproached the Muslims of Tibet for not proselytising amongst the Buddhist population where, in fact, conversion to Islam remained very rare. They were also accused of confining themselves into too much of a reserved attitude, especially in the cultural domain. Apart from the small artefacts which they often made, they had no real artistic or literary activity.

I am nevertheless still convinced that the existence of these small Muslim groups in the immense Buddhist domain which made up Tibet, was in itself something admirable. Their daily life, within the faithfulness to their traditions and the respect for those of others can be compared, in my opinion, with deeply moving and living poetry. It was a veritable *art de vivre* which, judging from many eminent or humble persons whom I knew, produced genuine masterpieces of the human state.

~

In the months following my arrival in Lhasa with the Lopchak, I envisaged happily integrating myself into this community whose lifestyle agreed with my tastes. Although my uncles' shop did not attract me very much, I realised that it was possible, as a Muslim merchant, to have a more interesting activity and to build up for oneself a good position, especially if one were introduced into the circles of the nobility. The Tsakurs, and especially Khwaja Abdul Aziz, were well integrated into these circles even though they did not take full advantage of it. Thanks to such relations, several other coreligionists floated in these aristocratic spheres and they shared its comfort and pleasures.

Contacts with people of the upper class who came regularly to the bazaar were frequent and easy. At this time when there were neither newspapers nor any other means of obtaining news, the bazaar was a place where news was exchanged more often than merchandise was sold. The aristocrats, calling out to passers-by whom they wished to speak to briefly, called the Muslims 'bhailas', an expression derived from the Urdu bhai, which we used amongst ourselves. They called the Nepalese 'sodalas' *so* meaning 'wealth' and *da* 'property' because the subjects of this kingdom were said to be wealthy. As for the Khampas, they were called 'abolas' after the term *abo* (brother, like bhai) which they added to the beginning of their name. We would sit in one of the numerous tea houses in the bazaar and were soon up to date on everything that went on in the town. My uncles' shop was also often a place where these types of conversations took place, often in 'bazaar Tibetan', which most of the Muslim merchants spoke. However, conscious of a level of culture which my university training had given me, I wanted to learn good Tibetan.

It was easy to get to know members of the nobility and I had the good fortune of being welcomed into the Tendong household, a renowned family from Shigatse. They had belonged to the leading classes for generations. The head of the household, a man of less than thirty years whom I soon became friends with, was surrounded by his wife and children, a brother and two younger sisters as well as several other relatives amongst whom often appeared an uncle who was a monk. His father, after holding high positions in the government of the Thirteenth Dalai Lama, had been governor of Chamdo in the east of Tibet and had died a few years previously.

I was always received with much kindness in the Tendong household where I became a regular figure, and the children began to call me 'Uncle'. The bonds of friendship which I forged at that time with this distinguished family were to be even more strengthened over the years, because later I had the opportunity to meet several family members in Kalimpong and do them some favours, in particular, helping one of the daughters to get into an English school in Darjeeling. She acquired an education which was extremely useful for her when she found herself reduced to the state of a refugee. I also accompanied my friend, as well as his brother and sisters, on the pilgrimage which they made to the Buddhist sanctuaries of India. More fortunate than other families of a similar rank, several Tendongs escaped the cataclysm of the Chinese revolution and two of them immigrated to Switzerland and lived in Appenzell in the village of Pestalozzi.

Their friendship was especially valuable to me at a time when I wished to transfer our business from Leh to Lhasa without too much delay and see my wife again, and I didn't know how to organise my collaboration with Khwaja Abdul Aziz and the Tsakurs. In any case, I found more pleasure in the company of my new friends than with my uncles. Thanks to the Tendongs, I cultivated relations with other young people belonging to the most important families, especially with the sons of people as important as Kapshopa, Tsarong, Taring. Their education was similar to mine since most of them had studied in India and spoke good English. Another frequent visitor to the house was Thangmay, the engineer responsible for the central electricity of Lhasa, and the same one who three years later was so kind to the Austrian mountain climber Heinrich Harrer, the future author of *Seven Years in Tibet*. He helped him, along with his companion Peter Aufschnaiter, to escape a British confinement camp in India and got him accepted by the Tibetan authorities.

At a time when the nobility really controlled all the political life in Lhasa, frequenting such circles and the unending conversations which we had there provided me with first-hand information about the situation in Tibet and the most important episodes in her recent history. I, obviously, could neither guarantee the authenticity of all the statements that I then heard nor the objectivity of those who upheld them, but these conversations permitted me to get a fairly good idea of the main events which had taken place since the death of the Thirteenth Dalai Lama.

The latter had been called the Great Thirteenth because, since the Fifth in the sixteenth century, he had undoubtedly been the most remarkable figure of the lineage. The way in which he had stood up to the English troops of Colonel Younghusband, then to the Chinese troops who had invaded his country time and again, strengthened his authority within the country and at the same time won him respect from abroad. Fairly open to the modern world, he consented to send four young people to study in England. He had also re-organised and modernised his army, inspired by the Western and Japanese models. Within the country, he managed to unravel the intrigues of the nobility who for so long had poisoned political life in Lhasa and he imposed his authority everywhere.

The promotions which he promised to men of plebeian origin were proof of the power which he exercised over the nobility and they had to resign themselves to this. Tsarong and Kunphela were the most well-known examples.

The story of Tsenser, an insignificant peasant who became a high aristocrat, is worth recounting. From a village north of Lhasa where his father crafted arrows, he entered the service of the Thirteenth as a river jumper and was recognised for his resourcefulness. In 1904 when the Dalai Lama was escaping from the English invasion, and retreated to Mongolia, Tsenser had already distinguished himself for his devotion and courage, but the events of 1910 made him into a sort of national hero. Since the Chinese were marching into Lhasa with the intention of kidnapping the Dalai Lama and taking him hostage, he decided once again to escape, this time, towards the south. But the invaders were at his heels. Leading a handful of brave men,

Tsenser managed to stop them at the monastery of Shaksam not far from the place where the ferries crossed the Tsangpo river, allowing his master time to reach Indian territory safely.

After this eventful interlude when Tsenser had reached his capital for the second time, the Dalai Lama compensated him by making him a noble and marrying him to the eldest daughter of the Tsarong family. This daughter had become a widow in her first marriage. The young man was thus adopted by this famous family whose name he took, and from then on when one mentioned the name Tsarong, everyone knew that it could only be him that was being spoken of. Remaining illiterate, he never spoke refined Tibetan. This, however, did not prevent him from taking charge of the highest responsibilities of the state for a long time where his intelligence, political sense and energy were felt.

Placed by the Thirteenth at the head of the army, which he was in charge of reorganising, Tsarong also entered the *Kashag*, the council of ministers where his influence was considerable. At the same time he consolidated his position at the centre of the aristocracy by multiplying his marriages with the daughters of important families. He had many children from them and thus found himself related to a good number of the most powerful figures in the country. That is why the intrigues contrived against him were never able to bring him down. Of course, his enemies were able to reduce his power and several years before the death of the Dalai Lama, he had to resign from his ministerial post and as commander of the army, but he remained influential in the close circles of the court and the sovereign continued to consult him.

His position was such that the sudden death of the Thirteenth in 1933 was not, as it was for the others, the signal for his downfall. Distancing himself somewhat, he remained one of the most respected figures of the capital and his opinions carried much weight. For a man of such a simple background, his everlasting success sparked the imagination and the expression 'Clever as Tsarong' became proverbial.

This exceptional destiny can be compared to that of Shensay Kunphela, who has already been mentioned in connection with the Tsakur brothers' cinema. Also of a peasant background, he came from the village of Talung, to the north of Lhasa and was but an unknown young monk when he was employed as a messenger in the offices of the Dalai Lama. He made himself appreciated and His Holiness, who had noticed him, gave him more and more important responsibilities making him his 'patron', that is, his confident and his right-hand man and gave him the nickname Shensay which means 'close to the eyes'(of the sovereign). But, unlike Tsarong, Kunphela was not integrated into the nobility and remained a monk all the time he governed Tibet on his master's behalf until the latter's death.

According to traditional custom, the Dalai Lama never entered a private home without it being thereafter considered a palace and called Phodang. Now Kunphela built a beautiful home for himself and invited His Holiness who deigned to go there. I often noticed the silhouette of the building located in the same quarter as the Tsakur house and I thought then of the extraordinary career of this man whose prodigious rise was followed by a dramatic downfall. I was to meet him many times later in India and in China, where he was exiled.

The death of the Thirteenth in 1933 was, for some circles of the nobility, the signal for new intrigues. They plunged into them with all the more ardour because the deceased sovereign had for a long time been able to keep the intrigues in check. During the first weeks, Kunphela managed to keep his position. But the more influential members of the *Kashag* did not delay in manipulating his downfall and spread rumours which were meant to compromise his reputation. It began to be whispered around Lhasa that the Dalai Lama had been poisoned and that the guilty one was none other than Kunphela.

On the basis of this terrible accusation, Kunphela was arrested and taken before the *Kashag*. The various eye-witnesses who reported to me are all in agreement in recognising the admirable courage and dignity shown by this man, alone and defenceless, confronted with a gathering of snarling figures who, having feared him for so long were determined to get rid of him. He had an answer to all the accusations which they tried to topple him with and it was impossible to prove anything against him or to make him lose his poise. It was thus decided to banish him and this was done in the most humiliating ways: thrown out of the palace, he was carried in the streets to the jeering of the crowds before being taken to Kongpo in the south where he was relegated for several years before being able to cross the border and reach Kalimpong.

A much more dramatic episode marked the first year following the death of the Dalai Lama. Its protagonist was Lungshar, one of those whom the late sovereign had sent to study in the West and this was no doubt the reason why so many revolutionary intentions were attributed to him. He was also said to be resolutely pro-Chinese which also won him many arch enemies.

Lungshar, who was from the upper nobility but not very wealthy, succeeded Tsarong as commander of the armed forces. The elimination of Kunphela, which he had contributed to in a decisive way, made him one of the most powerful figures in Tibet. This was when the so-called republican affair broke out.

At that time Tibetans who could explain the meaning of 'republican' were undoubtedly very rare. But the term was used to implicate the conspirators and uphold the idea that they were impious men, enemies of the religion and resolved to upset the traditional and sacred order. It seems that, in fact, Lungshar would have liked to modernise Tibet and reform her institutions but in a more moderate and less revolutionary manner than it was said of him. One thing is certain: he was against the *Kashag* and the old Trimon who presided over it, and tried to break up its power.

Lungshar was supported by a small group of young aristocrats who, like him, were open to modern ideas. The two most notable were the Khyungram, who were related to the Tendong, and

Changlochan, a refined literary man who had edited most of the texts defining their ideas and political objectives. It is difficult to say what sort of action they planned to take because Trimon, continually informed that some scheme was being hatched, had Lungshar and his friends arrested, accusing them of wanting to assassinate him.

Judging him without an appeal, the *Kashag* condemned Lungshar, the main guilty one, to being blinded and then imprisoned until the end of his days. He had his eyes torn out, but after several years, he was permitted to leave prison. He finished his life in a park serving as an asylum for old animals which the Buddhists did not want to kill. He had a cabin there and that is where I met him. At the depth of his suffering he maintained a strength of soul and patience worthy of much respect and admiration.

Khyungram was only deported. Placed in a residence under surveillance at Rudok, a journey of three months from Lhasa, he lived for several years until his death in this lost place in western Tibet. Crossing these desert regions, my relatives who were able to meet him were impressed by his attitude, full of dignity.

As for Changlochan, he was ordered to have both hands cut off according to the *Kashag*'s sentence. He had the good fortune of escaping this terrible punishment which was commuted to exile. He thus set off on the Kalimpong route where Kunphela was to meet up with him. It was there that I had the opportunity to meet him and hear him tell of the events which he had been involved in.

During the years following the death of the Thirteenth Dalai Lama, all Tibetans had their attention fixed on the search for the Fourteenth. The traditional procedure, overseen by Reting Rimpoche, the regent, had taken the searchers farther and farther east and was to end up with the discovery of the sacred child in a peasant family from the village of Taktser, not far from the celebrated monastery of Kumbum in the Chinese province of Tsing-hai (capital Sining). Its governor was a famous 'warlord', Ma Pufang, a Muslim general who was practically independent but recognised in principle the authority of the Kuomintang. He knew how to take advantage of the situation by not authorising the departure of the child who was recognised as the reincarnated Dalai Lama, except against payment of an amount in dollars representing a fortune. The transaction was preceded by interminable bargaining and followed by a no less interminable journey to Lhasa. In October 1939 the Fourteenth Dalai Lama, who was not yet five years old, solemnly entered his capital, greeted with an enthusiasm which witnesses still speak of with emotion.

The holy child arrived accompanied by his father, his mother and two older brothers. They soon became important figures and were lodged in Potala with honours showered on them and surrounded by toadyism. The high society of Lhasa continually put themselves out for them by inviting them to sumptuous receptions and presenting them with magnificent gifts. Even their servants were treated with special regard.

Reting, the regent, had established especially cordial relations with the father who, as has been mentioned, tended to take advantage of his sudden promotion. A modest farmer who had attained such glory in one lucky stroke, he liked to make others aware of his newly acquired power or at least this was the impression that certain aristocrats had of his behaviour. When he went into town followed by his escort, all the passers-by had to bow before him and horsemen had to alight. The pride of several nobles of high birth was ruffled and intrigues began to be plotted.

However, it is important to note that the political mix-ups which went on during those years were not totally exempt from international prolongations. In effect Tibet—positioned between the British empire of India and China who had successively invaded Tibet at the beginning of the century—oscillated between the two great powers, each of whom had partisans in the political circles of Lhasa. The very origin of the new Dalai Lama and his family, from a province under the Kuomingtang administration constituted a trump card for the pro-Chinese party who obviously wanted to take advantage of the situation and compensate for the failure they had suffered in the Lungshar affair.

The government of Nanking realised perfectly well that this was an excellent opportunity for re-establishing Chinese influence in Tibet, which had been much compromised since the revolution of 1911. In place of the *ambans* who had represented the emperors in Lhasa, the government had assigned there a liaison agent with a poorly defined official status. This representative established close relations with Reting, the regent, and according to widespread opinion, bribed him copiously.

True or not, this fact was undoubtedly not unknown in the powerful intrigue, which in 1941 ended with the wiping out of this too good a friend to the Chinese. The regent was then forced to give up his functions and return to meditate in the monastery which, eight years earlier, he had left to handle the affairs of the State.

Reting carried the name of this monastery located three days' walk to the north of Lhasa and which had recognised him as a great *tulku* or reincarnated lama. He was only nineteen when the *Tsongdu*, or national assembly, choosing by lot amongst three candidates, decided to make him the regent who would exercise power in place of the deceased Dalai Lama until the latter's successor be identified and become of age. Undoubtedly ill prepared for such weighty responsibilities, the young man was under the influence of a group of nobles open to modern ideas who convinced him to introduce into Tibet innovations such as electricity which were considered revolutionary. This already made him a certain number of enemies but his popularity suffered mainly from the fact that he was seen as a puppet of the Chinese faction. Moreover, since the discovery of the Fourteenth and his arrival into Lhasa, his compliance towards the father and the sacred child was considered excessive. The result was discontentment at Dekilinga, seat of the British mission, then directed with much distinction by Hugh Richardson. They were perhaps not too upset to see this discontentment grow.

To save appearances, it was claimed that Reting, on the advice of the State Oracle, had freely decided to abdicate in order to devote himself to the contemplative life. Such a story is hardly likely. In any case, the new regent was in many ways the opposite of the preceding one. Also a *tulku* from an important monastery, Taktra was seventy-five when he ascended to power. Hostile to innovations and modern influences, he had orthodox views conforming to the tradition about everything, which won him the favours of the most influential circles of the nobility and clergy. In addition, he was very well regarded by the British resident.

As for the China of the Kuomingtang, she was much too involved in the war against Japan to be able to react as she would have liked, but she nevertheless managed to re-establish herself in Lhasa, thanks to the new liaison agent sent from 1944 on, Shen Tsing Lien. A first class diplomat, he had studied in America and spoke fluent English. Very open-minded, he had real sympathy for Tibet and knew how to manoeuvre prudently and wisely there, directing the regent Taktra and knowing how to take advantage of the fact that the Dalai Lama and his family could speak the Chinese dialect of Sining, their native place, better than Tibetan.

Although calm seemed to return to the political life in Lhasa, a certain tension remained because Reting retained his supporters. His openness to modern ideas had made a good number of young people sympathetic to him and the pro-Chinese faction accepted his eviction badly. The question of him often came up in conversations that I had with my friends in the nobility, but the subject was delicate and was only broached with circumspection.

As later events were to prove, a plot was forming from this time on in view of rendering power to the fallen regent. It was to end up with a crisis in 1947 and risked degenerating into a civil war. Many aspects of it remained obscure. This was a veritable revolt which the monastery of Sera, housing 6,000 monks, gave the signal for. For several days the situation was uncertain and it was not known which party would take over. The old Taktra, who showed an unexpected firmness and resolve, managed to get the situation under control. But there were quite a few deaths on both sides.

As for Reting, he lost his life in Potala under circumstances which were never entirely clear. No trace of violence was found on his body. According to a version of the facts which I heard, he was killed by a son of Lungshar, who never forgave him for being unable to protect his father. He suffocated him by stuffing a scarf (*kathak*) down his throat.

Whilst introducing me into the arcane of Tibetan politics, my friends shared with me their hopes and worries. All the neighbouring countries were then at war. Although theirs was still fortunate to escape this, it was clear that the world conflagration was preparing for upheavals which it would be difficult not to suffer repercussions from. Rare foreign publications and faint radio broadcasts allowed us to follow the development of the events on the Asian continent. What would Tibet's position be when peace returned? All our friends, even those who remained sympathetic to Reting and the pro-Chinese faction were in agreement on the basic necessity of making Tibet totally independent. In this respect, Afghanistan, whose geographic location was comparable to Tibet's was an example which they often pointed out. Situated between two great imperialist powers, Afghanistan had been able to resist their pressure and intimidation, fully assuring her liberty and individuality. The primary objective of Tibet should have been international recognition of a similar status of independence. Only after this would the time come for domestic reforms and modernisation.

However, not everyone was unanimous on this second aspect of our worries and our discussions could go on all night. To tell the truth, the ideas which we debated then were neither revolutionary nor very 'advanced' and no one dared to envisage, for example, violating the powers and prerogatives of the Dalai Lama. And yet these young 'educated' aristocrats began to open a door to secularising influences, which others later made use of, overthrowing the domestic order of Tibet and making her dream of liberty vanish.

Frequenting such a world, I now spoke Tibetan better than my uncles. In the meantime, the business that I had to settle with them hardly progressed and when the year 1944 came round, we had not yet taken any decision on the means of our collaboration and on the transfer of the capital coming from my grandfather's estate.

CHAPTER 7

THE ENCOUNTERS AT KALIMPONG

Since the beginning of 1943 when we arrived in Lhasa with the Lopchak, Khwaja Abdul Aziz and I realised that the traditional caravan traffic between Ladakh and Tibet along the tracks of the Trans-Himalayas was doomed to an irreversible decline. Despite the detour that it meant from then on, communication via India was faster, safer and more profitable thanks to paved roads and railway lines. In addition, the life of a caravaneer hardly attracted young people anymore. They found it too severe, demanding and dangerous.

What, then, would become of Leh, the warehouse of Central Asian commerce, if the caravans ceased to converge there? The township was undoubtedly condemned to impoverishment and decline. It was an unavoidable process and no one could do anything about it.

On the other hand, the traffic between India and Tibet by the large track passing through Kalimpong, Sikkim and Gyantse continued to develop and was very profitable for the merchants of the Lhasa bazaar. The best thing for us to do was to try and find a place for ourselves in this trade.

These arguments furthered our resolve to proceed with the great move of our goods and business to Lhasa. It was finally decided that I would return to Leh where I would organise the transfer of our capital and other movables with Muhammad Asghar Tsakur, who had gone there ahead of me. Before accomplishing this, we had to come to a compromise solution with my cousin Abdul Haqq, who possessed part of the fortune but absolutely refused to leave Leh for Tibet. After having sorted out these material questions, it was agreed that I would return to Lhasa, accompanied by my wife, aunt and sister and we would settle there for good.

So I set off to accomplish this difficult mission. Thanks to excellent mules, I arrived in Kalimpong quickly and without fatigue. I stopped a few days in Calcutta to settle some business deals that my uncles had put me in charge of and soon found myself back in Srinagar where I was put up by my great-uncle Abdullah Shah, the *aksakal* who had peacefully retired in the capital of Kashmir. A mere two weeks on horseback along familiar tracks separated me from Leh, which I had left with the Lopchak more than eighteen months ago.

The happiness of seeing my wife again was quickly dampened by the complications of my task. My uncle, Muhammad Asghar Tsakur, was in a hurry to settle the issues at hand and my aunt, who already knew Lhasa, could only think of the pleasures of the big city and looked forward to seeing so many cousins there again. My sister, on her part, who was barely an adolescent, was impatient to see the world that lay beyond the Ladakhi horizon. I met another uncle, Mukarram Shah, a younger brother of my father's, who normally resided in Sinkiang and who had crossed the formidable passes of the Karakoram in order to get into contact with the family again. When he found out that we had decided to leave for Lhasa, he was so upset that he was unable to speak to me for several days. For him, having lived in a country often shaken by troubling events, my grandfather's house in Leh had always been a symbol of security. And he didn't share our infatuation with Tibet.

Mukarram had to share his doubts and regrets with me. It suddenly appeared to me that the task I was charged with in Leh was equivalent to destroying the very foundations of the house of Haji Muhammad Siddiq. I had the impression that I was going to commit a sacrilege. This brusque impression made me so ill that I had to stay in bed for an entire week.

Finally, I declared myself incapable of organising the move. Very unhappy, Muhammad Asghar didn't dare take things into his own hands when I, as legal holder of most of the goods, hesitated. It was then decided that we should leave for Kalimpong where Khwaja Abdul Aziz was staying for business, and we would examine the situation together. We thus saddled up once again, leaving my wife, sister and aunt in Leh.

After an unpleasant journey with a surly companion, the meeting I had in Kalimpong with Khwaja Abdul Aziz was even more unpleasant. The two brothers held me responsible for all the disastrous consequences which they said my hesitation had inevitably caused and they showered me with reproaches. I suffered greatly from such a situation and felt torn between Ladakh to which so many memories were attached, and Lhasa to which I was attracted by the call of a promising life.

I finally had to attend to our business under the supervision of my two uncles who continually expressed their unhappiness with me. I accompanied them on their visits to several merchants of Kalimpong and assisted them in purchasing various articles, especially textiles and cottons, cosmetics and construction supplies. And the three of us finally left for Lhasa.

The discussions soon ended with an agreement: Khwaja Abdul Aziz, head of the family, would go to Ladakh himself to carry out the task which I had been incapable of undertaking. A few weeks later, he arrived in Leh. Free of the scruples which had held me back, he put all his energy into organising the big move.

Soon I received a telegram summoning me to Srinagar to lend Khwaja Abdul Aziz a hand. I thus returned to Kalimpong and from there only a few days were necessary to reach Kashmir. My wife was waiting for me there, accompanied by my sister. I then took care of expediting thirty to forty cases which were already in Srinagar and which represented most of our heavy furniture.

We were to collect them in Kalimpong. Unfortunately, three of the most precious were lost en route. They contained a splendidly illuminated Qur'an, magnificent ivory objects, old gold sovereigns dating from the time of our ancestors, Chinese silverware as well as all the notebooks in which our grandfather had kept a detailed diary of the Lopchak caravans that he had led. Thus was lost an irreplaceable source of information on western Tibet and the Trans-Himalayas at the beginning of this century.

When we had all arrived in Kalimpong, the discussions with Khwaja Abdul Aziz and his brother Muhammad Asghar Tsakur were resumed in earnest. The uncles had wanted me to participate in their trading business in Lhasa. After the unpleasant scenes which had taken place between us I had no desire to work under them. Moreover, the Tsakurs, whom I found ignorant and inefficient, led the life of small-time shopkeepers which didn't attract me at all. Their eldest brother, Abdul Aziz, was of a different calibre, but his conception of trade seemed mediocre compared to the big business I had seen my grandfather head so successfully.

Finally, a compromise was found. The family business which we would try to reorganise and make more efficient, would have its main office in Lhasa under the trade name Tsakur Ladakh-khache which in Tibetan roughly means 'Muslim Ladakhis of the Tsakur house'. It was agreed that I would open a branch office in Kalimpong where I would live with my wife. Seemingly satisfied with the agreement that was reached, the uncles set off again for Lhasa.

The solution that was thus found marked the beginning of a new phase of my life. Kalimpong was not an unpleasant place. Located against a beautiful backdrop of mountains and enjoying

Seated in the middle is the author's maternal grandfather, Haji Muhammad Siddiq, with Abdul Karim, his son-in-law, (the author's father) to his left. (circa 1930)

Haji Muhammad Siddiq with the Moravian missionary, Reverend 'Peter Sahib', in front of the Radhu home. (Leh, circa late 1920s or early 1930s)

A family photograph. From the left, standing: the author at age 10, his elder cousin Abdul Haq, his uncle Mukarram Ahmad and his father Abdul Karim. Seated on the chair is Abdullah Shah, one of the Radhu clan who favoured a positive engagement with the modern world. He was an Aksakal, or 'white beard', a British appointment under which he kept records of trading and other movements by non-citizens of the J&K State. (Leh, circa 1928).

Haji Abdul Aziz, the author's uncle, whom he accompanied on the Lopchak mission of 1942. (Photograph circa 1970s)

Haji Abdul Aziz's two brothers, Muhammad Asghar and Sirajuddin, on one of their business journeys in eastern Tibet, towards Kham. (Circa early 1940s)

Abdul Wahid Radhu's family. On the far right is the author, with his uncle, Mukarram Ahmad, who had to flee Yarkand and migrated via Leh to live with his nephew in Kashmir. On the far left is his wife holding their youngest child, Ghafoor, with their daughter Farida standing to her right, and son, Siddiq, seated on the ground. The other girls are the author's neices, visiting from Leh.
(Rajbagh, Kashmir, 1955)

Abdul Wahid and Ruqayya Radhu, his wife.
(New Delhi, circa 1970)

Abdul Wahid Radhu, second from left, with Gyalo Thondup, the elder brother of
His Holiness the 14th Dalai Lama, to his left. They are flanked by US army personnel.
(Nanking, February 1948)

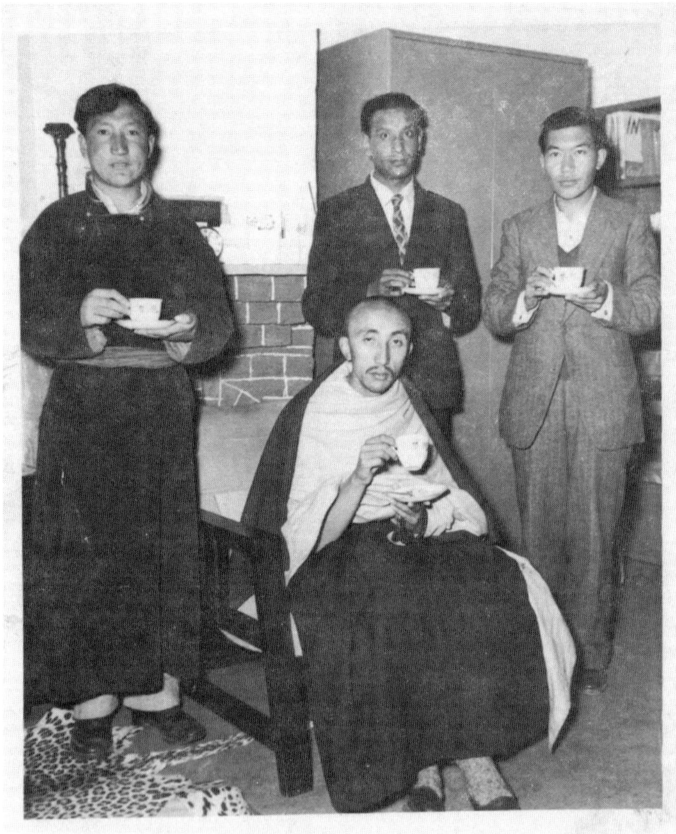

Abdul Wahid Radhu, standing in the centre behind Kushok Bakula, seated, the incarnate abbot of Spituk Monastery and its estates. At the time the author was Managing Director of the Ladakh Wool and Pashmina Syndicate. (Kashmir, 1953)

A rare reunion photo in the author's orchard. (Kashmir, circa late 1970s) Abdul Wahid Radhu, middle; to his left, Muhammad Asghar and to his right, Ataullah Khwaja, the cousin with whom he spent several years as a student at Kashmir's Tyndale Biscoe Mission School in Srinagar and at Aligarh Muslim University. Ataullah Khwaja joined the Pakistan Foreign Service in the late 1940s and retired after serving in several countries as the ambassador of Pakistan. The two cousins passed away within ten days of each other in February 2011.

Abdul Wahid Radhu
(Srinagar, circa mid-1980s)

an ideal climate, it was the terminus of the main trading track connecting Lhasa with the outside world and enlivened by an endless traffic of people including Nepalese, Sikkimese, Bhutanese and, inevitably, the Chinese, as well as Indians and Tibetans. The British still reigned over this variegated world and no one seemed to have any complaints about their administration.

My job from then on consisted of ensuring that Tibetan products, in particular raw wool, yak tails and musk, were expedited and sent to Calcutta or elsewhere in India. In the reverse direction I organised the shipping to Lhasa, according to the orders that my uncles sent me, of Indian merchandise of which textiles made up the largest part. This business provided me with the opportunity to collaborate with Indians of the merchant caste of the Marwaris. Natives of Rajasthan, they had an innate sense of business and went to any length in order to please their trading partners. Several of them had acquired an excellent knowledge of Tibetan, and were able to correspond in this language with their clients in Lhasa even from their offices in Calcutta. The Marwaris were the ones who furnished most of the textiles that my uncles ordered.

My contacts with these efficient and ingenious men helped give a good start to my new business career and to penetrate the most reputable 'business circles' of the place. In effect, Kalimpong was the seat of powerful and prosperous companies which, in relation to the financial centres of India and the world, represented the interests of the leading circles and the nobility of Tibet.

Amongst these establishments, those of the Khampa merchants occupied a leading position. The most well known of them were the Sandutshang, the Andutshang, the Gyanaktshang and especially, the Pangdatshang whose reputation was widespread. They were the masters of the Tibetan wool trade and exported wool in great quantities to America. They knew how to be generous and were open-armed and determined to maintain their prestige. Apart from their warehouses, they had built large beautiful residential buildings in Kalimpong where they vied for hospitality in receiving the Tibetan nobility who frequently visited.

The Pangdatshangs were three brothers, Yamphel, Topgay and Rabga. The first, head of a veritable business empire, was a great personality whose influence was felt in the political circles of Lhasa and he was not a stranger to a number of intrigues. He had worked himself into the nobility, and had adopted their customs as well as attributing their prerogatives to himself but did not have the official status of nobility—something that no Khampa had achieved yet. His wife, who was intelligent and gave good advice, also knew very well how to adapt herself to the rank he had raised himself to. However, curiously, Abo Yamphel had short hair, whereas Tibetans, if they were not in the ecclesiastic state which obliged them to shave their head, wore their hair long.

In this respect I can recall that with the nobles the hairstyles varied according to the rank of each one in the hierarchy, the highest having an amulet box fixed in their bun, the others wearing various sorts of plaits, hats and bonnets according to their rank. Certain young Tibetans with 'progressive' ideas began to rebel against these old customs and one of them was even of the opinion that, in order to modernise their country, they should begin with cutting the hair of all these dignitaries. This, in fact, was what finally happened, but under the force of the Chinese occupation.

There were also Nepalese merchants in Kalimpong. One of them, Shamokabo, rivalled the opulence of the great Khampas. He bore the name of 'White Marble' which his grandfather, founder of the family fortune thanks to the trade with Lhasa, had carried. At this time he worked with Shakabpa, a figure whose influence continued to grow within the entourage of the regent and, having acquired the title of Tsipon, became a sort of minister of finance.

Coming from a family of the lower nobility, Shakabpa had first been a monk and then returned to the laity. He owed his political rise to Taktra, the regent who had succeeded Reting in 1941, but Shakabpa had made his fortune by himself. I heard him tell of the first big project which founded his financial power. He had noticed in Lhasa that the mint which produced pieces of copper threw out the scraps after minting. It was Shamokabo who gave him the idea of gathering the debris and reselling it in India where copper had reached a very high exchange rate. The result was profits which made the great Pangdatshang himself jealous. From then on Shakabpa was rich enough to play his first roles in Tibet's political scene.

Such success stories whetted my own ambitions and perhaps caused me to lose a sense of the proportions and of the potential of our modest family enterprise. My relations with so many powerful people had given me the illusion of having penetrated a world very superior to that of the Tsakurs. I had become a member of the Association of Indo-Tibetan Merchants presided over by the eldest Pangdatshang. Shamokabo was its secretary and I was nominated to be his assistant. I was proud vis-à-vis my uncles with whom I was in constant contact and I hoped that they would finally consent to listen to me when I advised them to modernise their work methods.

At this time my cousin Ataullah, the one who had preceded me and introduced me to Aligarh University, visited me. He had arrived from Ladakh and was looking for work. During the war, he worked for a firm that constructed barracks and canteens for the army. As he had a taste for business, he wanted to launch into it now but didn't have enough capital to get started by himself. He therefore offered his services to the Tsakur Ladakh-khache house in hopes of going to live in Lhasa, his native town for which he was nostalgic. My uncles agreed to take him on and he left straight away to join them.

Despite his university education, the level of which was higher than mine, Ataullah did not scorn the Tsakur business nor joining them in their shop. He helped them make substantial progress with their enterprise. Continually in correspondence with him, I was happy to have him as a spokesman for me in Lhasa.

Our business seemed to go better and better from then on. We held an important position in the export of Indian textiles to Tibet. At the end of the war, the British authorities decided to put a limit on these exports as they considered them to have taken on an exaggerated volume. In effect, the great trade centres shipped bales of cotton by the thousands through Kalimpong and at their end the Tibetans sent them on to China, making enormous profits. Wanting to keep this traffic within certain limits, the administration established a quota system, dividing the trade amongst the various communities having an interest in it. In Kalimpong, Major Sheriff, a British officer in charge of assigning these quotas, designated me as a representative of the Muslims of Lhasa. This guaranteed me being able to regularly export great quantities of textiles to my relatives in Tibet and make an appreciable contribution to the prosperity of our business and to its good reputation.

Thus was accomplished the great merging of the family business, which, having abandoned the tracks of Central Asia, now tried its luck in direct exchange between India and Tibet. It had a promising beginning and the uncles seemed satisfied. Life in Kalimpong was so pleasant, varied and bustling that I didn't even regret not living in Lhasa anymore. My wife was also happy in this town where the climate was less harsh than in Leh and the bazaar always offered everything that the most demanding of housewives could require.

My business contacts permitted me to deepen my knowledge of Tibet. Abo Arabga Pangdatshang became a regular visitor at home and it was mainly through him that I made the most interesting acquaintances, beginning with Kunphela, the former mentor of the Thirteenth Dalai Lama and ignominiously banished after the death of the latter. He was the one who barely missed having his two hands cut off for participating in the so-called 'republican' plot.

I couldn't say how many evenings I spent listening to them discuss the then current situation. Although the war was over, the Asian continent had not yet recovered its equilibrium and remained threatened by new troubles. And the two figures obviously had not given up any active participation in political activity at a time when politics seemed to be taking a new turn. They seemed to have discrete contacts with emissaries of the Kuomingtang. Concerning this subject, it is necessary to recall that the pro-Chinese party had not disarmed in Lhasa where the attempted *coup d'état* was being prepared, aimed at overthrowing Taktra and re-establishing Reting, his predecessor, in the office of regent.

Also pro-Chinese but of a different bent, was a young and brilliant Tibetan intellectual whom I was attached to through a deep friendship. Phuntsok Wangyal, better known by his shortened name of Phuwang, had open sympathies for the Communism of Mao Tse-tung. He made frequent attempts, of course in vain, to make me share these sympathies with him. A genuine Tibetan nationalist, he also laid out 'pan-Tibetan' theories aiming to regroup all the ethnic and cultural regions of Tibet into a sort of federation, therefore including Ladakh. Our discussions at that time friendly, though with their differences, were to be extended later in Lhasa where destiny had it in store for us to meet under unexpected circumstances.

A frequent visitor of the same house, Gyendum Chombel was undoubtedly one of the most knowledgeable and cultured Tibetans of his time. Native of Amdo in the east, he had studied in the monastery of Drepung, near Lhasa, for a long time where he was the disciple of an eminent learned man, Sherab Gyaltso Rimpoche, who had already made himself known for his non-conformist ideas. After obtaining the degree of *geshay* (doctor of theology) he became involved in political activity which put him in opposition to the power whose methods he criticised. He also denounced the disastrous custom of intrigues so widespread in the circles of the upper nobility. But unfortunately for him, he was unable to avoid getting mixed up with them himself. Author of good works on the history, literature and arts of Tibet, he modernised the language and introduced new technical terms in it. It is to him also that the Tibetan national anthem is due.

Of a remarkably open mind, he spent long periods abroad and was interested in religions other than Buddhism, in particular Christianity and Islam. I recall that he had a genuine understanding of Islam and rose up against the idea upheld by the British who claimed that this religion had spread wide in the world through the strength of weapons and force. And he added that, without being a man of the faith himself, he could understand Muhammad, our Prophet.

Gyendum Chombel maintained relations with Europeans residing in Kalimpong at that time, in particular with the Tibetanist of Russian origin, George Roerich. Chombel helped him translate the *Blue Annals*, a famous religious text recounting the life and asceticism of the great lama Taglungpa. According to what was told to me, the documents and manuscripts which he had left in Lhasa also served as sources for Hugh Richardson, a British political agent and author of a history of Tibet.

However, this remarkable man was unable to avoid the trap of politics during his stay in Kalimpong. Abo Rabga, whose association with the Kuomingtang was notorious, persuaded him to carry out information-gathering missions first in Bhutan, then in Lhasa. There he was arrested as soon as he arrived and was put into prison after being publicly flogged. His library was seized. He was set free again in 1950 it seems after the regent Taktra retired in order to entrust the real power to the young Dalai Lama. But Chombel's health was ruined. In any case, those who accused him of having Communist sympathies and claimed that he applauded the Chinese invasion slandered him. He surely was a sincere Tibetan patriot and his unfortunate end was as much due to his imprudence as it was to his non-conformism.

The most important encounter that I made in Kalimpong was alien to the domains of business as well as politics. This encounter was to give me access to the unlimited avenues of the Spirit.

The Tibetanist, Roerich, was part of a distinguished group of Europeans who studied Orientalism and ethnology in Kalimpong or more simply, took advantage of the inexhaustible resources that the region offered amateurs of mountain climbing. They met in the Himalayan Hotel, an establishment run by David Macdonald—in theory anyway because in practice he left the actual administration to his daughters—a former officer of the British administration. His father was English and his mother Sikkimese and he belonged more to Asia than to Europe. He had written a book on Tibet which was very highly thought of. It was always a pleasure to spend evenings in his company and listen to him speak of the Himalayan world which had become his true homeland.

It was in this colonial-style setting that I one day found myself in front of Prince Peter of Greece whom I had curiously met by chance a few years earlier on an isolated plateau of the Ladakhi Rupshu. At that time he was doing research into the recent history of Tibet and, needing a collaborator for certain translations, asked me to help him. Within the time allowed to me by my professional obligations, I did various translations for him for several weeks, working as a secretary-translator. I was then able to get an idea of the extent of his contacts. A friend of Lord Mountbatten who had been named Viceroy of India in order to make India comply with conditions of independence, he had also been introduced to Jawaharlal Nehru.

One day the prince introduced me to another member of the group of European regulars of the Himalayan Hotel, Marco Pallis. Born in England of Greek parents, he was a remarkable person from many points of view. Well versed in Orientalism, and especially knowledgeable of Hinduism and Buddhism, he was also—and still is because, thanks to God he is still living at the time of writing[1]—musician, mountain climber and writer. He had just published a book which caught the attention of the public, *Peaks and Lamas*. Already having a rich experience of the Himalayan world, he was preparing a new expedition which would take him as far as Shigatse, the second largest town of Tibet.

Upon learning that I was a native of Ladakh, Marco Pallis spoke to me of his stay there before the war and we soon realised that one of the homes he had been received into was none other than that of my grandfather, Haji Muhammad Siddiq, whom he had known well. (The English edition of the book *Peaks and Lamas* contains his photograph.) He hadn't met me at that time because I was following classes in a college in Srinagar. There must have been an understanding between my grandfather and the European visitor and they spoke to each other at length in Tibetan, each one undoubtedly recognising in the other a lively interest in values of the Spirit.

This reminder probably urged my interlocutor to think that the grandson of such a man might be capable of understanding ideas which were dear to him. A few days after our first meeting, he brought me the English version of a book which he himself had translated from French. It was *A General Introduction to the Study of Hindu Doctrine*, by René Guénon.

Reading this book was to radically transform my thought patterns. Putting into its proper perspective the relationship between the traditional East and the modern West, the book was to help me find answers to the great questions I had been asking myself since my university years and finally to reintegrate myself intellectually and spiritually into the East and into my own tradition.

In fact, the book discussed much more than Hindu doctrine and I found in it the greatest metaphysical questions to reflect

---

[1] (Translator's Note: Marco Pallis died in June 1989.)

upon. René Guénon gave me insights which made all the academic culture that we had to assimilate at the university seem singularly narrow. René Guénon invited me to reconsider the spiritual possibilities of the human state and the meaning of civilisation.

I must confess that this reading was often strenuous. I didn't give up, however, because from the first pages I felt myself in a current of thought capable of providing me with the certainties which, consciously or not, I had always sought. And I often took the book with me on solitary walks in the neighbouring valleys of Kalimpong as well as later in China or in the vast desert stretches of Tibet. I sometimes re-read passages which I had made note of and wondered why I was indebted to Westerners for rediscovering the traditional values of the East.

It was also an opportunity for me to realise to what extent I had been impregnated by Western thought and concepts in spite of the Oriental environment of my education. The notion of Western superiority had in fact infiltrated everywhere, 'backward' Tibet being undoubtedly still an exception because of its geographic isolation, and no one to my knowledge had yet dared to contradict this notion.

To tell the truth, in my early years I had but little direct contact with Westerners and, apart from the Reverends Driver and Biscoe, all my teachers had been Orientals. But, whether they were conscious of it or not, their teaching transmitted values which were more Western than Oriental and their attitude generally upheld an implicit admiration for modern civilisation.

At the end of World War II, the British still maintained much of their prestige in the eyes of Indian intellectuals. It is important to point out that the very political movements fighting against colonial domination made reference to notions of Western origin such as Anglo-Saxon liberalism, nationalism or various sociological ideologies which inspired Nehru and other leaders of the Congress. The majority of those who led this fight did not at all question the values of modern civilisation and, on the contrary, wanted to facilitate access to it for their people. In any case I had never been placed in the presence of a criticism of this civilisation in the name of intellectual or spiritual principles. It was in this respect that this initial reading tore away a veil and allowed me to gaze upon unlimited horizons.

Amongst the fundamental notions which I retained from this initial stage was first of all the primacy of traditional and universal metaphysics 'the unique centre of all the doctrines of the East'. Guénon emphasised that the West had rendered itself foreign to this metaphysical knowledge and had developed a philosophical thought which was not situated at the same level of universality. This very important argument was the basis of his criticism of Western civilisation, denouncing its lack of higher principles and its incapability to understand those principles to which the East remained attached.

He also pointed out the essential traditional nature of Oriental civilisations, contrasting them so strongly with that of Europe which, since modern times, has been so bent on instability and change. And he found fault with the idea of progress, the basis of supposed Western superiority, showing how illusory it is with regards to true intellectuality.

Although he more particularly proposed to define the spirit in which he approached the study of Hinduism and its doctrines, this work, in fact, was of a more general nature and a good part of his thoughts could also be applied to other sacred traditions of the East. Moreover, the author demonstrated a wide knowledge of these traditions, including Islam, backing up his arguments with remarks which I welcomed as if they were addressed to me personally.

Islam, pointed out Guénon, had a double essence, religious and metaphysical: 'the religious side of the doctrine can be exactly qualified as esoteric which in fact is its more outward side and within the reach of everyone, and as esoteric the metaphysical side of Islam which constitutes its deep meaning and which is moreover seen as the doctrine of the elite.'

The memory of my grandfather's face came back to me and I said to myself that he would have approved of such notions. I also thought of my earlier ideas on the concepts of *zahir,* 'outer', and *batin,* 'inner'. They then seemed to me to take on a clarity which gave them their full meaning and I finally understood the reasons which had allowed a Dara Shikoh in the seventeenth century to affirm that there was essential agreement between the non-dualist Vedanta of the Hindus and *Tawhid*, the Islamic doctrine of unity, as understood by the Sufis, the people of the *batin*, in its deepest meaning.

Having presented me with the masterly proof of the superiority, in an absolute sense, of metaphysics and traditional wisdom over the pragmatic and relative thought of the modern West, this reading re-ordered my thoughts, renewed my certitude and deepened my understanding of Islam. At the same time it provided me with the proof that this one Truth was also expressed in other traditional forms, one of the most obvious examples being precisely the Vedanta. And it especially pleased me to think that this Truth was also present in Tibetan spirituality with which I had always had affinities.

It appeared to me then that the real kafir, the unfaithful disbeliever, was not, as narrow Muslims of the *zahir* thought, the Hindu or Buddhist. He was rather the secularised Westerner, frequently an unbeliever or agnostic who, under the pretext of his supposed progress, had come to upset the values and traditional order of the East, thus also of Islam.

Finally, the book that Marco Pallis gave me had the unexpected result of reshaping me into a true Oriental from the Westernised intellectual that I had been since leaving Aligarh. Such a return certainly could not have taken place all at once and it took me months, even years to really deepen and assimilate these principles. I was to be aided in this by other works of the same author, especially *The Crisis of the Modern World*, which reinforced my conviction of having rediscovered, along with this train of thought, the straight path towards the Truth.

I was naturally curious to learn something of the personality of René Guénon. Compared to the latter, the philosophers whom I had studied at university seemed to me from then on as propagators of illusions compared to him. What a happy surprise it was for me to learn one day that this Westerner had 'Orientalised' himself in becoming a Muslim, that he practised Islam faithfully and had adhered to a *tariqa*, a Sufi order! I also learned that his Muslim name was Abdul Wahid, 'Slave of the Unique One', and since this is also my name, I have always tried to be worthy of it since then.

Marco Pallis, who had provoked this intellectual revolution in me and to whom I often came seeking clarifications in my reading of Guénon, himself appeared to be penetrated by the traditional wisdom of the East and by the teachings of the Tibetan masters whom he had frequented. He shared an apartment with his friend Richard Nicholson and both had a calm, discreet, thoughtful and detached manner, very different from that of most Europeans. I always found a refreshing, peaceful atmosphere of recollectedness with them in contrast with the agitation and tension of the business circles where my professional activity went on. In their home, I had the impression of arriving in an oasis after having crossed a desert or gone through a high mountain pass.

Other Tibetans frequented the apartment of the two 'wise men', in particular my friend Tendong, who was often called from Lhasa to Kalimpong on business. Marco Pallis introduced him to the works and thinking of Guénon. Unfortunately, too absorbed by Tibetan politics and its intrigues, he did not draw all the intellectual benefit from the reading that he would have been capable of and remained half-committed.

These were the most important encounters that came my

way in Kalimpong. I have always had a deep gratitude to this valuable friend who allowed me to discover the domain of 'traditional' thought which, apart from Guénon, whose writings in a way opened the way for them, is now represented by a series of eminent and remarkable authors. Of these, Frithjof Schuon, A.K. Coomaraswamy, Titus Burckhardt, Martin Lings, Seyyed Hossein Nasr, not forgetting Marco Pallis himself, should be mentioned because they provide the best keys for an in-depth understanding of the traditional East and the various forms of its spirituality.

Meanwhile the business of the Tsakur Ladakh-khache house continued to expand relatively satisfactorily. The presence of two 'educated' persons, my cousin in Lhasa and myself in Kalimpong, represented a positive element and carried a certain prestige within the business circles where our activity went on. In virtue of the quota system, I regularly followed up the expediting of bales of textiles which caravaneers loaded onto ponies and mules destined for Lhasa. In the capital, the exploitation of the cinema which the uncles looked after alongside their shop, also brought in a significant income so that the family business appeared to thrive under happy auspices.

Under these conditions, Khwaja Abdul Aziz decided to accomplish the Haj. He thus departed for Mecca accompanied by his octogenarian mother and stopped in Kalimpong. Obviously, we had meetings about the business during which we discussed the sale of Tibetan products in India, in particular musk, wool, and yak tails. This latter article was easily sold whereas musk was less in demand. I went to Bombay to try to dispose of this merchandise but I didn't manage to liquidate all the musk, part of which I had to bring back to Kalimpong. Soon afterwards my uncle re-appeared on his return from the pilgrimage, bearing thereafter the title of 'Haji'. He showered me with reproaches for the musk affair, holding me personally responsible for its failure. I then realised that despite the success I had had in many other transactions which I had undertaken, Uncle did not entirely trust me and retained mixed feelings towards me.

At this time Khwaja Abdul Aziz had entered into relations with a certain Wangdola, a former close acquaintance of the Thirteenth Dalai Lama, whom he had served in a domestic capacity. I had noticed this person who frequently travelled between Calcutta and Kalimpong but had never paid any attention to him until the day my uncle introduced me to him, assuring me that, thanks to him, we would be able to carry out one of our most profitable transactions.

In fact, we knew that merchants who were well introduced into the British administration could sometimes obtain customs reductions from them for Chinese merchandise to be sent to Tibet. Thanks to an English officer who Wangdola said was his friend, he affirmed that he could give us such an authorisation without difficulty. The deal which he flaunted to us concerned silks especially, brocades, which were always in demand by Tibetans for their formal dress, because in the administration every officer of rank, even if he were not very highly placed, had to wear this official dress. We were now assured that it would be easy to negotiate the purchase in China and the transit via India of two huge bales of these valuable articles that were snatched up in the market of Lhasa.

Wangdola claimed that a short trip to China would suffice to guarantee the success of the deal and he suggested that I accompany him. Khwaja Abdul Aziz, who often let himself be taken in by the cajoling of highly placed persons, strongly pressed me to accept. However, since I had travelled to Bombay I felt rather weakened physically and the idea of leaving for China, even for a short time, did not appeal to me at all. It seemed to me preferable to carry on with my usual activities whilst at the same time deepening my spiritual insights. Also, it hardly pleased me to be dependent on a man I hardly knew and whom I didn't take to very well, and this for a business deal which seemed to me to be full of imponderables. I was also busy with the necessary supervision of expediting the cotton bales in virtue of the quota which had been allotted to us, but Uncle assured me that I would have nothing to worry about and that he would take care of everything. His insistence was such that I found myself obliged to give in.

The year 1947 was coming to an end when I left Kalimpong, accompanied by Wangdola. We had to wait some time in Calcutta to get our papers in order. As a Tibetan, my companion did not need a passport to get into China where he was considered a national. As he knew the Chinese consul general well, he thought it would be simpler to have me pass for a Tibetan as well, instead of getting me an Indian passport.

I had no idea what an enormous mistake I had made by letting him do this. And I had no idea that this 'brief trip' was to last more than two years.

CHAPTER 8

THE CHINESE TRAP

A commercial aeroplane took Wangdola and me from Calcutta to Shanghai in only one day, a very strange means of transportation for a caravaneer accustomed to the gait of mules along Tibetan tracks. We stayed at the Metropole Hotel, one of the most well known in this immense Chinese city.

Already on the day after we arrived, my companion took me on a tour of visits of protocol. To my great surprise, I already knew the first person whom he introduced me to: it was Dr Shen, the former Chinese resident in Lhasa, and recently a member of the Shanghai municipality. I could see from his face that the surprise was reciprocal.

This first meeting, where I served as an interpreter with Dr Shen expressing himself in English and Wangdola in Tibetan, had nothing to do with the commercial transactions for which, in theory, we had come to China. My companion spoke only of personal affairs, bringing up episodes from the past that took me back to the most muddled intrigues within the circles surrounding the throne of the Dalai Lama in Lhasa.

On the following days he proved that this was his sole concern. Certainly, I was happy to have the experience of being in China and this beginning of the trip was interesting, but Wangdola's attitude caused me increasing uneasiness. I quickly realised that he was insincere and inefficient and, more seriously, he had flagrantly lied to us in leading us to believe that a profitable business in silk was within easy reach. In the first stage of the journey I still wanted to hope that we could carry out the planned transactions, but each day only deepened my disappointment and after we had left our luxurious Shanghai apartment I had very mixed feelings when I took my place in the train destined for Nanking.

In what was then the capital of nationalist China, Wangdola ignored the commercial objectives of our trip just as he had done in Shanghai. As I found myself through force of circumstances associated with his activities, it did not take me long to understand which matters preoccupied him so much and were in reality the unique objective of the trip.

In reality, Wangdola had been bitterly disappointed at not having drawn greater benefits from his closeness to the Thirteenth Dalai Lama and in particular, at not having obtained the status of nobility. The death of his master did not put an end to his ambitions and, under the regency of Reting, he had exerted great efforts towards being well viewed by the prime minister upon whom he showered gifts. For this it was said with certainty that he had dipped deeply into the deceased sovereign's heritage, to which he had access thanks to his former position. It was in this way that priceless *thanka*s, silver, rugs and magnificent brocades came to grace the presence of the prime minister. In exchange, the latter had promised our man the title of *kutak* which would confer nobility. But then came the downfall of Reting, immediately followed by the designation of a new head of the government.

Taktra Rimpoche, the new regent, was not well disposed towards Wangdola who, frustrated once more in his ambitions, cultivated deep rancour and spite and looked for ways to avenge himself. These were his feelings when he arrived in Nanking where he presented himself to the leaders of the Kuomingtang as a supporter of the Chinese policy in Tibet. He claimed to represent an influential section of the opposition to Taktra's regime and my presence provided him with the opportunity of pointing out the highly placed contacts that my family had in Lhasa.

He never stopped talking to me about Tibetan politics and when I tried to bring his attention around to the purchase of silk, he answered with allusions to the even greater profits to be made by his openings into official Chinese circles, adding that great changes were probably coming soon in Tibet and he himself would have the best chances of getting a high position there, and even of becoming a minister. Wangdola then alluded to the recent attempted *coup d'état* in Lhasa which nearly overthrew the regent Taktra and gave power back to Reting. He wanted to read into these events proof that the pro-Chinese party remained powerful in Tibet and retained all its chances of bringing the situation back into its favour, whereas, in my opinion, it proved just the opposite. It became more and more obvious to me that, under the effect of a fixed idea, he lived outside of reality.

From then on, I was anxious to separate myself from this burdensome companion. Already a week or two after our arrival in Nanking, when his behaviour had assured me that he would not make the slightest move to establish commercial contacts, I had decided to seize the earliest opportunity to be rid of him. But a very unpleasant problem presented itself: we were both short of money.

This situation forced me to put up with the company of Wangdola for even longer and to accept, as he suggested to me, the hospitality of the Department of Mongolian and Tibetan Affairs dependent on the government. This bureau had a guest house where we were put up free of charge. I was determined to stay here only a short time and organise my return trip without delay but, alas, I was not master of the events.

First of all, to whom should I address myself in order to get repatriated? There was an Indian representation in Nanking which had recently been upgraded to the rank of an embassy, whereas the British embassy still represented Pakistani interests.

I did not know which one to go to because the fate of Kashmir, under whose jurisdiction I was as a Ladakhi, was still hanging between India and Pakistan. In any case, the chances of something happening with any foreign representative in China were almost nil, since I had arrived with papers, furnished by Wangdola, making me a Tibetan.

I then told myself that the Chinese authorities would perhaps let me go to Tibet but I very quickly realised that I shouldn't even dream of this. Because, by putting us up in the guest house, the authorities treated us like other Tibetan residents of the establishment who, not being prisoners, were not completely free. We were very conveniently kept by the government who even gave us the opportunity to study and amuse ourselves, but our movements were limited and supervised. It was obvious that the Department of Mongol and Tibetan Affairs wanted to keep us, with the idea that maybe one day the Chinese government could use us to an advantage for its Central Asian politics. The fact that I was not a real Tibetan changed nothing in this regard. On the contrary, the authorities seemed to have a special interest in my being a Ladakhi and my knowledge of English.

This situation totally perplexed me and I didn't understand what I was doing there or rather what I wasn't doing, because I spent my days in idleness and this weighed on me. Vis-à-vis the other boarders whom I hardly knew, caution imposed upon me an attitude of reserve and I didn't know which way to turn to seek advice.

Soon after settling into the guest house I made the acquaintance of a young Tibetan who was both eminent and kind. This was Gyalo Tondup, the elder brother of the Fourteenth Dalai Lama by seven years.

Before leaving the Tibetan capital, the representative of the Kuomingtang, Dr Shen, had persuaded the family of the Dalai Lama to entrust the young boy to him so that he could be educated in the best Chinese establishments at the expense of the latter's government. He was inspired by the example of the British who had had sons of Tibetan leaders, such as Tsarong, Kapshopa or Surkhang, come to English schools in India, in particular Darjeeling. It was obviously a means of exercising some political influence. Gyalo Tondup's coming to Nanking was to have reinforced the links between China and the family of the future spiritual and temporal sovereign of Tibet. By arranging this, Dr Shen had brought about an undeniable diplomatic success.

In the Chinese capital, the young man received princely treatment. Lodged in a luxurious villa, he had his own servants and driver with the latest model jeep and the possibility of receiving many friends. Nearly twenty years old at that time, he was already composed and thoughtful. Right away it seemed to me that he was gifted with a remarkable independent judgement and the Chinese had not really succeeded in indoctrinating him.

Although he seemed to feel mainly distrust towards Wangdola, he immediately showed kindness to me and invited me to join his circle of friends. He showed interest in my university education and my knowledge of English, at the same time being sensitive to the attachment I felt, as a Ladakhi, for Tibet and her culture.

Thanks to him, I was able to break all relations with Wangdola who was responsible for the impasse I was entangled in. Certainly, from the material point of view I couldn't complain, but I suffered from being forced into inactivity. In any case it was useless to rebel against destiny and there was nothing for me to do but to imitate the other 'guests' of the Chinese government—Tibetans, Mongols, Turkestanis from Sinkiang, who peacefully existed, just waiting for events to unfold. Guénon's book helped me pass the time. Gyalo Tondup's friendship was also a great comfort.

In his house I met a Chinese Muslim, Ma Yugi, whose family had lived in Lhasa for a long time. In a way, he fulfilled the function of a bodyguard and the brother of the Dalai Lama much preferred his company to that of the 'guardian angels' whom the Chinese authorities placed around him. The three of us became excellent friends and impassioned for conversations that the long hours permitted us.

It was thus that my forced stay in the capital of nationalist China plunged me back into the tangle of Tibetan politics. These politics were connected to Nanking by numerous threads and, through the intermediary of various delegates, projected the opposition in the Chinese capital.

First of all there was a mission which, in principle, represented the Dalai Lama and the regent Taktra Rimpoche. In fact, its presence in Nanking was the result of a misunderstanding which was very significant of the status of Tibetan–Chinese relations. To the *Kashag*, the council of ministers of Lhasa which had decided to send it in 1946, the mission was merely one of goodwill in charge of making a gesture but a gesture that was without real political value towards the Kuomintang. It was also sent to establish personal contact with the Kuomintang leaders. Now the latter, who had invited the mission, wanted to consider it the official delegation of Tibet to the Peoples' Congress which was supposedly made up of all of China.

When the Congress assembled, Tshator Khenchung, head of the mission, and his two assistants, refused to attend and sent their servants to occupy the places which were reserved for them. This showing had mainly the effect of provoking general laughter in the political circles of the capital.

The three Tibetan delegates then wanted to return to Tibet but the Chinese authorities, refusing to give them travel documents and facilities, prevented them from leaving. Therefore, they found themselves detained in Nanking in a situation very similar to mine and used their forced leisure time mainly to spy on their compatriots who resided in the city, beginning with Gyalo Tondup, the brother of the Dalai Lama. The doings of all those who could be suspected of being hostile to the regent Taktra and his regime kept their attention and I felt that they had an eye on me too. But they were not really feared and nobody took them very seriously.

The Tibetans of the opposition party were grouped mainly around the official representation of the Panchen Lama. There was always one such representative in the capital of nationalist China despite the fact that the Panchen Lama had been dead for twelve years and his reincarnation had not yet been officially recognised.

Since the time of the emperors, the Chinese have continually sought to use the Panchen Lama as an instrument of their politics in Tibet, taking advantage of every opportunity of discord that might oppose him to the Dalai Lama. On the personal level, however, the two hierarchies always maintained proper, even cordial relations. In 1918, the visit of the Panchen Lama of that time to the Thirteenth Dalai Lama had been really warm, the first having declared to the second, who was seven years his senior, that he considered him his guru. But this was not enough to diffuse the conflict, which was hardly of a spiritual nature, opposing the court of Shigatse to that of Lhasa and which went back to a tax affair. Intrigues amongst the nobility, poisoned by sly manoeuvres by the Chinese, aggravated the conflict which ended up with the flight of Panchen Lama to China in 1923. He was still there in 1933 when the Thirteenth died. At that time he showed his goodwill by praying for and having many prayers said for the prompt reincarnation of the Dalai Lama. But the Panchen Lama himself died suddenly in 1937 whilst negotiations were being made for his return to Shigatse. However, his own reincarnation was very slow in manifesting itself and the attempt by the Chinese to impose a reincarnation who served their interests did not sufficiently conform to traditional criteria, and failed.

Since then, the function of Panchen Lama, even deprived of an official title, never failed to polarise the trends of Tibetan politics in favour of the Chinese for whom it remained a useful instrument. And the office of the Panchen Lama in Nanking was active. Its members, more business-like and efficient than the three delegates of the regent, were educated and cultivated men who knew how to impose themselves on the Chinese as well as on their compatriots residing in the capital.

Closely connected to this office were three remarkable figures who, a short time earlier, were still part of the circle of my best relations in Kalimpong where their pro-Chinese attitude had annoyed the British. The latter, undoubtedly at the request of the regent and his government, had asked them to leave. Those involved were Shensay Kunphela, the former 'patron' of the Thirteenth Dalai Lama, Changlochan, the friend of Lungshar, who abetted with him in the 'republican' conspiracy, and Abo Rabga Pangdatshang, the most active of the three. Exerting an influence reinforced by the commercial success of his brothers, Abo Rabga Pangdatshang had pulled the two others into the Chinese orbit. Comfortably settled in Nanking, he had influence on the leaders of the Kuomingtang who soon made him a sort of advisor to the Department of Mongol and Tibetan Affairs.

~

I often went to Abo Rabga where I was always very cordially welcomed. Curiously enough, his wife, Chomola, was one of my relatives. Born in a family of the Chumbi valley in the north of Sikkim, she first of all married my uncle Khan Sahib Faizullah who had been seduced by her great beauty, and she followed him in Islam. The two of them lived several years in Lhasa and had a daughter, Salimala. One day Chomola asked her husband's permission to go with her daughter and visit her parents. Faizullah accompanied them to Chumbi, but Chomola found a way to give him the slip and never reappear in his presence. People then wondered if she were not happy with her husband or if she did not feel at ease in Islam. The fact remains that she left, taking with her all the jewels which her husband had given her and which represented a fortune. The latter soon made up for his misfortune by marrying a wealthy Muslim. Salimala, who hadn't left him, remained in Islam. I had met her in Tsethang in central

Tibet during the tour of the monasteries which we made with the Lopchak. She was to marry there and have several children who now live in India and Pakistan.

Abo Rabga frequently questioned me about Faizullah, his wife's first husband, and about Salimala, the latter's daughter, taking care to only speak to me in private. However, Chomola showed much consideration for me, in particular making sure I was only served food in conformity with Muslim customs which she obviously was very familiar with. So, in this home where Kunphela and Changlochan also lived, I felt as if I were in a circle of old friends. However, Gyalo Tondup, with whom my links were reinforced, did not mix with this group.

There had been a political disagreement between Abo Rabga and the brother of the Dalai Lama which did not, however, exclude the cordiality of their personal relations. Although Abo Rabga was clearly the man of the Chinese, Gyalo Tondup remained, in spite of his young age and in spite of the attempts at indoctrination which he underwent at the Political Academy of Nanking where he studied, a firm supporter of the complete independence of Tibet. I can affirm that he never swayed on this point because, since he still didn't know English, I served as an interpreter for him many times.

India at this time had just gained her independence. Circumstances were thus favourable for making progress towards the cause of Tibetan independence. But the leaders in Lhasa did not know how to best take advantage of this.

During my previous stays in Lhasa, I had noticed that the aristocratic class often expressed reserve towards the national Indian movement and the democratic movements which manifested themselves there. There were exceptions of course, like my friend Tendong who was a sincere admirer of Gandhi, Nehru, and on the Muslim side, of the great thinker Maulana Abul Kalam Azad. But, generally, the circles of the nobility felt rather disdain for the ideology which inspired the fight for the freedom of India. And these feudal landlords saw neither greatness nor power in non-violent action, the Indian nationalists' main weapon. On the contrary, they continued to look upon the British with admiration and respect. As members of the ruling class of Tibet, they considered that the English were, like them, born to lead others.

However, amongst the leaders in Lhasa, there was one at least who had enough sagacity to see where the wind was blowing from; this was Shakabpa, thereafter the main inspirer of the regent's policies. He had understood perfectly well that if Tibet wanted to be really independent, she could do no better than to evoke the same principles as Gandhi, Nehru and the national Indian movement which had triumphed to the applause of the United Nations and world opinion.

Within this perspective, Shakabpa decided to personally lead a new mission of goodwill which would attempt to make his point of view known to the Chinese government. Accompanied by several figures, the most notable of whom was Abo Yamphel Pangdatshang, the Khampa elite, Shakabpa went through India and arrived in Hong Kong. A particularly thorny problem detained the delegates there for several days: would their status, upon entering China, be one of nationals of the country or of citizens of a foreign state? Finally, they crossed the border, furnished with identity cards endorsed by the British authorities. This was regarded by Shakabpa as a success and he considered himself to be the bearer of the first Tibetan passport.

Upon their arrival in Nanking, the three members of the preceding delegation of the regent spent copiously to organise receptions in their honour. But the contacts with the government were rather disappointing and hardly helped advance the cause of an independent Tibet.

Amongst the delegates, none spoke a foreign language, with the exception of Surkhang who knew a little English. And the interpreter who accompanied them was not even a Tibetan but Nepalese. His services were undoubtedly considered to be inadequate since I was called upon to serve as an interpreter. I deemed it prudent to refuse, accepting only to fill this office during the meeting which the Tibetan emissaries had with the ambassador of India, Mr K.P.S. Menon. The eminent diplomat listened to them, then answered with courtesy, tact and subtlety. Shakabpa Tsipon seemed very satisfied when he left him.

The mission shortened its stay in Nanking, because the nationalist administration, already threatened by the Communist advance, had other concerns. As for my own troubles, they only increased as time went by but I still saw no escape from the trap I had fallen into. The absence of news of my family, whom I wasn't even able to correspond with, caused me particular worry.

The main obstacle to any attempt at escape was my total material dependence upon the authorities of the Kuomingtang, because apart from the small subsidies that I received from them which permitted me to survive, I was deprived of financial resources of any kind. Moreover, most of the boarders who received stipends from the Department of Mongol and Tibetan Affairs were in an analogous situation and were no less perplexed.

The uneasiness soon became widespread and anxiety weighed upon the entire city. The news was alarming. Each day it was felt that the distance separating Nanking from the Red Army of Mao Tse-tung was decreasing. Numerous Communist agents were at work passing out pamphlets and spreading rumours. At the same time the economic situation degenerated rapidly and rampant inflation made the life of the people more and more precarious. It became clear that the regime, which until then had functioned after a fashion mainly to serve the interest of the two Soongs, brothers-in-law of Chang Kai-Shek, was completely rotten and on the verge of collapse.

There was one thing certain: the downfall was close at hand. The rest was mere doubt and speculation. The administration became progressively paralysed and many government employees disappeared, seeking refuge elsewhere. One of them suggested that I evacuate with him to Taiwan. I absolutely refused because that would have kept me in the power of the Kuomingtang who had already given me enough to complain about.

As the brother of the Dalai Lama, my friend Gyalo Tondup, obviously was also going to get himself evacuated and repatriated but I couldn't think of benefiting from the same facilities. One possibility would have been to remain where I was and await the arrival of the Communists. However, the aversion I felt towards Marxism and materialism removed any desire to try the experience.

It seemed to me interesting in any case to get the opinion of a few Tibetans who I knew had Communist sympathies and who were grouped around Sherab Gyaltso, a reincarnated lama. This erudite man had had Gyendum Chombel for a disciple, one of my acquaintances from Kalimpong. Settled for many years in China, he had served the interests of the Kuomingtang and then let himself be seduced by the ideas of Mao, some of whose writings he had translated into Tibetan. He was also the author of an interpretation of Buddhism in Marxist terms which was to be published shortly after these events. I met him several times but on each occasion, this learned old man, then seventy-five years old, seemed to me intellectually enslaved to an ideology foreign to his own culture and left me with a poor impression.

I also made contact with Abo Rabga Pangdatshang, a very cunning man who had certainly laid out elaborate plans to get himself safely out of the predicament in Nanking. But he didn't let anyone know to which side his leanings were and, recalling the political flexibility which he and his brothers had already displayed, I told myself that it wasn't entirely excluded that, after everything, he was thinking of going over to Mao's camp.

I had made several good friends amongst the Muslim government employees and students, who sometime earlier had arranged for me to meet the famous Ma Pufang, 'warlord' and master of Tsing-Hai, the native province of the Dalai Lama. He had then returned to his capital of Sining, putting a good thousand kilometres between himself and the Red Army of which he had killed so many soldiers at the time of the Long March. For a moment I envisaged the possibility of slipping away in the same direction.

Other Muslims, Turkestani natives of Sinkiang, absolutely dissuaded me from this. Thanks to them, I ended up finding a way out.

A few of them, some merchants, had had business relationships with some of my relatives. Authentic Muslims of Central Asia, they were anti-Communist although without ever really being in favour of the Kuomingtang and were foreign to China. These new friends introduced me to members of a troupe of dancers and musicians from Sinkiang who had just carried off a great success in Nanking. Amongst these kind artists gravitating around the star dancer, Qamar Jehan, was the son of an important political figure, Issa Effendi Beg. As an adolescent, he had sojourned in Ladakh with his father who had sought refuge in Kashmir during the Muslim revolt of Sinkiang between 1931 and 1934. Both of them had even been guests of my grandfather in Leh and I remember that we had played ball together.

Issa Effendi then made up with the Kuomintang and took over the office of secretary general of the provincial government of Sinkiang in Tihwa. My unhoped for meeting with his son opened for me the way to save myself. Upon learning about what a mess I was stuck in, he didn't hesitate for a moment.

'You are going to join up with us. There is no other solution. We have a debt of gratitude towards your family and I would be only too happy to be of service to you. You shall no more worry about problems of money or passport or visa. You are now one of us and you shall accompany us on our return journey to Tihwa. Every facility will be granted to you so that you can return home. I will guarantee this.'

~

Destiny had appeared to me in the form of this warm-hearted interlocutor, a tall man with an open face often seen amongst the Uighurs of Sinkiang. I immediately began preparations to leave, and fearing that an obstacle might loom up at the last minute, I avoided taking leave of most of my comrades in semi-captivity. A few days after my meeting with the son of Effendi Beg, we left together for the airport.

Amongst the costumes and musical instruments of the troupe, I took my place with my new friends in the Dakota which permitted us to cross in two days the enormous distance separating Nanking from Tihwa, the administrative capital of Sinkiang. Seated cross-legged on blankets spread out on the floor of the cabin, we traversed the entire breadth of China. The relief I felt in leaving the capital of the crumbling Kuomingtang is difficult to describe but at each stop, especially in Lanchow where we spent the night, the fear of an incident or snag risking to compromise this veritable escape came over me.

Issa Effendi was waiting for us on the runway of Tihwa. He welcomed me like the representative of friends of the family. I could but congratulate myself for the hospitality he offered me as well as the facilities he granted me so that I could continue my journey in good conditions.

Located in a green oasis on the northern foot of the Tian Shan mountains, Tihwa in Chinese or Urumchi in Turkish Uighur, was a town of some 150,000 inhabitants of very diverse ethnic origins. The governor, appointed by Nanking, was Chinese but the provincial government as well as most of the officers, were made up of the ethnic majority of the Uighurs. Various aspects of local life bore witness to the Chinese influence, in particular the signs in Chinese characters and mural newspapers which were quite common in public places. They were most often written, not in Chinese, but in Uighur, which is written with letters of Arabic origin like classical Turkish.

The town was then an important commercial centre and the

bazaar was very lively. Besides Uighurs and Chinese, one came across most of the human types of Central Asia: Mongols, Uzbeks, Kirghiz, Tajik, Huis, or Chinese Muslims, as well as sometimes people of the European race. These were white Russians who had fled the Bolshevik regime. They seemed to be well adapted to the country and most of them spoke the language fluently. However, the turn taken by recent events in China filled them with worry because there was no doubt that if the Communists succeeded in occupying the region they would find themselves treated like rats; turned over to the Soviets they would be bound for Siberian concentration camps. I met a few of them, young men who were discussing the best means of leaving this country where they soon risked being trapped. The itinerary which they preferred and which was moreover, the only possible one, went through the deserts of the south, then through the Karakoram or Pamir passes. I prepared to follow this route myself.

~

In Nanking, shortly before my departure, I had been introduced to some French people, Monsieur and Madame Dominique Fourcade who were going to Tihwa, whence they intended to go on by land southwards towards the Pakistani border. I confided in them that I myself was just going to leave on a similar journey. A rendezvous was thus set in the capital of Sinkiang, where we agreed to undertake the rest of the expedition together.

M. Fourcade, a learned, erudite sinologist, was attached to the cultural services of the French embassy and had a diplomatic status which allowed him various privileges which he obligingly was also going to let me benefit from. On my part, as soon as we had met again in Tihwa, I was happy to introduce him to Issa Effendi whose help was to turn out to be invaluable for crossing Sinkiang. However, at this meeting, it seemed to me that he was not as cordial as he was when I had come to see him alone. I wondered about the reasons for this more reserved attitude, which I finally learnt was due to the leftist political opinions which were attributed to the two French people, for Issa Effendi must have received information about this and he suspected Fourcade of having had contacts with Burhan Shahidi, the Uighur Communist leader trained in the USSR and at that time living under surveillance in Nanking.

Although my association with this Frenchman of suspicious political opinions somewhat cooled the warmth of my relations with the authorities, I could but congratulate myself otherwise, because during the long and fairly adventurous journey which was to take us from the heart of Asia to the shores of the Indian Ocean, the Fourcades' company was a continual pleasure, thanks to their kindness, good humour and culture. Moreover, their diplomatic status gave us advantages which ordinary citizens would not have benefited from. It was for this reason that they were given an official escort, Mr Wu Shansay, an official in charge of assisting us and obviously of watching us as well. Free transportation was put at our disposal: it was a Russian lorry loaded with various merchandise which we were authorised to hoist ourselves up upon.

Leaving Tihwa for Kashgar, we had absolutely no idea of the fatigue and danger which was awaiting us during the three weeks which our expedition was to last in this uncomfortable but surprisingly sturdy vehicle. These regions were totally deprived of anything worthy of calling a road, and we rode along caravan tracks across immense deserted stretches where, in case of a breakdown, no help was to be hoped for. But, bumping along on thin tyres, the lorry held out for the entire trip and didn't have any serious mechanical problem.

The first days, during which we crossed the Tian Shan mountains on rocky tracks, were not the most difficult, and as far as Karashahr where the roof of a caravanserai sheltered us for the night, the areas we went through were sparsely inhabited, mainly by nomads. The country became even more desert-like the more we went in a southwesterly direction to approach the Soviet border. Although we had the lorry to transport us at a certainly faster speed than the mules of Tibet, I had the impression of going back to my former life of a caravaneer. At night we camped out in much the same way. As it was summer, and it was hot, we didn't always have to put up our tents for the night. And thanks to the tins which the Fourcades had brought along, the food also was more varied than that of ordinary nomads.

Although we were still in China, in fact, the regions we travelled through were less and less Chinese and more and more Turkish Muslim and Middle Eastern. The place names marking out our itinerary—Karashahr, Kusha, Aksu—reminded me of the stories of my uncles who, before the war, went regularly to trade in these districts which they reached by the 'Treaty Route' crossing the Karakoram. This was sufficient to give me the feeling of being no longer completely in a foreign country.

Thanks to my companions who were travelling as guests of the Chinese government, and to the presence of Mr Wu who never left our sight, the authorities granted us many kindnesses everywhere we stopped. In Kucha, a small party was held in our honour in a garden where we were served a succulent meal of rice and meat in Turkish style followed by a show of folk dancing performed only by men; wearing brightly coloured traditional clothes both young and old men, some with white beards, participated in the dancing with a catching liveliness. The women kept to their own side without mixing with men. In the streets they were strictly veiled.

Between these oases, the jolting of our tireless Russian truck continually seemed to me incomparably more trying than all my earlier rides through the highlands of Asia. But the morale of our little group remained high even though the company of Mr Wu imposed upon us a certain reserve and sometimes seemed rather heavy to us. He was not an unpleasant man, and we didn't have any real reason to complain about him. He had long conversations with my friend Fourcade who spoke fluent Chinese, but Mr Wu was also able to speak in Uighur Turkish with the local people.

Three weeks after our departure from Tihwa, night had already fallen and we were given some relief from the bumping of the endless track when our lorry finally rumbled into Kashgar. We went straight to the residence of the general consul of Great Britain, Eric Shipton, who welcomed us with the greatest kindness and for an entire month was to extend to us unforgettable hospitality.

Once the capital of sultans who reigned over the Roof of the World and had even occupied Ladakh, Kashgar had lost its former glory but remained an important caravan crossroads and commercial centre specialising in rugs, leather and skins. The town was not without charm. Its location on a mountainous plateau and even sometimes its architecture, reminded one of Lhasa. However, the presence of Islam strongly affirmed itself everywhere and the Turkish-style mosques, often very beautiful, were numerous. The crowds of the faithful participating in the Friday prayer lent an air of festivity to the bazaar and foreigners were welcomed with engaging smiles. Hospitality was bountiful and we were constantly invited, even by people we didn't know, to share in generally delicious meals. The Fourcades, who were refined gourmets and connoisseurs of Chinese cooking, made warm and apparently sincere compliments to the food.

The hospitality which the consul general of Great Britain extended to us was also customary of Central Asia. With the absence of any place worth calling a hotel, the official foreign representatives never failed to invite the rare travellers of international status, and they even disputed over them since it was a question of prestige. In Kashgar, where there were two consul generals, the British and the Soviet, any foreigner could present himself at the door of either, and regardless of his nationality, his origin or his political or ideological leanings, would find shelter and food. Rivalling each other for prestige, the two consul generals observed each other rather in the same way as the two empires in

Central Asia which they represented had done for so long. There had been all sorts of intrigues in the past and each one in its turn had been mixed up in them. The Russians in particular had bribed local 'warlords' so that they would be totally independent of the Chinese government. Mr Shipton often recalled how all this took place and how he had intervened on behalf of these formidable figures and had flattered them so that they wouldn't fall completely under the sway of the Soviets.

On his part, the consul general of the USSR, to maintain his prestige in the vast dimensions of his residence, counted on the magnificence of his carpets and the stocks in his cellar. He welcomed us into his sitting rooms in a very friendly manner because, in spite of the political differences, there existed personal relationships of courtesy and even cordiality between the two consuls. It was the rule that each one should invite the guests of his colleague and rival at least once. During one of these receptions of the Soviet consul cockfighting took place, a spectacle that was very popular in these regions and that the master of the house seemed particularly proud to be able to present to his guests.

However, one of the most enjoyable aspects of our stay in Kashgar was the company of Mr Shipton himself. A remarkable mountaineer who had scaled many difficult summits of the Himalayas without an oxygen mask, he had been a pioneer in demonstrating the advantages of proper equipment for this type of expedition. Moreover, he was probably one of the most knowledgeable Westerners of Central Asia, of its geography and its inhabitants. His conversations helped us to better grasp the significance of the events which were upsetting the equilibrium of the continent. On a more practical level, his advice was extremely useful in determining our itinerary across the immense barrier of mountains which we still had to cross

We had a choice between two possible routes: one to the east going through Yarkand then through the Karakoram pass would have been more direct to get to Ladakh, but Mr Shipton strongly advised us against this route because, after crossing inhospitable deserts and climbing through perilous passes, it would have brought us into the state of Jammu and Kashmir which was still in a state of armed conflict. The route to the west, which followed the Soviet border and climbed the Pamir to the Mintaka pass to come out in the Hunza and the Gilgit, thus seemed much preferable and less risky, besides the fact that, according to our guest, it would be more interesting and would put us into contact with a wider variety of inhabitants. The best thing my French friends and I could do was to follow his advice.

~

A journey like this required the organisation of a caravan and this prospect filled me with excitement. The preparations took place under the auspices of the British consulate. Mr Shipton had sent word to people in the surrounding area of Kashgar who had good horses and were familiar with the tracks which we proposed to follow. Guides and servants were assigned to us. Upon meeting them, I knew that we could trust them completely.

We now rode directly southwards and, ascending the slopes of the first foothills of Pamir, we had penetrated a region mainly inhabited by Kirghiz nomads. Riding across plateaus which reminded me somewhat of Tibet, in spite of the lower altitude, and where I even spotted yaks, I had the impression of reliving my life as a caravaneer. However, the white felt tents of the Kirghiz encampments were very different from those of the Tibetan Drogpas which were much coarser and made of black yak hair. The interior of the tents, often decorated with geometric motifs typical of popular Muslim art, was more comfortable and bore witness to an existence which was less severe, somewhat more refined and, from our experience, with a superior diet. When we approached one of these encampments, the Kirghiz hailed us so that we would stop and with the natural kindness of nomads, invited us to share their meal. We then were treated to white flour pancakes, mutton, curdled milk, melons, apricots and fruit, delicious things, but my nostalgia for Tibet made me miss *tsampa*.

In general, the country was less austere than Tibet, the mountains less gigantic and on the often green plateaus, flocks grazed on grass that was not as sparse. The higher the altitude became, more similarities with Changthang and the Trans-Himalayan regions, which we had crossed during the time of the Lopchak caravan, appeared and the scenery became almost as grandiose.

We were now very close to the Soviet border of Tajikistan which, if one believed the nomads, was not at all shut off. They assured us that, on the contrary, we would cross the region easily and unknown to the Russian as well as the Chinese guard posts. They also assured us that they maintained continued relations with the inhabitants on the other side who led an existence very similar to theirs and the Soviet regime did not too openly oppose their traditional customs and in particular, the practice of the religion.

In the encampments where we stopped, Islam was fervently practised in the very orthodox form of Hanafite Sunnism. The Friday prayer took place either on carpets laid out in the open air or else in a large tent set up like a mosque where the Imam gave his sermon. I spoke several times with mullahs responsible for the cult and found them educated, open and kind.

As in most of the regions of Asia where foreigners are rare, Europeans were said to be in possession of medicines which were quasi-miraculous and the Fourcades were constantly assailed by men, women and children who clamoured for pills and tablets or displayed their injuries. My friends did their best not to disappoint them too much, distributing aspirin and above all, cleaning, disinfecting and bandaging numerous wounds. They received gifts in gratitude for their cares, especially blocks of butter and meat. We almost never noticed money whilst crossing these regions.

The most important location between Kashgar and the Pamir is Tashkurgan. This meeting point of several groups of nomad tribes is also, according to a well-established reputation at that time, a nest for spies and various political agents. In fact the frontiers of the three largest empires of the world—China, the USSR and India, for whom Pakistan had recently assured troops, not counting Afghanistan whose band of territory borders on Sinkiang—came together in these highlands to create one of the most sensitive regions of the globe. In Tashkurgan, one came across people from these countries and heard a variety of languages like Tajik, Pashtu and even Urdu besides the Turkish and Chinese dialects.

The authorities were careful to strictly check travellers which was normal but this made me very uneasy because I still had no identity papers and the British consul in Kashgar, Mr Shipton himself, was unable to issue me with any, not knowing whether, as a Ladakhi, I should be considered an Indian or a Pakistani. Thanks to Mr Wu, our official Chinese companion, to my great relief, the police let me go through without difficulty.

After granting ourselves as well as our horses two days of rest in this rather worrying place, our little caravan, still escorted by the indispensable Mr Wu, set off again. The track going up to Mintaka took us zigzagging through valleys and plateaus surrounded by immense mountains whose shapes were not as rough and jagged as the peaks of the great Himalayas or of Karakoram. The Pamir massif seemed less impressive, less overwhelming, also less dangerous for travellers and we noticed many patches of green watered by the streams flowing from snowy heights of rounded summits.

I don't remember anymore exactly how many days it took us to reach the culminating point of the pass which is at 4,700 metres of altitude. I retain above all, the memory of a relatively easier climb than the crossing of the mountainous massifs separating Tibet from the rest of the world. It was also this less rigorous nature and climate which allowed us to use horses, whereas in Tibet it is preferable to have mules as they are sturdier and better adapted to high altitudes.

As we approached the point which supposedly marks the frontier, Mr Wu declared that his responsibilities as an official companion came to an end. After exchanging gifts, thanks and compliments with a courtesy worthy of old China, he returned in the direction of Tashkurgan and Kashgar. Upon seeing him disappear I told myself with immense relief that at last I was out of an impasse where I had lost two of the best years of my life.

~

The highest point of the Mintaka is made up of a vast plateau marked by pillars of rocks to which were attached little flags fluttering in the wind, something like the prayer flags of the Tibetans. And it is a curious fact that the custom of setting up these pillars, which must go back to primitive cults, is not limited to regions of Buddhist influence but is practised in all of Central Asia, even within the domain of Islam.

Whilst crossing this plateau, our Muslim caravaneers expressed their joy and gratitude with the cry 'Allahu Akbar' (God is the Greatest) and by the testimony of their faith: 'La ilaha illa 'Llah, Muhammadun Rasulu 'Llah' (There is no divinity but God; Muhammad is the Messenger of God). As I undoubtedly had even more reason for gratitude and I shared the same faith, I joined in with them and our invocation was addressed to Him for whom the Roof of the World, whose silence we thus broke, is but a speck of dust.

CHAPTER 9

A DISILLUSIONED HOMECOMING

Having crossed the Mintaka pass, we began our long descent towards Hunza, Gilgit and the Punjab plain. Walking alongside our horses, we followed a track which zigzagged around huge rocks in damp, muddy ground, proof that we had left dry Central Asia and penetrated the area watered by the monsoons. We went down into Misgar, the first stop on the southern side of the Pamir in the principality of Hunza, formerly a vassal of the Maharaja of Kashmir and now part of the new state of Pakistan.

The telegraph office which was known to be the northernmost of the entire former empire of India was located in Misgar. I went there immediately to inform my family that I would be returning soon. The office employee was a real Kashmiri and in talking with him, as well as with other residents of the village, I had the feeling that I was in a familiar country or in an antichamber of my homeland.

In order to follow some strong advice from Mr Shipton as well as to conform to a long-established custom, we still had to send a telegram to the highest authority of the country, the Mir of Hunza, Jamal Khan. His father was placed on the throne of the principality by the English in 1891, following a war which put an end to the constant incursions caused by the Hunzas into Sinkiang as well as into neighbouring territories belonging to India. Restless warriors, the Hunzas had also just participated in the military operations against the Hindu regime of the Maharaja of Kashmir, who had declared himself in favour of India, the Hunzas being in favour of Pakistan.

Besides the telegram, we sent a polite letter to His Highness Jamal Khan who had a reputation for acting like the absolute sovereign of an independent kingdom. It was, therefore, essential that we treat him with the greatest respect if we wanted to cross his state.

After several days of waiting in Misgar we got the green light from His Highness and our little party was able to set off again on its downward hike. However, a little lower, the valley narrowed so much that we had to go back up along the side of the mountain and go through a pass close to a glacier. Finally, we made our entrance into Hunza, or Baltit, 'capital' of the little state.

The prince was very friendly. He gave the two French people a gift of two brown woollen hats of the region and a comfortable warm coat to me. And even more appreciated, he offered us hospitality in his guest house, the hotel for travellers of distinction. It is difficult to describe the pleasure we had in staying in rooms furnished with real beds and having adjoining showers, then sitting down to an evening meal at a table laid out in a modern-style dining room.

During the three days that we were his guests, the Mir was very kind to us and in particular entertained us with a picturesque folk dance show. During our conversations, however, I sometimes felt uneasy because, upon finding out which family I came from, he expressed sharp criticism with regard to my great-uncle Khwaja Abdullah Shah who, according to what he had heard on the Pakistani radio, had gone to welcome the passengers of the first aeroplane to land in Ladakh. These people were highly placed officers and military personnel sent by the government of Delhi to take possession of the country in the name of India. And Jamal Khan cried out:

'Shame on the Muslims who have given Ladakh over to the

kafirs (infidels) of India and have not made it a part of Pakistan!' I thought it prudent not to react.

Before setting off again in the direction of Gilgit and the great plains of the south, we would have liked to cross the Hunza river to visit the principality of Nagar located on the left bank. A rivalry stirred up by religious differences opposed the two little states and their inhabitants who nonetheless were Shiite Muslims on both sides of the river. But the Hunzas being Ismailians, recognised the authority of the Aga Khan, whereas the people of Nagar were Twelvers or Imamites like the Persians. I would have much preferred to visit the neighbouring principality where a Mir who had been a classmate of mine in Srinagar reigned. We had to give up this plan because Jamal Khan made it clear to us that he did not approve of our crossing the river to go and offer our respects to the rival Highness.

Our host insisted on the fact that he himself was a much more important person. According to what he said, he maintained official relations with China and every year sent an expedition somewhat similar to the Lopchak caravan to Kashgar. In fact, it seems that he had an emissary in Kashgar who was more or less connected to the British consulate. Be that as it may, all we could do was set off again, showering him with gratitude.

Besides my family ties which seemed compromising to him, Jamal Khan must have been disconcerted by my association with the Fourcades, suspecting perhaps political implications or relations with some foreign information service. In any case, our next crossing was announced to the political agent of the Pakistani government in Gilgit, advising him to watch us closely.

Without being warm, the welcome we found in Gilgit was nevertheless polite and the political agent did not put off receiving us. He bore witness to the changes that were taking place in his country. Instead of the modern look we were expecting of the highly placed officer, our interlocutor was an authentic representative of the Muslim inhabitants of the frontier regions with a thick moustache, fur cap, *sherwal* (baggy pants) drawing smoke from a beautiful hookah.

In addition to the reservations he must have had towards us that were of a political nature, he obviously was unfamiliar with Western customs and stared at his female French visitor as if he had never seen a European woman in his life. This did not prevent him from granting us the hospitality of the official guest house and inviting us to dinner that very evening. Probably recalling a legacy going back to one of his British predecessors, he extended his friendliness to the point of asking the Fourcades if they wished to drink some wine. Upon their affirmative answer, a servant soon arrived with a bottle covered with dust. My friends considered the contents excellent but the disapproving look of our host spoilt their pleasure in tasting it.

After Gilgit, several days of a relatively easy track, first along the Indus, then through the Bahasar pass, were sufficient to get to the foot of the mountains, at the edge of the great Punjab plain. The police detained us in Abbotabad to question our identity and the reasons for our movements. Everything was cleared up after several hours and we were able to continue without hindrance until Peshawar.

~

The long adventurous journey was now over. It left us with a deep fatigue which made us greatly appreciate the few days of rest spent in this beautiful city. I took advantage of this to see two or three former classmates from Aligarh. They helped me re-establish contact with the reality of the subcontinent which had changed in two years. From then on it was divided, or rather torn, between two states which had not yet learnt to live side by side.

Where was I to go and what did I have to do to rejoin my wife? I didn't even know where she was. It seemed unlikely to me that she would be in Ladakh, which would be difficult for me to get to because of the conflict that had still not calmed down in Kashmir. The best thing to do then was to try to get back to Kalimpong and then go into India. But with the state of tension that persisted, crossing the border was a real problem. A special permit, sometimes difficult to obtain, was necessary in western Pakistan, especially for travellers who, as in my case, were arriving from such an unusual direction. On the other hand, in East Pakistan, now Bangladesh, no permit was required to cross the Indian border. And as there was no special formality to go from one 'wing' of Pakistan to another, I was determined to take a plane to Dacca or Eastern Bengal, whence it seemed it would be easy to reach Calcutta and then Kalimpong.

Since most of the flights to East Pakistan left from Karachi and my French friends were about to leave for that city, I decided to accompany them. Our long Asian expedition, therefore, ended with a train journey to the large port city of Sind. Suddenly promoted to the rank of the capital of the new Muslim state, Karachi was overflowing with refugees from all over the most diverse regions of India, and the city seemed to be surviving in an improvised manner. After the great silence of the deserts and mountains where we had spent so many long weeks, our heads were spinning as we mingled in the thick crowds that hurried through the streets. The Fourcades were nevertheless glad to get into contact with their embassy and be amongst their French countrymen again.

For my part, I did not delay meeting up with Ladakhis of Baltistan and it was a pleasure to converse with them in my native language. They advised me to go to the Ministry of Foreign Affairs where they said they would be particularly interested in hearing about my crossing of Sinkiang. I went there but, undoubtedly because of the Kashmir crisis, it was mainly my being a Ladakhi which attracted the attention of the government officials whom I was introduced to. They presented me to the Secretary, States Department, Mr Ikramullah, who invited me for tea.

Several other highly placed officials were there too. After

answering their questions, they offered me entrance into the diplomatic service of their country.

The offer was tempting. However, I didn't easily imagine myself as a diplomat and besides, I was afraid that this would prevent me from seeing Tibet again. The nostalgia for that country had not left me. I, therefore, asked for some time to think about it and consulted my French friends who, by the end of our journey knew me well. They didn't hesitate an instant before answering me.

'You are foreign to the countries south of the Himalayas,' they said. 'You belong to Central Asia. You should live in Tibet, Sinkiang or Kashmir. You have the most in common with people of these regions.'

Their opinion struck a chord in my heart. I, therefore, refused the offer. At the time the decision hadn't been difficult to make. In any case, I felt the call of Tibet more strongly than the desire to serve the new Islamic state whose ideology was based on Iqbal and other modernist reformers. And I was in even more of a hurry to return to Lhasa since I had learnt from a telegram that my wife was there then with her parents.

After bidding farewell to my French friends, I flew to Dacca. As the Pakistanis did not yet possess long-range planes that could fly over the vast territory of India, there was a technical stopover at the airport of Safdarjung in New Delhi. This was remarkable when one thinks that at the time the two countries had just barely stopped fighting with one another. The trip to Eastern Pakistan was no problem. Neither was there a problem crossing the frontier and arriving by train to Siliguri at the foot of the Himalayas. A few hours later, a car let me off in Kalimpong.

~

Upon the news of my return, all my old friends expressed their joy and had a party for me. However, I was about to face cruel disappointments.

The trade projects I had set up in Kalimpong and which were

so promising seemed to be in complete decline. One of my uncles who was supposed to be taking care of them, Muhammad Asghar, had not known how to take full advantage of the quota system that I had organised for the benefit of the Muslim community of Lhasa and had evidently neglected this work for the cinema, the management of which demanded less effort and in which the profits were perhaps more immediate.

On a more personal level, even more distasteful trouble was in store for me. I very soon came to realise that gossip circulated throughout the entire family, all my relatives, implying that during my stay in China I had been unfaithful to my legitimate spouse, that I had taken a Chinese woman as a second wife and that I had abandoned the rules and traditional customs of our religion. In short, that I could no longer be considered a true Muslim. It was also said that I had adapted the habit of showering in the Chinese way and that I had stopped doing the ritual ablution prescribed by Islam. They also added that I used towels to wash my face like the Chinese did, something reprehensible because a Muslim, as everyone knows, is supposed to wash with his bare hands.

~

It didn't take me long to identify the source of all this slander; it was a woman who was part of the court of the Thirteenth Dalai Lama and who knew Wangdola. The latter, by communicating these libellous rumours to her and suggesting that she pass them on to the ears of my uncles, had wanted to take revenge on what he considered my treason when in Nanking I had decided to break off all relations with him. This procedure, unfortunately, was typical of certain Tibetan circles who did not fear spreading discord and dividing families in order to advance their own interests or take personal revenge.

After all the trials and tribulations that I had endured for more than two years, after giving up a brilliant and lucrative post in Pakistan in order to rejoin my family, their attitude caused me bitter resentment. I could not understand how my uncles could take such calumny seriously and I was indignant to think that they had discredited me to my wife. As for the practice of Islam, I certainly did not blame them for being so firmly attached to their religion, but after the spiritual enrichment which I owed to my recent reading, it was certainly not from them that I expected lessons.

Soon after my return to Kalimpong at least some good news reached me: my cousin Ataullah who had worked for two years with our uncles from Lhasa decided to return to India and look for a job which corresponded to his university training, now that the country was independent. He hoped to find a position which would allow him to work for the welfare of his homeland, Ladakh, whose attachment to the Indian union he did not question. He had already published correspondence in Indian newspapers from Lhasa expressing his views, as a Ladakhi, on the great political problems of the times.

He had left the Tibetan capital and set off on the southern route. When he arrived in Gangtok, he went to see Harishvar Dayal, the first political agent of India to Sikkim. He asked him to convey to his government the offer of his services, expressing the desire to work in a ministry, preferably that of Foreign Affairs. Dayal laughed in his face, stating very frankly that, as a Muslim, he would have no chance of being recruited into the diplomatic service of India. My cousin, however, had all the desirable qualifications; equipped with a relatively high university degree, he had served in the British administration for some time and had a rare experience of Tibet. He was full of goodwill and his loyalty was unquestionable. But he found himself face-to-face with a wall of incomprehension and disdain.

The disappointment he shared with me was not designed to illuminate the dark mood I was plunged into. We obviously had a thousand things to talk over. When I told him about the offer that was made to me in Karachi to enter the diplomatic service of Pakistan and that I had declined it, Ataullah listened. After the brush-off in Gangtok, this gave him something to think about. In any case, he had no desire to continue in business with the Tsakurs whom he already had barely put up with for the three years he worked with them in Lhasa.

Neither did my cousin hide from me the fact that the Tsakurs held me in distrust. He added that after all their slander, my wife wondered if I still cared about her and if she should consider us as still married. As for Rabia, my sister, she wasn't happy in the Tsakur household either.

My reaction then was to want to leave immediately for Lhasa to clear up this nasty situation. Ataullah strongly advised me against it, considering it more advisable to wait in Kalimpong for the arrival of Khwaja Abdul Aziz, head of the family, and engage him in a discussion which his brothers would not be able to interrupt. I insisted at least that my sister accompany him and I let this be known in Lhasa.

In effect, I soon had the happiness of seeing her again. Then eighteen years old, she was very mature and assured me that she had never given credence to the gossip that had circulated about me. However, her formal education left much to be desired and she didn't know a word of English. I made arrangements for her to enter as a boarder at the school of the St Joseph convent in Kalimpong. She was to acquire knowledge there which was very useful to her later as she was to marry a man who made his career abroad and both still live in the Near East.

~

After some thought Ataullah got himself an offer, with the references he had, to serve the government of Pakistan. He then left for Kashmir, intending to go to Ladakh and wait for events to unfold. As there was no other way of getting to Leh during this season, he wanted to take a plane and left to find Bakshi Ghulam Muhammad to request air transportation from him. As vice prime minister, his power was beginning to eclipse that of Sheikh

Abdullah, head of the government. The answer was that there was a shortage of food supplies in Ladakh and that it would be better to load a bag of rice onto the plane instead of a man like him. So my cousin remained in Srinagar not knowing what to do until one day a message came to him from Pakistan informing him that he was expected at the Ministry of Foreign Affairs in Karachi for an interview and that he should go there as soon as possible.

A few days later in Karachi, Secretary, States Department, Ikramullah welcomed him warmly and courteously but was surprised not to find me there. It was me whom he had expected, thinking that I had changed my mind about the offer. Ataullah was nonetheless recruited on the spot into the Pakistani diplomatic service. After several months he was posted as a counsellor of Pakistan in India. He took up his post in the Calcutta office. His wife and children soon joined him in this city whence it was easy for him to remain in contact with Kalimpong and Lhasa.

~

For my part, I had left for Lhasa again with Khwaja Abdul Aziz. We were in a grim mood during the three weeks of the journey and as we rode we hardly exchanged a word.

When I finally found my wife again I was happy to learn that she hadn't taken the gossip that had spread to discredit me any more seriously than my sister had. But I was astounded when she told me that the Tsakur uncles had constantly urged her to begin a divorce procedure against me.

The attitude of these two fellows hurt me deeply, all the more so since they were largely indebted to me for their prosperity. They worked from the capital which came from Haji Muhammad Siddiq, my grandfather, and which I had put at their disposal. And the quota system I had set up in Kalimpong had also permitted them to make great profits until their incompetence caused it to go to seed. What finally seemed clear to me was that they wanted to prevent me at any price from heading the family business. I was never really able to find out the reasons for this but it is a fact that they did everything in their power to get rid of me. And they were to succeed.

During the first weeks following my return to Lhasa and before finding out what had happened during my absence, I decided to avoid all discussion and to keep quiet. My silence itelf displeased my uncles and they tried to put me up against a wall and make me accept an arrangement under their conditions, which would have amounted to excluding me purely and simply from the family association. They had not yet succeeded in bringing their eldest brother, Khwaja Abdul Aziz, around to their point of view. Being my father-in-law, he always treated me with circumspection. The discussions went on and on and I myself did not care to let them end too abruptly before seeing things more clearly.

~

The pleasures of Lhasa brought welcome compensation for the troubles I went through in the family circles. I was happy to return to the Tendong household where the hospitality was just as warm as ever and I also found consolation with cousins who had resolutely taken my side in the conflict opposing me to the Tsakurs. Moreover, since I was linked to Gyalpo Tondup by friendship in Nanking, I was received with the greatest kindness into the family of the Dalai Lama and since then I have never ceased to maintain excellent personal relations with them.

At this time I also happened to make the acquaintance of Heinrich Harrer, an Austrian mountain climber famous for his 'firsts' in the Alps and in the Himalayas. Along with his friend Peter Aufschnaiter, he had escaped from the concentration camp in northern India where the British had placed them during the war, since they were nationals of an enemy country. After an adventurous crossing of the mountains, they had reached Tibetan territory and with luck had ended up in Lhasa where the protection of several aristocrats, especially of Thangmay, the first to welcome them, had granted them the exceptional privilege of being authorised to stay.

Harrer, who was later to relate his experiences in a successful book, *Seven Years in Tibet*, had then been in Lhasa for three years. He had succeeded in working himself into the most influential circles of the aristocracy and was sometimes seen at the Tendong home. But my friend was somewhat reserved towards Harrer, finding him indiscreet and talkative. Others disapproved of the rise of the 'German' into the family of the Dalai Lama. He had become a regular visitor there and his opinions were listened to. It is true that political circles must not have been totally ignorant of the criticisms circulating against him because the presence of the two escapees was not seen in a favourable light from either the British or the Indian side. They were suspicious of the bad influences that the two foreigners could exercise in the close spheres of the government.

Be that as it may, it is a fact that Harrer attracted criticism to himself, even on the personal plane. On the other hand, only good was said of Aufschnaiter, a hardworking, discreet and calm man whom everyone respected. People were grateful to him for having directed work on the digging of an irrigation canal which, in memory of him, had always been called the 'German canal' in Lhasa.

Whilst I was taking in the charms of Lhasa, the Tsakur uncles never stopped backbiting about me to my father-in-law. The latter, finally giving in to their pressures, began to mix his recriminations with theirs. Voices were raised amongst us, giving way to regretful scenes with lively quarrels. Finally, Khwaja Abdul Aziz declared to me: 'If this is really the situation, then it is better that we go our own ways.'

This meant that there was nothing left for me to do but to leave. This was a painful shock for me. My first reaction was to point out that if I lay claim to my part of the inheritance, there would not be much left of the Tsakur business. But Khwaja

Abdul Aziz was the head of the family and the uncles held all the cards. They had formed our association in such a way that I was practically without power. Besides, we had reached the point where I didn't even have any more desire to talk to them.

The best thing to do then was to attempt to set myself up independently. Now this did not seem to be a very desirable thing to do in the proximity of my uncles so I was obliged to return to Kalimpong where my best business relations lived. I was heartbroken at not being able to stay in Lhasa and to have to start from square one again, but I found encouragement and comfort from my wife, who, having strongly resisted my uncles' pressure, preferred to distance herself from them and was happy to accompany me.

Before leaving, I tried to obtain some funds. The uncles stubbornly refused to give me any sort of advance on the pretext that all the family capital was invested and could not be touched. So I borrowed 10,000 rupees from a Muslim friend, and this was all that I had at my disposal for my new resettlement.

~

Accepting our destiny, my wife and I, therefore, climbed back into our saddles to set off again on the route towards the south. My cousin Abdul Salam, the brother of Ataullah and my sister's fiancé, accompanied us. He had also worked for the Tsakurs and they were very sorry to see him leave because he was a dynamic and efficient young man.

We had left Lhasa and were peacefully riding along, struck by the beauty of Nechung, the residence of the state oracle very close to the great monastery of Depung, when my wife's horse tripped up. She lost her balance and with her foot caught in the stirrup was dragged some 20 metres. Alarmed, I rushed to pick her up and was able to see that, fortunately, she had not broken anything. However, she didn't feel well during the entire journey and it was very difficult for her. As soon as we arrived in Kalimpong, I took her to the mission hospital where she had a miscarriage. This incident was hardly what we needed to boost our morale at a time in our lives when we particularly needed it.

Without losing time I began to work on setting myself up again in business. For this I thought of renewing contact with Ladakh where I still had some goods and whence high quality wool was exported, called pashmina and *shahtush*, which had given Kashmir a worldwide reputation and was still much in demand on the Indian and international market. I, therefore, got in touch again with Abdul Haqq with a view towards going to Leh to work out the details of an eventual commercial collaboration. Prior to this it seemed indispensable to me to consolidate somewhat my position in Kalimpong by doing some business and my young cousin Abdul Salam participated actively in this, not hesitating to set out again along the Tibetan tracks to collect merchandise in Shigatse.

To meet my expenses, I started giving English lessons to Tibetans and spoken Tibetan lessons to English-speaking people. Amongst my students were some Americans belonging to a missionary organisation, a sister of my friend Tendong, as well as some aristocrats and other important Tibetans from whom I learnt almost as much as I taught. This was all very interesting, but my wife's condition forced me to give up plans of going to Ladakh. She was pregnant again and because of her recent accident the doctor, a Scot, Dr McLochlan, remarkably competent and devoted, ordered complete rest for her under medical supervision for the entire duration of the pregnancy.

Our stay in Kalimpong lasted until 1951. The birth of our first child, Muhammad Siddiq, named in memory of his great-grandfather, the patriarch of Leh, brought us great joy. I thus had nothing to complain about my lot. Moreover, I was surrounded by good friends and I frequently met such eminent figures as the Russian Tibetanist George Roerich, Prince Peter of Greece, and especially, Marco Pallis.

On the business side I saw new possibilities opening up thanks to my encounter with a remarkable Tibetan, Lobsang Yeshay, also called Shondon. From a modest peasant family, he had acquired an influential position in the circles of the regent thanks to the protection of Shandzo, the regent's attendant and favourite. This did not imply a 'special' relationship with this powerful figure but was in conformity with the customs of Tibet where friendships amongst men could be strong without being equivocal or passionate. Lobsang Yeshay had taken English lessons in Lhasa with my cousin Abdul Matin who had recommended that he come see me in Kalimpong.

When I met him I had no doubt that this young man was one of the most influential figures in leading Tibetan circles but his appearance and his speech made me realise immediately that he was very intelligent. Although he was powerful thanks to the favour of the Shandzo, right-hand man of the regent, he distinguished himself from most of the other leaders of his country by his sincere and disinterested patriotism.

Having arrived in Kalimpong for a fairly long stay, he often came to see me and we had long conversations about the political situation in Tibet. Black clouds were piling up on her eastern horizon since the victory of the Communists in China. My interlocutor was clear-headed enough to evaluate the seriousness of the threats but he insisted on the necessity of trying everything for the Tibetan cause at this time when decolonisation was beginning, taking advantage of the principle of self-determination of peoples which was being so loudly proclaimed on the international scene.

The relationship also involved business. In the manner of so many highly placed figures in the leading classes of Lhasa, Lobsang Yeshay made plenty of important deals and was usually successful with them. He proposed that I collaborate with him in this domain and I had little difficulty accepting because the conditions he offered me were really tempting and above all, he insisted that I return to Lhasa.

~

Thanks to my new friend, happy prospects appeared to open up to me with the possibility of working in big business as I had always wanted and to collaborate within the most interesting circles of the Tibetan aristocracy. I rejoiced at the idea of soon returning to Lhasa after being chased out by my uncles, and I found it scintillating to undertake a commercial venture there which might overshadow their own.

~

The plans for our collaboration were carefully drawn up and my wife and I began preparations for our next move. But before this, Lobsang Yeshay was determined to visit the principal holy places of Buddhism in India and asked me to accompany him.

The tour began with a stop in Calcutta. I, of course, hurried to go and see my cousin Ataullah who was much at home in his diplomatic post of third secretary of the Pakistani high commissioner. We spent several excellent evenings together exchanging news of relatives and reliving old memories.

Then as interpreter I escorted Lobsang Yeshay to the places where Buddha had once lived and taught. Naturally pious like all Tibetans, my companion withdrew there in prayer and meditation. But then, when he rejoined me it wasn't spirituality and religion which he spoke of, but politics and particularly the threats which seemed to be building up in his country. This was the autumn of 1950 and the most worrying rumours had begun to circulate. It was said that the Red Army of Mao Tse-tung had gone through Shamdo attacking people and that the Communists were in combat with Tibetan garrisons.

At first, official Indian sources claimed that these were only false alarms. Alas, the invasion, odiously disguised as 'liberation', was all too real. It had made Tibet enter the darkest phase of her long history.

CHAPTER 10

THE INVASION

Once we were back in Kalimpong, the news and rumours coming from the north were so worrying that we were urged to remain in that city until it was possible to discern what was happening on the other side of the border. In any case, the invasion of eastern Tibet by the Chinese Communists was confirmed and appeared to have provoked a serious crisis in the leadership circles of Lhasa. These events began to preoccupy world public opinion and correspondents from important Western newspapers were seen arriving in Kalimpong and Darjeeling. But the information they were able to gather was contradictory.

On the one hand, the Indian authorities tended to systematically minimise the seriousness of the events. On the other, Tibetans who claimed to be 'well informed' dramatised events as much as they liked or reported anything to make themselves sound interesting. The reality of the facts only appeared gradually during the final weeks of the year 1950.

On 7 October, the Chinese launched their decisive attack against Chamdo. The governor of the province, Ngabo Ngawang Jigmay, an aristocrat of high lineage who had been assigned to this post only a short time earlier, evacuated the Tibetan garrison and gave up the town without putting up any resistance. The route through central Tibet was then open to the advance of the so-called Liberation Army.

Informed of these facts one week later, the first reaction of the Lhasa government was to launch an appeal to India, Nepal, Great Britain and the United States. Only evasive and disappointing answers were received. As early as November, the Tibetan government addressed itself to the United Nations. They found no serious support there. From the outbreak of the crisis, it was clear that no one in the international community would lift a finger to help Tibet.

In Lhasa, decisive changes had just taken place in the governance of Tibet. The regent Taktra Rimpoche had stepped down to hand over power to the Dalai Lama, who at sixteen, was declared to have come of age, two years earlier than the legal age.

One of Taktra's really important final decisions, inspired moreover by Shakabpa Tsipon in July 1949, had been to expel all Chinese representatives and citizens from Tibet. In theory, these latter still included Kuomintang members but in Lhasa there were still reasons to believe that many of them were disguised Communist agents. This harsh measure was a means of demonstrating that Tibet acted as a fully independent state.

At the same time, the Communists, conquerors in China, openly proclaimed their will to 'liberate' Tibet and to reunite her to the 'mother country'. From then on, the threat became more and more real. The government of the regent did not really do anything to act against it. When the invasion, easily foreseen, really began in October 1950, Taktra, old, tired and discouraged, felt himself incapable of shouldering the burden of power any longer. His decision to abdicate was opportunely endorsed by the state oracle which also suggested entrusting the responsibilities of the government to the Dalai Lama.

The *Tsongdu* or National Assembly, officialised these decisions right away. So at the gravest moment of her history, Tibet turned her lot into the hands of an adolescent who was more educated in metaphysics than in politics and was entirely ignorant of the modern world.

However, no one could deny that the young sovereign's first important decision was particularly judicious: as prime ministers, a double function according to custom, he designated a monk, Lobsang Tashi and a layman, Lukhangwa, a choice which could not have been better. Shortly afterwards, conforming to the pressing opinion of the *Tsongdu* and of his ministers who feared he would be captured by the invaders, the Dalai Lama left for the monastery of Tungkar, near Tatung in Chumbi, where it would be easy for him to get into Indian territory in case of danger.

Lukhangwa, remaining in Lhasa, took up the main responsibilities of power. Sometimes called the Gandhi of Tibet, he was surrounded by the unanimous respect of his co-patriots who knew him to be of perfect integrity and uncompromising patriotism. This landed aristocrat represented the best of the feudal nobility of Tibet. Deeply religious, he was known for his kindness towards his serfs. Unlike so many other high-ranking nobles, he lived from the income of his land and never ceded to the temptation of easy profit in business deals. He was fundamentally attached to the traditional order and its institutions and had already shown his opposition to modernising influences coming from the outside. He held these influences responsible for the corruption of morals, which was spreading amongst the upper classes. I had several opportunities to be near him and I felt his radiance. Wearing a beard and moustache, which is rare amongst Tibetans, he had harmonious features and a deep look in his eyes. His venerable aura was imposing on everyone. The Chinese Communists were to find him an unfaltering and unbending interlocutor in the face of all their attempts at intimidation. They did not delay getting him into their grip and calling for his dismissal.

In the eastern regions occupied by the so-called Communist Liberation Army, Ngabo, governor of Chamdo, the one who had capitulated without a fight, accepted playing the game of the invaders who had taken him prisoner. This was to cost him his reputation, being considered by his co-patriots as the principal traitor or 'collaborator' in the service of the occupying power, an expression used in Europe since the last war. But he was a complex character and the possibility couldn't be totally excluded that he sincerely believed he was acting for the good of his country. A worldly, cunning aristocrat, this had not prevented him from admiring Lukhangwa and adhering to his ideas. It was said that shortly before leaving Lhasa for Chamdo where he had been named governor, he had had a difficult meeting with Lukhangwa who, aware of his weakness of character, perhaps foresaw the disastrous effects that were to result from it.

In effect, as soon as he had fallen into the hands of the Chinese Communists, Ngabo became the main pawn of their political game in Tibet. And the government of the Dalai Lama, with a knife at its throat, was forced to rely on him and to officially designate him as a plenipotentiary entitled to act in the name of the government. As demanded by the Chinese, the decisive negotiation took place in Peking. All that the legal authorities of Tibet could do was to send four high-ranking officials to join Ngabo as consultants. Travelling by way of India, they met up with him in the Chinese capital at the beginning of 1951. The Panchen Lama, who had been recently proclaimed but did not satisfy all the traditional criteria, was then barely thirteen years old. He attended the parleys, which in reality were no such thing since the Tibetan representatives could do nothing but ratify the conditions dictated by the Chinese.

Therefore, on 23 May 1951 the Seventeen-point Agreement was signed for 'the peaceful liberation of Tibet'. The main clauses of this treaty, the foundation of Sino-Tibetan relations in the years that followed, can be summed up as follows:

- The Tibetan nation, one of those constituting the whole of China, having undergone the influence and provocation of imperialist forces, will be restored to the mother country.

- The right of national regional autonomy is guaranteed to the Tibetan people.
- The political regime of Tibet will be maintained as well as the status and powers of the Dalai Lama.
- The Panchen Lama, presently in China, shall be reinstated in Shigatse with all his prerogatives.
- Freedom of religion shall be respected and monasteries protected.
- The regional government alone will itself decide reforms to be introduced into Tibet and these will not be the object of constraint on the part of the central authorities.

In addition, it was specified that Tibet's foreign relations would be assured by the Peking government and that Tibetan armed forces would be re-organised within the framework of those of China. Finally, there was a clause relating to encouraging Tibet's economic development.

This treaty was a model of perfidy. As soon as the text was made known in the circles of the Dalai Lama and amongst his ministers, no one had any illusions about this. But the Tibetan leaders could do nothing but play the game that the Chinese imposed upon them. Some wanted to give themselves reasons for hope by saying that, if the treaty were truly and honestly applied and respected, it would be possible to preserve the essential, that is, to maintain conditions permitting Tibet to live her own life without overthrowing her traditional institutions. To foster this hope, or rather its illusions, the Chinese government made several mollifying declarations. These were believed by some who really wanted them to be true because the Chinese announced the sending of an emissary who was in charge of studying the means of applying the treaty with the Dalai Lama. The inexorable process set up by the Chinese giant was released. Nothing was to stop it anymore.

However, in Kalimpong we refused to see things too darkly

and we were encouraged in this by the attitude of the Indian government of Mr Nehru who, under the influence of her ambassador to Peking, Sardar K.M. Panikkar, a good historian but less of a good judge of current events, affirmed his conviction that the Chinese would exercise great moderation in Tibet. In fact, initially, they did try to give this impression.

~

As the situation seemed to be stabilising, Lobsang Yeshay thought there was no longer any reason to postpone carrying through with our projects. He, therefore, set off on the road to Lhasa asking me to join him there as soon as I had settled some unfinished business. To facilitate my trip he had a document issued to me by the Tibetan authorities conferring upon me an official status and the right to freely use state transport. Carrying this document, which I still possess, I set off again with my wife and our child. We would be returning to Tibet at a particularly crucial point in her history.

After crossing the territory of Sikkim, we arrived in Yatung. The Dalai Lama was still sojourning at the neighbouring monastery of Tungkar where he was awaiting the arrival of the Chinese general announced by Peking. In the streets of the township, which reminded us a little of Leh in Ladakh, we met up with several officials, monks and various courtiers.

The business I had in Yatung kept me there for a few weeks during which time, thanks to the introduction of Lobsang Yeshay, I lived in the closest entourage of Taktra Rimpoche, the old regent who had been stripped of his function several months earlier but who maintained a status of protocol almost as high as that of the Dalai Lama. He continued to have himself called, as the latter was, Yeshay Norbu, the 'Jewel of Certitude'. He was always surrounded by dignitaries clothed in shining brocades and precious furs but as he was no longer the holder of supreme power, some courtiers abandoned him, preferring to bustle around the young sovereign and his family.

However, Taktra retained considerable influence and his opinions were always listened to attentively. Although I had never been a great admirer of his policies as their pro-British tendencies brought no real benefit to his country, I was very interested in approaching this man who, remarkable in many respects, had held the destiny of Tibet in his hands for nearly ten years. Despite his advanced age, he still had a robust stature and maintained a presence. Being a reincarnated lama, he had a shaved head and wore ecclesiastic clothes. His dark face, dominated by a large nose, most often expressed reserve. In fact, he had a cautious nature and in the presence of interlocutors, he nodded his head, which allowed him to defer his response while signifying to them that he had understood.

It was certain that Taktra Rimpoche loved power and was receptive to the flattery of aristocrats. Having known him well, I could not question the sincerity of his patriotism and his attachment to the throne of the Dalai Lama. His policies were undoubtedly debatable in many respects and were not capable of preparing his country to face up to the threats which were building up. But who could have done better in the post-war world? This was a world that was throwing off as contrary to progressive ideologies, the traditional and sacred values to which Tibet, isolated and misunderstood, intended to remain faithful.

~

In the meantime the imminent arrival of General Chang Ching-wu was announced. He was appointed by the Communist government of Peking as 'Commissioner and Administrator of Civil and Military Affairs in Tibet'. More out of curiosity than any desire to welcome him, some inhabitants of the region went to meet his retinue. They were disappointed. The great figure and his escort, wanting to demonstrate 'Communist simplicity' had given up all formal attire. This was incomprehensible to the Tibetans who found these people dressed in dark uniforms devoid of any ornamentation and wearing Mao caps, completely insignificant. Dignitaries of the Dalai Lama's court waited for the retinue at the entrance of Yatung and led them to the monastery of Tungkar where His Holiness was residing.

According to what filtered out, the meetings of the Communist general with the young holy sovereign seemed to take place in a cordial atmosphere. It was assured that the two interlocutors had forged a good personal relationship which augured well for the future. To confirm these optimistic impressions, the general demonstrated affability, smiling at people in the street, especially those of modest state, and patting children. However, he was not able to fool anyone because his attitude smacked of the pride of power.

Soon the big news spread. His Holiness had decided to return to Lhasa, his capital, and General Chang would accompany him there. This announcement aroused great hopes and at the same time, fear and perplexity. It was said that the Dalai Lama was forced to give way to the pressure of the Chinese envoy and it was added that opinions were very diverse amongst his closest advisors, some considering it dangerous and inopportune to go and give oneself up to the power of the invader, others considering this move, on the contrary, as the best means of lightening the yoke of foreign occupation and avoiding greater misfortunes.

Undoubtedly, not only political motives dictated this decision. As a reincarnation of the compassionate Bodhisattva, Chenrezig, the Dalai Lama, traditionally exercised the function of protector of Tibet. His presence amongst his people was thus a sacred duty from which no other consideration could turn him away. This is the best explanation for his return to Lhasa in the summer of 1951 when the Chinese Communist army was approaching central Tibet. And this was how the event was interpreted by the populace who manifested their relief and joy.

The preparations for the great return enlivened Yatung and the entire region. They caused several problems for me just as I was preparing to return to Lhasa because all the available saddle and pack animals were requisitioned for the official caravans of the Dalai Lama, the Chinese general, dignitaries and all their personnel. Thanks to the document which granted me the use of state transport, I was finally able to obtain several mules and we were able to set off again on the road up the Chumbi valley towards Phari Dzong.

The Dalai Lama had left several days before with a procession in conformity to traditional custom. Depending on the lap, he either rode horse-back or in a palanquin sheltered by the symbolic parasol held by a servant. His bodyguards walked around him and the high-ranking figures of the court followed behind. They were glitteringly bedecked, with hairstyles corresponding to rules of protocol and their hierarchical order. The former regent Taktra and his people formed their own caravan which was just as opulent and imposing and usually went along at the head. As for General Chang, he left Yatung following close behind the Dalai Lama. Like the officers of his escort, he was dressed in the gloomy clothes of the Communist Chinese. The general not only presented a striking contrast to the magnificent processions which had just passed, but he also personified New China's scorn for traditional Tibet, whose destruction he was in charge of preparing. In any case, General Chang made a poor impression on the populace. They found his expression too dour and saw bad omens in his appearance on the scene.

Because the long procession walked at a slow pace, it only took us a short time to catch up with them. We were crossing the high Phori plateau when I caught sight of the general and his grim-looking horsemen. In this desolate part of the world they seemed to surge up out of nowhere. During the entire journey to Lhasa they very carefully observed every topographical peculiarity, especially, it seemed to me, places which could have a strategic importance. Fleeing their proximity, we soon distanced ourselves from them and were able to mix with the escorts of His Holiness.

In the more populated regions, crowds had come to greet their sovereign and protector. To welcome him, villages were decorated and incense was burning. Often the inhabitants lined up along white lines drawn in lime on both sides of the track and everyone bowed when the Dalai Lama passed by, sticking out their tongues as a sign of respect. Their emotion was all the more intense since a few months earlier they had already paid homage to him when he was travelling in the opposite direction. Many tears were shed then because his departure towards the Indian frontier was an indication of the seriousness of the events and it was said that perhaps he was leaving Tibet for good. Relief had now followed sadness but the joy was mixed because as soon as the general and his officers appeared, the atmosphere became heavy, and in spite of their displays of 'democratic' cordiality, the Chinese were looked upon with suspicion and their passing through left a poor impression.

The stops were frequently prolonged to permit the Dalai Lama and the Chinese general to pursue their talks. As a simple merchant amongst so many important and powerful people, I had no reason to remain integrated into the official procession and in Gyantse I decided to accept the hospitality offered to us by a friend who was a native of Sinkiang, Abdul Ahad, the son of Daoud Khan. He was a clothier in Lhasa after serving a British officer and was also the cousin of the devoted guide who two years earlier had led me through the tracks of Pamir. A radio operator serving the Tibetan government, he was up-to-date on important events concerning Tibet and in particular could indicate the points reached by the Red Army who were working their way along the ancient trade routes of the East. This allowed us to calculate that, if the troops continued to advance at such a slow pace, they would not enter Lhasa for a few weeks. We, therefore, had no need to hurry.

Hanging out their beautiful prayer flags, all the townships along the Lhasa road celebrated the Dalai Lama's passing with joy. The capital also celebrated the return of the young sovereign with enthusiasm. On the other hand, they pulled long faces at the Chinese general. Despite the courtesy of the ministers assigned to officially welcome him, he didn't think that he was received with enough respect and admonished them in harsh tones contrasting with the friendliness he had feigned until then.

For my part, I took up lodgings with my wife and child in the apartment that Lobsang Yeshay had put at our disposal in a property recently purchased by Taktra from Abo Yamphel Pangdatshang who had held it from Tsarong. The ex-regent had entirely restored it, and the annex where we lived was really comfortable. Soon after our arrival I didn't neglect visiting my relatives, in particular the three uncles whom I had separated from on fairly bad terms. I sensed their surprise when they realised that I was returning to a prosperous position and I was asking nothing of them.

The business I was involved in with Lobsang Yeshay was interesting and looked promising. But from the first days following my return to Lhasa I felt that the atmosphere, hitherto happy and relaxed, was no longer the same. The expectation of the arrival of Chinese troops caused anxiety and nervousness, which was understandable, but at the same time I had the impression of a decline of the former upper class as well as a weakening of the traditional ethic. As if sensing the immanence of a catastrophe, those who were well-off and even sometimes the highest-ranking aristocrats seemed to have nothing more important to do than to earn money and enjoy life. Greed, avarice and suspicion changed human relationships and people began to be suspicious of one another, even of their best friends. Lobsang Yeshay himself noticed the effects of this deterioration of mentality even in the immediate entourage of the old regent and he suffered because of it.

Since the failure of the action taken in the United Nations and in the international community, the government had lost all hope of being able to put up any obstacle at all to the unrelentingly progressing foreign invasion. But the ruling circles sought to at least limit its disastrous effects. With this intention, the government began to prepare to receive the Communist Chinese troops marching into the capital. General Chang Ching gave instructions to the government as to the manner in which he expected the reception to be organised and, with his officers, participated directly in the preparations. He especially insisted on having portraits of Mao Tse-tung, Chou En-lai and Liu Shao-chi and other great Communist leaders set up everywhere but he must have been quickly persuaded that the inhabitants had no desire to decorate their town with them, agreeing only to have the face of the Dalai Lama posted up.

The Chinese Communists and their officers already present in Lhasa sought above all to give an air of festivity to the arrival of the 'Popular Liberation Army'. They wished to avoid at any price that it resemble the entrance of occupation forces into a conquered town. The staging was to correspond to the proposition proclaimed in the Seventeen-point Agreement according to which Tibet was being returned to the mother country after being under the influence of foreign imperialism.

When an adequate number of military contingents had reached the outskirts of Lhasa, an impressive revue took place on the large plain east of the city. Units of the infantry, cavalry and artillery participated in it. There was not a single motor vehicle because communication between China and Tibet would not have permitted them to go through. Civilians belonging to the Communist hierarchy also paraded on horseback and I had the great surprise of noticing that one of them was none other than my old friend Phuntsok Wangyal, called Phuwang. He was also making a show of returning to his homeland where he had been recently banned by the government of the old regent.

Out of curiosity, many inhabitants of Lhasa came out to the plain. They mingled freely with the Chinese soldiers, examining the details of their clothing and feeling their weapons. Because the Communist leaders intended to prove their friendliness and promote brotherhood, the men had orders to maintain great calm and let themselves be approached without losing their composure. However, after this experience, a certain number of rifles disappeared and from then on the Chinese soldiers attached their weapons to their wide belts with small chains.

Finally, this great demonstration, intended to display military power as well as friendship, left bad impressions because it was marked with signs of bad omens: a violent wind rose up, tore up the banners and overturned the portraits of Mao and other great leaders. The Tibetans were amused and applauded but this was too much for the Chinese. Some of them, despite the orders for restraint, let their anger explode. If the day proved anything in the end, it was above all, that the population refused to collaborate with the invader and intended to oppose them with non-violent resistance. All the events which followed confirmed this.

It must be recognised that the first phase of the occupation did not create an intolerable situation for the population of Lhasa and did not submit them to a regime of tyrannical oppression. They certainly did not hesitate in manifesting their fundamental opposition to the armed presence of the Chinese and it became commonplace, for example, to ostensibly spit on the portraits of Mao and then bow with hands together in front of the portraits of the Dalai Lama. All this did not prevent the occupying forces from persisting in their policy of moderation and brotherhood, feigning to respect the traditional institutions and not to intervene in the direct administration of the country. Sporting forced smiles, the Communist officers vied with each other for courtesy and in town the soldiers had received special instructions to avoid any incident with the populace. It cannot be denied that in these first weeks of the occupation they were irreproachably polite, never displaying their weapons and maintaining an imperturbable self-control in every situation.

There was tension, however, because the Tibetans were discerning enough to foresee that the occupying forces would not persist indefinitely in this attitude of moderation. They knew perfectly well that Communism was the enemy of all religions and that the Buddhists in China were already being persecuted. They, therefore, looked upon the invaders not only as foreigners but as infidels bent on the destruction of that which they held most sacred.

In reality, behind the screen of the Seventeen-point Agreement and the feigned respect for Tibetan autonomy, the Communist Chinese had already begun their methodical work of undermining and this was destined to ruin the regime of the Dalai Lama by secularising his administration and gradually reducing his power. They used men like Ngabo for this. He was soon reintegrated into his ministerial functions as was Phuwang. They even used the Panchen Lama whose return was being prepared under conditions designed to harm the Lhasa government.

After seeing him in his new glory with the arrival of the Red Army, I was curious to meet Phuwang and learn how he had been led to collaborate so closely with the Chinese Communists and to hear him speak of the situation in Tibet and the perspectives for the future. However, considering the position he was in, I did not want to take the initiative for a meeting. Eventually, he was the one who came to see me having learnt I was in Lhasa and greeted me with great displays of friendship. Eventually, these visits were awkward for me because he never moved about without an escort of Chinese soldiers. When he came to my home, two armed men were posted on the roof and two others guarded in the street in front of the door. This displeased my servants very much.

However, I don't believe Phuwang was such a bad man. There was a sincere idealism in this former teacher in the Kuomingtang Chinese school in Lhasa who later let himself be seduced by leftist theories and Maoism. After our links of friendship in Kalimpong where he was involved in politics as much as he was in business, he had returned to Tibet and in 1949 was chased out as a spy by China—in principle still the China of the Kuomingtang whose representatives were simultaneously expelled. His return to Lhasa now was a sort of revenge and, although for obvious reasons he was not loved here, he could at least say of himself that he was feared. When he went through the streets surrounded by his escort, everyone bowed before him and ministers themselves got down from their mounts to greet him. It didn't take me long to realise that the friendship he diligently showed me also forced me to reconsider my position. Far from being happy about this friendship, I already sensed the difficulties it was to cause me later.

In their relationship with the legal government of Tibet, the Chinese used constant pressure to force it to adopt and carry out a series of 'reforms' which corresponded to their political interests. But they came up against obstinate resistance from Prime Minister Lukhangwa who, insensitive to their intimidations, unyieldingly defended the prerogatives of the young sovereign and the traditional regime which guaranteed the liberty and identity of its people. All Tibetans knew very well and felt that he had stood up to the Communist invaders and they were proud of him. Never had a prime minister been so popular.

In order to be rid of him, the Chinese stepped up their manoeuvres with the Dalai Lama. He resisted them for several months, but was finally obliged to give in and during the year 1952 had to ask Lukhangwa to step down. Thus was taken a new step in the enslavement of Tibet.

In any case, the occupying forces had ignored the government agreement in order to undertake a series of projects that would progressively reinforce their influence on the country and change the face of Lhasa. They began by building large barracks in the immediate outskirts of the town and at the same time, they acquired several houses for their officers in the town centre. Next they built a hospital for the benefit of the Tibetan people, and then a school.

~

Sensing dislike on the part of the Tibetans, the Chinese Communists increased their efforts to reduce the distrust of the people and gain their sympathy. One is forced to recognise that they succeeded to a certain extent, at least during the first two or three years of the occupation and this mainly thanks to the open air theatres and cinemas they opened and which were a real success.

My uncles, the Tsakurs, who until then were owners of the only cinema in Lhasa, were obviously much annoyed about this, but in fact they suffered no prejudice from it, at least in the beginning. Instead of making them shut down as the uncles had expected, the licence permitted them to run their theatre. They obtained an assurance from the Communist authorities that they could continue under the condition that they not show films which were contrary to 'progressive' ideas.

This still relatively liberal policy was accompanied by intense propaganda. Signs, public meetings and loudspeakers placed in the streets broadcast radio programmes as soon as the occupying forces had set up a transmitting device in the region. It was always the same tireless repetition: China, the mother country to whom Tibet had returned, was here to help her develop and progress in all fields. Added to this were more and more insidious attacks against traditional institutions. Religious beliefs were called prejudices as were old customs, for example, the habit of sticking out the tongue as a sign of respect. However, this propaganda still avoided clashing with the very deep religious convictions of the Tibetans and always claimed to respect the famous Seventeen-point Agreement.

After the arrival of the first units of the Liberation Army, the presence of military personnel very soon increased considerably. Soldiers often seemed more numerous than civilians in the streets of Lhasa. Their attitude remained proper: they were polite, and scrupulously paid merchants for what they bought. My uncles did excellent business with them in their shop.

This swelling of the population of Lhasa caused a shortage of certain food products and in the bazaar practically all the prices rose to heights never seen in the past. Merchants rubbed their hands together and many said that the occupation had its good side. As for the people, they may not have suffered from this kind of inflation as much as some claimed they did. A business sense is innate with Tibetans and most found a way to take advantage of the sudden influx of Chinese dollars caused by the occupation. Be that as it may, this situation was the equivalent of an aggression against the Tibetan economy, an economy which was overturned and never again found its equilibrium.

At the same time exchanges between Tibet and India developed as never before. Merchandise such as textiles, food products, and notably vegetable oils, construction material, watches, medicines, surgical and scientific instruments abounded south of the Himalayas. The merchants resold a good portion of these items to the Chinese army and made good profits on them.

A certain euphoria spread through quite a few circles in Lhasa where people began to say that, after all, the Chinese occupation was more tolerable than one would have believed in the beginning. My relatives congratulated themselves because their business had never been so lively and they pursued fruitful transactions with the Chinese. One of them brought in two lakhs (200,000 rupees), a considerable sum for the Tibetan market. This was advanced to them for the import of medicines and construction supplies. Their Chinese partners paid them punctually, leaving them with a large profit.

In fact, the occupying forces developed and encouraged construction. To facilitate credit they opened a bank in Lhasa dependent on the same financial organisation which already had a branch in Calcutta.

It was the heyday of the politics of rapprochement and fraternisation between India and China and the expression attached to it was *Hindi-Chini bhai bhai*. Nehru, a supporter of Asian solidarity, warmly encouraged this. The villain then was Pakistan, labelled an instrument of American imperialism. Such an attitude on the part of India could not fail to have its effects felt in Lhasa where it helped the Chinese fight against the mistrust and prejudices of the Tibetans. And the latter often let themselves be put to sleep.

For my part, I led a fairly happy existence carrying on with an interesting business project and seeing good friends. I had then forged closer links with the family of the Dalai Lama, in particular with Lobsang Samten, a brother younger than Gyalo Tondup with whom I had been friends since my stay in Nanking. He was at this time sojourning in India. I was admitted into the presence of the Dalai Lama himself on several occasions. He addressed me with a word of welcome, smiling each time. However, I did not have real conversations with him. I found him beautiful and his face bore witness to a state of sanctification. Not yet polluted by the modern world, he seemed to possess inner peace, innocence and purity. I was moved to think that he had hardly gone through childhood when he was already confronted with overwhelming and unsolvable problems. The entire future of Tibet and her people depended on this adolescent. He was completely aware of this, as were his brothers, but the pleasant mood reigning in the family was unchanged.

Lobsang Samten, his younger brother, who had formed a friendship with me despite a fairly tangible difference in age, insisted that I come regularly to see him at Potala. Of a thoughtful and cheerful nature, he liked to joke and laugh but we also had serious political conversations. Mixing laughter and seriousness is typical of the Tibetan mentality. We didn't notice time go by and my young friend then kept me for the evening meal and often even for the night. In fact, it was customary in Tibet to have a visiting friend or simply any guest lie back on a sofa and stay there until the morning. I think I was the only Muslim to spend nights like this at Potala.

I went only once to Norbulinka, the summer palace of the Dalai Lama, but I was often received in the Takla home, especially built for members of his family. Gyayum Chenmo, the mother of His Holiness, his sister Semo Kusho, since passed away, and whose husband is presently a member of the Tibetan Council in exile in Dharamsala, his younger brother, Ngari Rimpoche, the lama recognised as reincarnated from a monastery in Ladakh, all lived there. I underwent a lasting influence from the members of this harmonious milieu and even now I remain entirely devoted to them although I have abandoned the hope which they want to cling to, of a certain Tibetan restoration. For me, alas, Tibet represents a totally completed past.

When my uncles, the Tsakurs, saw I was received into the family circle of the Dalai Lama, they felt very proud. They took advantage of it to increase their credit and carry out their most brilliant real estate bargain by making people believe that our family was close to the palace.

In the meantime, Phuwang became more insistent on trying to interest me in the 'Democratic Youth League' for which he was in charge of organising a big conference. He had taken up lodgings in the Yuthok house, one of the most beautiful in Lhasa and he wanted me to visit him there regularly. Given his position, I hardly dared refuse.

I felt a contradiction between my frequenting of this auxiliary—or 'collaborator' if one wishes—of the Chinese occupation and my familiarity with the brothers of the Dalai Lama. However, on neither side were remarks made to me about this subject. Moreover, it happened that Phuwang himself went to Potala. And every time he prostrated before the Dalai Lama, which a true Communist would never have done. Though he called himself a convinced Communist, he always seemed to me impregnated with Buddhism and in the depths of himself he remained Tibetan.

On several occasions he tried to share his Maoist convictions with me. I was absolutely impermeable where they were concerned, especially since my discovery of the writings of Guénon but caution ordered me not to express my opposition to him too openly. Moreover, it would have been difficult for me to contradict him on some points, especially when he denounced the attitude of certain figures of the high nobility who were obviously corrupt and prepared to do anything to earn money. He had got back into the disastrous game of their intrigues and even though it was the Chinese occupation that put an end to this, I could obviously do nothing but approve.

When Phuwang came to my home, I took care to lay out the works of Marx and Lenin on the table and in addition, I led him to believe that I was an admirer of Stalin. I didn't like this game at all but I felt the necessity of playing it because one could already feel that too strong an opposition to the ideology of the occupying forces risked leading to very unpleasant problems. And it was noticed that 'educated' people, which I no doubt was, were the object of special surveillance on the part of the authorities of the occupation and their informers.

Moreover, I didn't content myself with placing these classics of Communist literature on my table. I read them. It was not only a wise precaution to be familiar with their content but also these works were part of the tutoring that I had been doing for some time for the children of Ngabo, the great aristocrat who had capitulated at Amdo and then signed the Seventeen-point Agreement in the name of Tibet before being reintegrated into the government of Lhasa where he was the main instrument of Chinese politics. It was obviously Phuwang who obtained this job for me which I would have willingly passed up but it would have been risky to refuse it. So I had begun inculcating into the older children of this powerful figure who had two sons and six daughters, the rudiments of English to which I saw myself obliged to add some notions of didactic materialism! I had to measure my every word during these lessons because in the Ngabo household there were always Chinese government officials who certainly knew Tibetan and maybe even a little English.

Phuwang had married a Chinese Muslim of Lhasa and was very familiar with the customs of my religion. He seemed curious to know to what extent I myself remained attached to it and gauged my reaction when he attacked what he called the 'prejudices' and 'superstitions' of Islam or when he tried to make me eat pork. He must have understood fairly quickly that his scoffing had no effect. On the contrary, it was he who gave me the ever clearer impression that he was not a real Communist and would never be.

One day I said to him frankly, 'You are preparing yourself sooner or later for very big difficulties.'

'Why?'

'You have remained too Tibetan to be a real Communist.'

I could tell that he had kept his religious conscience. He didn't deny this when I remarked about it but remained silent.

Cruelly for him, the future was to confirm my suspicions. In the months following the great revolt of Lhasa in 1959 Phuwang, disheartened by the excesses of the Chinese repression, began to sympathise with the Tibetan resistance. This caused him to be arrested and placed in a concentration camp in China. He stayed there nineteen months. In the spring of 1980, it was learnt in the close circles of the Dalai Lama in India that he had got out and was seen in Beijing at liberty. He was then but a broken and bent over man. It was added that the Chinese would never authorise him to return to Tibet.

~

In 1952, Phuwang was especially busy preparing for the big 'Democratic Youth' conference which was to be held in Seshing, one of the properties of the Dalai Lama. It was an event to which the Chinese authorities attached the greatest importance.

There was not yet any question of converting young Tibetans to Communism because it was recognised that, since most of them had remained completely foreign to the modern world, they were not ready to understand Marxist and Maoist theories. The aim of regimenting them into the new youth organisation was to make them more receptive to new ideas and inculcate into them a critical attitude towards religion and the traditional social order. In order to do this, they attempted to incite them against the administration and the nobility, and monks were turned into objects of ridicule. On the other hand, interminable praise was showered upon the progressive spirit of Chinese Communists whose presence brought so much good to Tibetans and helped them to 'develop.'

The participants in the conference were divided into groups according to their professional, social, ethnic or geographical origin. Thus, the youth of Lhasa formed a group as well as those from Lokha for example, and from Kongpo, Amdo or Kham. There were also groups of peasants, merchants, handicraft workers and even the nobility of the Muslim community. All this was organised extremely carefully down to the last detail and there was little risk of finding oneself incorporated into a group which was not really one's own. The proceedings of the event demonstrated how efficiently the Chinese Communists had succeeded in sorting out the population of Tibet in only a few months.

Phuwang had insisted that I take an active part in the conference and that I even give a speech. I told myself then that I might be better off leaving Lhasa and regaining Indian territory, but once again I feared the repercussions of such a refusal which could also cause trouble for my family. I, therefore, composed a perfectly hypocritical speech and forced myself to calm my scruples by telling myself that such concessions might serve the

Tibetan cause and that the only chance for the survival of Tibet lay in the honest application of the Seventeen-point Agreement.

In the middle of the conference I thought I noticed my old friend from Nanking, Gyalo Tondup, the brother of the Dalai Lama, amongst the participants. His presence surprised me. Lobsang Samten confirmed that it was indeed him and transmitted a message from him to me asking me to meet him after the meeting.

When we were face-to-face, Gyalo Tondup addressed me in a loud voice so that everyone could hear his warm remarks, praising the work of the Chinese Communists. He said he was proud to have been received as a member of the Democratic Youth and expressed his gratitude to Chairman Mao. Winking, I answered him in the same voice and with the same grandiloquence but the looks we exchanged gave away our real feelings and we both knew that we had perfectly understood each other.

Despite his profession of 'democratic' faith, Gyalo Tondup, in whose company I had lived in Nanking in an atmosphere of perfect simplicity, now assumed the prerogatives that his status as the brother of the Dalai Lama confirmed upon him, wearing the traditional attire and insignia of his high dignity. Everyone bowed before him, even the great Communist figures. But I hardly ever saw him during the three weeks of his stay in Lhasa because he never had a free minute, running left and right meeting all sorts of people, especially high-ranking officials and Chinese officers. He informed no one of his comings and goings, not even his brothers, who found him preoccupied and tense. Many years later, after I had stopped seeing him, I learnt from a reliable source that he had made this trip for the American CIA.

Although I had few occasions to see Gyalo Tondup, I was at least able to meet his wife, a Hong Kong Chinese whom he had brought with him so that she would have a direct experience of Tibet. This marriage had attracted many comments within his family and beyond. As the brother of the sovereign he could have set his heart upon any girl of the aristocracy, the most beautiful, the richest, the noblest. He had preferred this Chinese woman, a charming, highly educated woman who spoke fluent English and had already begun a serious study of Tibetan. She seemed to have adopted the homeland of her husband and I had the impression she was already a Tibetan at heart.

One fine day, Gyalo Tondup disappeared as suddenly as he had appeared. He had told the Chinese authorities that he was going to visit some property of the Dalai Lama in Kongpu in the southeast of Tibet and would soon return to Lhasa. In reality, accompanied by his wife, he kept on going east in the direction of Assam where he crossed the border to reach Indian territory again. When he didn't return, the Chinese realised he had tricked them.

CHAPTER 11

THE REFUSAL

I was feeling increasingly ill at ease since the 'Democratic Youth' conference. Furious at the role that Phuwang made me play, I had reasons to fear there would be yet many more compromising situations I would be placed in. In fact, it was clear that in the short run the Chinese Communists and their Tibetan counterparts were capable of working together to modernise the country. Now there was no more doubt for me that this modernisation was only the preface to a pre-prepared methodical subversion aimed at overturning the traditional and theocratic regime of Tibet, practically the last in the world. It was more and more repugnant to me to lend a hand to a policy which was so contrary to my convictions.

However, the Chinese presence also had positive effects. The construction of hospitals, progress in public hygiene, the development of communications and irrigation, the promotion of agriculture and animal husbandry, all of this could be credited to their work. Along with a growth in trade, there was undoubtedly a rise in the standard of living, especially in Lhasa. More varied merchandise flowed in through the Indian route: textiles, cosmetics, toothbrushes, the use of which tended to spread, American gadgets, Swiss watches. These objects, which until recently were not in demand outside the nobility, were now accessible to a more widespread social strata and the Chinese soldiers themselves sought them.

There was also progress in the field of education, at least on a quantitative level. The number of schools increased, and teaching methods were modernised. Until then children had come to school carrying big slates on which they spent all day covering with letters, as they had always done and still do in some villages in India and other parts of the Muslim world. Following the example of New China, the teaching of the written language was simplified and speeded up, obviously to permit an increase in readers capable of assimilating Communist literature and 'Maoist thought'.

At the secondary school level, the occupying power stressed the training of young intellectuals whom they attracted to their schools in Lhasa. The courses in these schools were generally of good quality, independent of the emphasis put on Chinese culture and Marxist ideology. Two of my young cousins followed some of these classes, apparently avoiding being indoctrinated, and learnt Chinese perfectly.

Young Tibetans of good families whom the English formerly welcomed into their boarding schools in India were now invited to continue their studies in Chinese universities and many took advantage of it. Training programmes or simple touristic trips aimed at showing off China's progress were organised for government officials, various important people and even monks.

In the domain of culture and popular education the Chinese occupying forces insisted on the use of Tibetan. They sought to make this language suited for modern and scientific concepts. To this end they promoted the introduction of new terms, preferably of Chinese origin, to designate technical inventions, especially those related to electricity, radio, motors and aviation. In this respect it must be recognised that there was a 'Tibetanisation' movement, which also found its expression in serious publishing projects, not only of Communist inspiration but also of general interest.

Towards this aim, a special translation bureau was founded which accomplished work of remarkable quality. This was even admitted by educated Tibetans most opposed to the Chinese presence. The translated texts were no longer written in the classical and archaic language, as most books and printed articles were until then and which only well educated people could understand, but in a modernised Tibetan that was accessible to all Tibetans who had been to school. To accelerate the printing of all this new literature, according to what Phuwang told me, they had recourse to an old press which a certain Tharchin possessed in Kalimpong where he published a journal in Tibetan, *Bod gyi Melonq* (The Mirror of Tibet), after having for a long time printed works ordered by Christian missionaries. Tharchin was called on to return to Tibet to participate in this work of 'progress'.

The inhabitants of Lhasa willingly recognised that all was not negative in the innovations brought in by the occupying forces. They had acquired a taste for cinemas and open air theatres and these were always full. One even had the impression sometimes that fraternisation was growing and relations between Tibetans and Chinese were becoming less tense.

In reality all the effort that the occupying forces exerted to win sympathy only gave meagre results because the Tibetans felt fundamentally different from the Chinese. The Tibetans had clearly expressed their desire to be totally independent from the Chinese for a long time and often had been treated as such by the British power in India. Now the prime objective of the Chinese was precisely to impose the axiom that Tibet was an integral part of China. The 'Peoples' Liberation Army' was, therefore, not in foreign territory and those who spoke of the 'occupation' were denounced as playing the game of 'imperialist' propaganda.

Although on the surface the situation still seemed relatively normal, one could feel the relentless opposition of the population to the presence of the 'brothers come to help us' as was said ironically. Jokes and songs ridiculing the Chinese were heard more and more in the streets where the practice became widespread of backing away from Mao portraits and other Communist emblems with ostensible disgust. Real and imaginary rumours were circulated and the agents of important figures of the aristocracy repeated them to one another in small inns and teahouses.

For example, in a domain which was close at heart to the Tibetans, it was said that the Chinese authorities were opposed to love and did not let men court women serving in the army, taking care also to separate lovers because the Party alone decided who was to be married. A case was even cited of a young Chinese couple who, in desperation, had thrown themselves into the river of Lhasa.

But what raised the most indignation and worry was to hear repeatedly that the Communist Chinese were enemies of all religions and that they had come with the intention of destroying the Tibetan religion. Every day one heard scandalous remarks about the impiety of these people who were capable of every abomination, even eating human flesh.

Without giving much credit to such talk it was clear to me that the Communist Chinese, in virtue of their ideology with which I was now familiar, were fundamentally opposed to traditional Tibet and that their moderation only represented a transitory phase of their policy.

The future seemed very threatening to me. The mounting tension felt between the occupying forces and the occupied populace increased my worries, which became even heavier with new advances made by Phuwang. I knew him well enough to see that he himself was not at ease in the role he had accepted to play but he was locked into a part that he had to play until the end, and for this role, he lacked support. This was why he sought to associate me in his activities. And as I didn't let myself be convinced, he once said to me:

'Wahid, your duty is to collaborate with us and if you don't, you'll regret it one day. I know your attachment to Tibet and you should take advantage of the opportunity to participate in the great emancipation of the Tibetan culture that has now started.'

Here he implied, like the Marxists did, that the traditional culture of Tibet was really worthless because it was feudal and aristocratic but once it came down to the level of the common people it would finally flower. It goes without saying that I fundamentally disagreed with this point of view but it wasn't the time to discuss this aspect of things at length. In effect, what Phuwang wanted of me was that I work in the translation bureau.

Very well-qualified Tibetan intellectuals were already collaborating with this bureau. One of the most eminent was Tshatu Rimpoche, a reincarnated lama but married and the father of very pretty daughters. He had opened a school for teaching Tibetan and the Chinese offered him large amounts of money for his service. Another was Horkhang Geshe, a scholarly man of Mongolian origin who was highly paid for his translations of Marx and other Communist authors into Tibetan. Changlochan, the former 'republican' conspirator in the time of Lungshar, had also been recruited by the bureau whose personnel also included a group of Chinese intellectuals who knew Tibetan and even sometimes English. The authorities of the occupying forces attached the greatest importance to the activity of this bureau, indispensable for their propaganda.

The Tibetan versions of the fundamental texts on Marxism were done by excellent translators but they had worked from Chinese texts. They were aware that these texts were farther from the originals in European languages than the English versions were. What was, therefore, expected of me was a revision of the Tibetan translations from English versions of the same texts. Another collaborator was to find himself entrusted with the same task from Russian versions.

This job that Phuwang urged me to accept infused me, above all, with repugnance. Certainly, I remained completely prepared to serve Tibetan culture but not the culture that the Communists were striving to deform. In short, I was horrified at the idea of contributing to the spread of revolutionary doctrines as they sought to oblige me to do, doctrines opposed to the teachings of Guénon and to ideas I was attached to with all my being.

To help me get over my misgivings, Phuwang made me a firm offer: 300 Chinese dollars a month and, as an employee of the translation bureau, membership in the 'commune' of officials which he himself belonged to. These very favourable conditions did not make me change my mind. However, I dared not refuse too categorically because I felt myself surrounded by growing threats and began to fear for my safety and that of my family. As a Muslim of Lhasa who had gone through university, I knew from a reliable source that the Chinese police had their eye on me. What complicated things more was my status as a Ladakhi, and therefore, an Indian citizen.

I risked finding myself taken into the Communist mesh without being able to get out again. This idea filled me with anxiety and I went so far as to tell myself that the best thing to do would be to pack my bags once again and leave Lhasa, the city of dreams where a nightmarish atmosphere had set in. Not knowing what decision to take, I asked the advice of the brothers of the Dalai Lama. They did not give me a real response, only advising me not to rush into anything and assured me of their understanding. Seeing my disconcerted face, they began to laugh at my confusion. I remarked to them that they themselves risked finding themselves sooner or later in a situation comparable to the one I was then debating.

It was still possible for ordinary people to travel more or less freely across Tibet and even to cross the frontier on the Indian side. Since the Communist administration was interested in me and watched me, I no longer felt freedom of movement and I could no longer envisage leaving Tibet without their permission. I knew that a number of aristocrats and other wealthy people began to emigrate quietly and the desire to imitate them was growing in me. But in my particular situation, I had to think up a pretext to be able to leave without being bothered. Which one? I decided to feel out my most important relationships in the Communist camp, beginning with Ngabo.

I met him fairly often at the lessons that I had had to accept to give to his children. This was an activity which I hoped would contribute to my security and that of my family because this figure was at the height of power. Thanks to the occupying forces, he had become the most influential of the members of government, and had assigned himself the task of making the Dalai Lama collaborate as closely as possible with the Chinese. Whenever I arrived at his home, he spoke a few words of welcome to me, sometimes asking of news of my family. I then began to tell him about my wife's poor health and the necessity of having her treated abroad. I also told him that I hoped to return to Ladakh where I still had some property. I had several conversations on this subject with Ngabo who in essence answered:

'You have come amongst us at a time when knowledge like yours is precious. Your contribution will help us build a new Tibet. You love this country and you have the duty to participate in the great work of reconstruction which has now started. If you leave us now, you'll regret it later because you will have missed a great opportunity which may never present itself again, to work in a useful way for the progress of the Tibetan people.'

The aristocrat who addressed me seemed sincere. But what a difference from the cheerful companion he had been some years earlier when he was not yet a star of politics but of the mundane life of Lhasa! My cousins had often taken part in picnics with him. He was known as an inveterate *mahjong* player and he put high stakes into the game. In fact, at this time, *mahjong*, of Chinese origin, was very widespread in high Tibetan society and during mundane gatherings it was often preferred to political conversations. Many lost their money playing it, within the aristocracy as well as the more modest classes of society.

Ngabo, the worldly man, the player, was not the same man after he returned from China. It was said that he underwent brain-washing. He didn't play anymore—except for the game of making his co-patriots believe that his politics contributed to their welfare. The conversations I had with him demanded caution, because they were undoubtedly heard by the Chinese agents. Nevertheless I didn't lose hope of obtaining his support.

Ngabo, Phuwang and the Dalai Lama represented three poles between which I tried to manoeuvre. What contrasts between them! Ngabo unconsciously played the game of the Chinese. Phuwang was consciously their instrument. As for the Dalai Lama, he retained an immense moral authority but his temporal power was constantly undermined by the occupying forces and I couldn't expect any concrete support from him.

My friend Lobsang Yeshay's position increased my troubles even more by creating complications for me in my business. He had separated himself from the former regent Taktra and his entourage to become closer to the Chinese, letting himself be tempted by the offers they made to young intellectual Tibetans to send them to study in Chinese universities. He, therefore, declared that he was ready to leave for Peking so that later, he said, he could better collaborate in the development of Tibet.

As he was a monk, to try to prevent Lobsang Yeshay from leaving, I had the idea of approaching Yiktsang, the highest administrative authority in the clergy, by making the most of a debt Lobsang owed me of 10,000 rupees. I claimed he shouldn't have the right to leave Lhasa without having reimbursed it. The amount of the debt did not hold him back at all and instead of discussing it, he gave it to me immediately and we separated and he left. I suppose the monastic state weighed upon him. In any case, it wasn't long before he married.

As an Indian citizen, I observed the attitude of the Delhi authorities in the face of the new situation created on their northern border. Having reacted only mildly to the invasion of Tibet which, moreover was not only against the law, but also contradicted the assurances given a short time earlier by the Chinese leaders of not resorting to force, the Indian government was not long in officially recognising the *fait accompli* by upgrading its diplomatic representation in Lhasa into a consul general. This diplomatic representation had been there since 1947 when it succeeded the former British mission. This act was of capital importance for Tibet. Besides Nepal, Great Britain was the only foreign power with which Tibet had maintained relations as a de facto independent state, entering into agreements with her such as the treaty of Shimla in 1914, in which China was not included. And the British had never recognised Tibet as an integral part of China, only admitting that the country was placed under her 'suzerainty'. This guaranteed Tibet great autonomy and obliged the Chinese not to intervene in her internal affairs nor to occupy her militarily.

Ever since the declaration of Indian independence, the government of India had officially declared that, as the successor and inheritor of British power in India, it would assume all rights and obligations towards Tibet. This meant that the Indians, like the British before them, considered themselves the guarantors of Tibet's autonomy.

However, events had just proven that India did not assume these responsibilities at all. India hardly reacted to the military invasion of Tibet and the nomination of a consul general in Lhasa amounted to recognising Tibet as a 'region of China' with the same status as any other region. What is more, India's ambassador to Peking, Sardar Panikkar, seemed anxious to conform to the views of the Communist Chinese using all his influence with Nehru to make him adopt a lenient attitude in this affair. This was to cause so much disappointment for Tibetans and friends of Tibet.

The senior official in the consul general of India in Lhasa was a certain Major Sen. Now I learnt from a reliable source that he had made suggestions to the Dalai Lama on behalf of his government. The main idea of these suggestions was more or less the following:

'By dealing with Communist China and showing moderation as she had done until now, India sought to win the goodwill of

China's leaders. Even if we appear to have given way to their demands on several points, our position towards Tibet remains in principle unchanged and carries with it the same obligations as during the time of the British, in such a way that we shall maintain the same relations with you.'

When these remarks were reported to me I couldn't believe my ears because they were in such flagrant contradiction to the facts. They demonstrated a strange blindness and at the same time risked fostering dangerous illusions with the Tibetan leaders. Such an attitude seemed to me disastrous for the prestige of India in Tibet.

Already in Kalimpong when rumours, alas, all too well-founded, began to circulate about the invasion of Tibet by the Chinese, I had been surprised at the reaction of the Indian authorities. They had been generally unwilling to recognise the seriousness of the facts and accepted fairly reluctantly the presence of foreign reporters. Since then this tendency had increased and the ambiguous attitude of the Indian government seemed to give implicit acquiescence to the Chinese intervention in Tibet to the point that the term 'liberation' was heard from the mouths of some of India's representatives. The Chinese Communists on their side never showed any gratitude to the Indians for their 'understanding', not offering them the least compensation in exchange for the rights they had given up on their northern borders and treated them very cavalierly until the ill-fated Sino-Indian war of 1962 put a full stop to all the illusions.

This sort of resignation on the part of India was to cause much bitterness amongst Tibetans because India was the country with which they had the most links. First of all, geographically, communications with India are easier than with China but above all, it was from India that Buddhism had come. All Tibetan culture bears witness to Indian influences. Tibetan writing is derived from Sanskrit. Many folk customs have their origin at the south of the Himalayas, even the habit of chewing betel leaves. Tibetans have never considered Indians complete foreigners because they feel so many affinities with them. By contrast, apart from Buddhism which created some bonds between Tibetans and Chinese over the centuries, from an ethnic, linguistic and cultural point of view, Tibetans have nothing in common with the Chinese who became even more foreign to them since Communism forced the Chinese to reject the sacred heritage of their own tradition.

Disappointed as so many others were by the development of Indo-Tibetan relations, I hardly wished to seek help and advice from the new consul general and undertook a new attempt with Phuwang.

First I emphasised that my wife's health gave us serious worry and necessitated treatment that she could only receive outside of Tibet. To this first reason for going to India were added others, relating to my property in Ladakh and my business which had been left hanging in Kalimpong and it was urgent that I take care of it. When all this was settled, I would hasten to return to Lhasa to begin my new job in the translation bureau. But Phuwang listened to me sceptically.

'You are trying to escape,' he answered. 'How important can this business be in Ladakh and Kalimpong if you are really devoted to the Tibetan cause and her development?'

This conversation took place over a meal to which he had invited me in his apartment at the Yuthok commune. We were eating an excellent hare dish. I recall mentioning that in my childhood we were forbidden to eat the heads of rabbits for religious reasons. Phuwang reacted sharply:

'You would do better to get rid of all these old-fashioned ideas about what is permitted and what isn't and learn to look ahead. The next generation will have no more religion at all.'

Upon leaving his apartment, I had lost all hope of obtaining any help from him.

However, three days later I received a message informing me that Rokia, my wife, was expected at the Tihmon hospital for a medical examination. It was the first of the hospitals built and managed by the Chinese in Lhasa.

We presented ourselves there the next day and the consultations took place in fairly good conditions. They revealed that my wife, who had recently given birth to a little girl, Farida Banu, should in fact undergo an operation and receive treatment abroad. Although there was nothing joyful about this medical problem, we were happy to learn of it because it opened for us the exit door of Tibet. Our relief didn't last long because the Chinese doctors quickly added:

'You won't go to India for this but to China where treatment is of much better quality.'

So there was the situation, singularly complicated, and we dared not look at each other upon leaving the hospital. In my distress I resolved to attempt a final approach with Ngabo:

'I beg you,' I said to him, 'to use your influence to persuade the Chinese that our trip to India is necessary, not only because of my wife's health but also because I have urgent business to settle in Kalimpong and Ladakh.'

When he heard Ladakh mentioned, Ngabo remarked that normally it should be part of Tibet. In effect, the Communists liked 'pan-Tibetan' ideas which due to past events, had already sometimes been used in Lhasa because the Chinese saw the possibility of spreading their domination in upper Asia. Aside from this not very encouraging political consideration for my homeland, he gave me no assurance and I left him in a fairly despondent mood.

I then returned to Potala in the hope of finding there not the solution to my problem but at least some consolation. I was in fact welcomed with the same kindness as usual and Lobsang Samten informed the Dalai Lama, his brother, of the difficulties I was struggling with.

At last the friendship of Ngabo and Phuwang worked simultaneously in the direction I had so eagerly hoped for.

Although with reticence, they finally gave in to my insistence and four weeks later I was informed that, taking into account my wife's health and the personal business I had to settle in India and in Ladakh, the occupation authorities had no objection to my departure, on the condition that I then return and take up the post which was awaiting me in the translation bureau.

My relief was immense and it was a day of celebration at home. Our preparations for departure began immediately and with my wife and children I went to take leave of my uncles and cousins. In fact, the family bonds remained stronger than the disagreements that had put us in opposition, and Khwaja Abdul Aziz, my father-in-law, was particularly sad to see his daughter and grandson leave. He asked me to at least leave my son, Muhammad Siddiq, the only male descendant of his generation. I replied to him that on the contrary it was he, Khwaja Abdul Aziz, who would have done well, given the impasse we found ourselves in Lhasa, to leave with me and to try to get at least part of his belongings out of Tibet. But neither he nor his brothers wanted to see my point of view because their business continued to prosper and the Chinese clientele always brought them great profits. They were not willing to see farther than their immediate commercial interests.

I also returned to the Dalai Lama's palace to take leave of him and those around him. I had the impression then that they already felt so ill at ease under the inquisitive looks of the occupying forces that they also would have liked to set off on the southern route towards the Indian frontier. In any case they expressed to me their complete understanding.

Leaving Lhasa with the few mules and ponies that carried us, a servant, and our baggage, we formed a very modest caravan. We took the now so familiar track which went through Gyatse and towards Phari Dzong, Yatung and the Chumbi valley. But I did not feel safe. I feared that the excuses for leaving that I had put forward had not convinced the members of the Chinese information service and that agents might be at our heels.

During the night at each lap the slightest noise woke me with a start. I thought I saw spies everywhere, in each village and at each turning of the track. At least I could have total trust in our servant, Memey Rigzin, whose devotion was perfect. This long ride with a woman in frail health and two small children was a difficult trial added to which was the sadness of thinking that we were going to leave Tibet perhaps forever.

However, I had to admit that the Tibetans we met along the way or in the homes where we spent the night remained as I had always known them: hospitable, helpful and smiling. The Communist occupation had not yet changed anything in their behaviour.

The anxiety did not leave me when our caravan entered the Chumbi valley and set off on the downward track in the direction of Tatung and the border of Sikkim because the Chinese army and administration were present there too and my imagination made me fear being arrested, sent back to the north and treated like a spy. Something entirely new, a checkpoint had been set up at the border and we had to have our papers examined. Formerly we had always gone through there without thinking of showing any official document.

The officials who inspected us were Tibetan but I noticed in the background Chinese soldiers who were overseeing the operation. The sight of them aroused my anxiety but, thanks to God, it was possible for us to go through without any other inconvenience except additional emotion.

We breathed more easily when we arrived at the first Indian post, also a novelty in this place I had so often gone through without even knowing exactly where the track crossed the border. We had nothing to fear, on the contrary, but its presence, like that of the preceding checkpoint, was significant of the end of an era, that of the caravans that slowly but freely crossed the immensity of Central Asia.

We soon arrived in Gangtok, capital of Sikkim. In ordinary times, I would have gone directly on to Kalimpong where I had so many friends to see and business to settle. However, it was known that since the Chinese occupation, the town had become a meeting place for spies and agents working for all the powers interested in this region of the world. Upon arriving there I would certainly have been spotted by informers who watched the movements of all travellers coming from or going to the north and I would have run the risk of passing for a spy myself. I preferred to avoid that.

However, I was keen to go on to Calcutta and get into contact with the Indian administration, considering it my duty to share with the authorities of my country information I had on the situation in Tibet and about various aspects of the Chinese occupation. I met a highly placed Indian official, native of Sikkim, Mr Lhatsering, head of the regional information service. He told me frankly that his government had a very staunch stance towards the Tibetan question and was not much in agreement with my own view of the facts, so that he didn't consider it worthwhile to transmit what I had to say to his superiors. I also sent a note to friends I had in the police service in Kalimpong, in particular Mr Namshu, who gave me a rendezvous on the Tista bridge on the road between that city and Gangtok. He listened to me attentively but also in a troubled way because the current politics of India directly contradicted the picture I made of the situation in Lhasa as well as for the dark perspectives of the future that I foresaw for Tibet.

There was no point in insisting. The era of the caravans having ended for us as well, I took a car for Siliguri with my wife and children and from there a train that let us off at the Sealdah station in Calcutta.

In the midst of the crowds of travellers getting off in the great city and the people coming to meet them, a police agent stopped me and enquired:

'Do you know a Mr Abdul Wahid Radhu, a passenger coming from Lhasa who should arrive in Calcutta today?'

The question set off a reflex of fear in me again and with only the thought about getting rid of this representative of the authorities as quickly as possible, I answered:

'He's an important man travelling in first class. You'll find him down there at the end of the platform.' And I slipped away.

During our week-long stay in Calcutta where we were in a hotel, the police appeared to be no longer interested in me. After Lhasa, where we felt constantly spied upon, it was a joy to find an atmosphere of freedom in India.

The 'Frontier Mail' that we took at the Howrah station took us to Delhi. My cousin Ataullah was waiting for us there. He was then second secretary to the High Commission (embassy) of Pakistan in the Indian capital. He had a pleasant apartment there where he offered us hospitality.

Thus mixing with the diplomatic society of Delhi for a few weeks I had the opportunity to meet many interesting people and in particular representatives of Oriental countries whose leaders were at that time all carried away with the principles of 'Asian solidarity'. I wanted to draw their attention to the situation in Tibet and to the tragedy that was building up there. But out of fear of drawing attention to myself by the Indian government, I hardly dared talk about it, and moreover, it was clear to me that in the diplomatic corps practically no one was concerned about Tibet. At a time when everyone was celebrating decolonisation, it was out of place to mention that Tibet constituted a typical case of 'recolonisation'.

Ataullah obviously took a keen interest in all that I told him about my recent experiences in Lhasa. But he only used the information for his personal documentation and not for a report to his government. As in every respectable administration he was not supposed to go beyond the bounds of his normal duties and these consisted mainly of receiving people at the airport and accompanying them back there.

CHAPTER 12

DIVERGENCES

For my wife and me our flight from Tibet was a veritable heartbreak. A whole part of our lives had slipped away. Helpless as I was, as a natural reaction I decided to return to Ladakh, my homeland, and to set off once again on the road to Kashmir.

Upon our arrival in Srinagar I got in touch with contacts I had kept up, in particular with Sonam Norbu, an eminent Ladakhi and good friend of the family. He immediately invited me to move into his house with my wife and children. Such were the bonds of trust and friendship that united Ladakhis despite the differences in religion because he was a Buddhist. He was then the most devoted and most representative of Ladakhi interests to the Kashmiri government and was to remain so for long years to come. His assistance and hospitality were an immense help during this period in which we found ourselves almost like refugees, having lost most of our possessions.

Politics in Kashmir had just gone through a troubled period. At the end of 1953 Sheikh Abdullah, the most popular political man of the country, had been at the head of the government since independence, was arrested at the instigation of certain Indian circles who suspected him of maintaining secret contacts with Pakistan. His successor was Bakshi Ghulam Muhammad, who until then was vice prime minister and who, because of popular support, inspired total confidence in the Delhi leadership.

It was based on this political background that Sonam Norbu and I began to explore the possibility of setting up a business which could serve the interests of Ladakh. Then Kushok Bakula appeared on the scene, the lama-politician whom I already mentioned in relation to the monastery of Hemis who was interested in exporting Ladakhi products. He was in the good graces of the new prime minister and he seemed to be able to obtain all the necessary support from him for carrying out important projects.

My cousin Abdul Haqq, whose experience and advice could be valuable, came from Leh to see me in Srinagar. We had lengthy meetings with Kushok Bakula about the economic situation in Ladakh.

Exports from Ladakh, principally made up of high quality wools, were at that time mostly in the hands of either Kashmiris of the valley or Hoshiarpuris (natives of Hoshiarpur in Punjab). They extracted profits which were much exaggerated in our opinion and it seemed to us desirable to set up an organisation that would allow Ladakhis to get a better retribution for their products and avoid the intermediary of these greedy merchants. Upon my suggestion, it was decided amongst us three to submit to the government a plan for the creation of a co-operative firm whose members and collaboration would be exclusively Ladakhi.

However, just as we were finalising our plans, a friend who held an official position offered me a job in the police of the state of Jammu and Kashmir. It was an interesting administrative post of a relatively high rank but having once already refused to be a diplomat, I didn't see myself as a policeman. I took the advice of Abdul Haqq who strongly dissuaded me. He thought that the projects we were planning were much more in accordance with the family tradition.

A company under the name Ladakh Pashmina and Wool Syndicate was established, a firm with a capital of five lakhs (half a million rupees) advanced by the state of Kashmir. Each one of us contributed funds to it and I was named director.

The question of the head office of the firm opened lively discussions. Should it be opened up in Ladakh itself or in Srinagar? In those days the road which allowed one to cover the distance separating Leh from the Kashmir valley in two days did not yet exist and the trip on ponyback took two weeks. Since air communication was irregular and perilous and because the most important clients of the firm would be foreign businesses, mainly English and American, we decided to set up our offices in Srinagar. This created a misunderstanding with the Indian authorities who perhaps did not understand why a firm devoted to defending Ladakhi interests wouldn't be established in Leh. In fact, our establishment in Srinagar did not at all imply a relationship of subordination to the government. Although we obtained most of our capital from the government, we were firmly resolved to remain independent of it and maintain our freedom of action.

Our trade involved the famous so-called pashmina and *shahtush*, which have given Kashmir a worldwide reputation. It is interesting to note that the fine material and shawls which are usually called 'Kashmiri' are made of a material not native to Kashmir properly speaking but to Ladakh, and are sometimes found in Sinkiang but mainly in western Tibet. Pashmina is taken from the stomach of goats living at a high altitude. Some herds live around Leh. *Shahtush*, the highest quality and a product of great luxury which no other wool can equal in both lightweightedness and warmth, comes from wild goats, types of gazelles of high plateaus that only live in Tibet. The suppliers of this product which was destined for a rich clientele were extremely poor and belonged to a social class which was scorned by the Buddhists because it was a class that hunted and killed the animals whose wool they sold and meat they ate. Moreover, *shahtush* has only ever existed in relatively small quantities on the market.

In Ladakh, two communities specialised in the gathering and trading of pashmina. First of all were the Arghons, who were usually Muslim descendants of immigrants from Sinkiang. They carried on a sort of trade with the merchants of Srinagar and in exchange for their precious wool, obtained various textiles, shawls, soap and utensils. They then distributed this merchandise amongst sedentary and nomadic Tibetans who obtained for them the raw pashmina and sometimes *shahtush*. But they hardly earned anything themselves from this trade, because they were accustomed to spending almost everything they earned in order to eat well and purchase beautiful clothing for themselves which gave them a proud look.

The Shammapas, Buddhists of lower Ladakh, were more prosperous. They were involved in both the pashmina trade and agriculture. They followed the practice of loading their bales onto donkeys and only travelling at night, resting during the day and costing practically nothing to their owners, whereas the Arghons normally rode horses or at least mules. The people of Shamma increased their prosperity over the years. There are now many of them in business and administration.

The transactions involving pashmina have never been easy and disputes having to do with quality were almost inevitable between Ladakhi suppliers and merchants of Kashmir and the Punjab, the latter never failing to complain about too many goat hairs remaining in the real pashmina. In fact, it was never possible to remove absolutely all of them but the fewer that remained, the better the quality. The elimination of these hairs was done in Srinagar where the merchandise was processed.

From the time of my grandfather, I had often been present in the courtyard of our house in Leh for the weighing of the wool, always accompanied by vehement discussions which could last entire days. But Haji Muhammad Siddiq was not specialised in this trade and didn't like the greed involved in it. He was content to occasionally purchase small quantities of pashmina from Arghons whom he knew well and then sell it in Srinagar.

All the raw material furnished by the Arghons and the Shammapas was classified according to the origin, length of the wool and the presence of goat hairs. There were three main categories of qualities. The first two were made up of wool of exclusively Tibetan origin with the exception of some import from Karakoram and Sinkiang. Ladakh, in particular in Rupshu and the neighbouring regions of Tibet, has hardly produced anything except third quality, which is already a very appreciated level.

The Chinese occupation of Tibet in 1950 did not at all stop this trade which represented an important source of revenue for the generally very poor inhabitants of these regions. But the events of 1959 delivered a hard blow to the commerce from which it has never really recovered. The Chinese closed the borders completely and they themselves bought up the production of raw wool to distribute on their own market. The Ladakhis and Kashmiris were deprived of better quality, which however, began to reappear after several years in small quantities and, therefore, at high prices. Some merchants even managed to obtain the authentic *shahtush* which from then on has been worth more than its weight in gold. It seems that this precious commodity arrived clandestinely into Indian territory because in these immense mountainous stretches it will always be impossible to completely block the frontier.

During the first year of the company's existence I tried to obtain the monopoly on the pashmina produced in Ladakh or coming from northern border regions where communications were still normal. To overcome the competition of Kashmiri and Hoshiarpuri merchants, it was necessary to raise the prices paid to suppliers and in this initial phase, we were thus prevented from earning any profit. Our Ladakhi partners were obviously satisfied but very soon we noticed a keen hostility on the part of powerful business circles who sought to harm us by using slander. We were wrong at that time not to take their provocations seriously enough and in particular to not sufficiently secure our position with the central government of India and its representatives in Kashmir. A court action was even taken against me but was reversed to the confusion of our enemies because they could not find anything reprehensible in my administration. Despite these difficulties, our enterprise was satisfactorily launched and I was happy to do something which conformed to the family tradition.

Naturally, I continued to follow closely the development of the situation in Tibet, and I learnt that my Tsakur uncles were feeling more and more uncomfortable under the Chinese occupation and had decided to leave. They envisaged coming to Kashmir and they counted on me to help them get set up.

After Lhasa, the idea of seeing them attempt to do business in Srinagar made me very wary because I was aware daily that Kashmiri business circles were considerably more demanding than those in the Tibetan capital. The conditions here were already those of modern business. In comparison, Lhasa was still the peaceful trade of the Middle Ages.

Soon after this, Khwaja Abdul Aziz, who had left the other members of his family in Kalimpong, arrived by himself in Srinagar and was anxious to meet his youngest grandchild, my second son, Abdul Ghafur, born the year before. With his mother of nearly ninety years, his two brothers, a sister-in-law and a niece, he had managed to leave Tibet under relatively good conditions, mostly thanks to the help of the general consulate of India. Their move had been facilitated by the recent, first passable road linking Lhasa to the Indian frontier. This was an extraordinary experience for people like them who had so often travelled the distance on muleback. After three days instead of twenty as before, they had crossed the plateaus and climbed the mountain passes, which formerly had made the trip so tiring, to find themselves miraculously on the southern side of the Himalayas.

Almost miraculously as well they were able to carry nearly all of their furniture, that is, a fortune of more than five lakhs (half a million rupees). In addition to their shop, this money came mainly from profits from the quotas that I had obtained for the import of textiles, from the running of their cinema which was tolerated by the Chinese for a long time, and from transactions with the latter and real estate deals that went through the brother of the Dalai Lama whom I had introduced them to. Khwaja Abdul Aziz had the means of guaranteeing the security of his family for many years on the condition, of course, that he used common sense in what he did with these funds.

Aware of the eminent position that our family had held in the economic life of Ladakh and knowing that its reputation had spread as far as Kashmir, and also impressed by the importance of my position at the head of the pashmina co-operative, my father-in-law was absolutely determined to re-establish himself in Srinagar and invest his money in a new business there. I tried to stress to him that he would be more successful as a merchant in Kalimpong or Darjeeling where conditions were not so different from those in Tibet and where other former Muslim merchants of Lhasa were established. But he did not want to understand that times had changed and that the family had no more the influence, nor the possibilities in the state of Kashmir that it had before the war. And the fact of holding large amounts of money also falsified his judgement.

I then suggested that he set himself up again in Ladakh. Finding conditions similar to those in Tibet, he would have lived peacefully with his family repatriated from Tibet and without problems, surrounded by those who could care for him. They were Himalayans who had always lived outside of modern civilisation and I could see that they would never be able to adapt to the lifestyle of a town like Srinagar.

Still just as determined to come back to Srinagar to start up a new business, Khwaja Abdul Aziz went back to Kalimpong where his brothers, mother, sister-in-law and niece were waiting for him. I was to soon see them all again on the occasion of the large family reunion that was the marriage of my sister Rabia to Abdus Salam, the brother of Ataullah, the Pakistani diplomat.

The latter, after being posted in New Delhi, was now consul and representative of the High Pakistan Commissariat in Shillong then in the Indian province of Assam. This is where the marriage took place in the presence of many relatives and friends.

On the way back I made a brief stopover in Calcutta with my wife and younger son. At the Grand Hotel where we stayed, I suddenly found myself in front of a well-known face: it was my old friend Gyalo Tondup, brother of the Dalai Lama. We had a thousand things to talk about, above all, the situation in Tibet.

In that autumn of 1956, great celebrations were being prepared for the Buddha Jayanti, the 2,500th anniversary of the birth of the historical Buddha, and the Dalai Lama himself was expected in India where commemorative ceremonies were scheduled in the principal holy places of Buddhism. Other members of his family were also staying in Calcutta. They were worried because it wouldn't be known until the last minute if the Chinese would allow the Dalai Lama to make this pilgrimage to Indian territory.

Gyalo Tondup thought that if his brother were authorised to leave Tibet, he should not return after the festivities but should inspire resistance to the Chinese occupying forces from outside the country. In fact it seems that during his stay in India, the Dalai Lama had seriously envisaged such a possibility and that he was strongly dissuaded by Prime Minister Nehru who at the same time received Chou En-lai in Delhi. He had excellent personal relations with the latter and was influenced by him. Be that as it may, the Dalai Lama returned to Lhasa at the beginning of 1957.

However, in the course of our conversations I did not hide from Gyalo Tondup the fact that my position as head of the pashmina trade company gave me many worries. He then made me a proposition which immediately arose deep echoes in me:

'So come work with us and serve the holy cause of Tibet. We are fighting for freedom against Communists who oppress us more and more severely. You can help us immensely in our great combat for Tibet and for the preservation of the unique value that it represents in the world.'

If I accepted he would guarantee me conditions that would

shelter my family and me from any material worry. My friend's offer was tempting, especially when I thought of all the emotional ties I had with Tibet, of my family who had always regarded Tibet as a second home, of my father who liked to dress like the Khampas, of the fascination of Lhasa, of the friends I had left behind, of the Dalai Lama and his sacred function. I saw in this a good opportunity to serve a great ideal and to contribute to the defence of the tradition in the sense understood in Guénon's works. What Gyalo Tondup didn't tell me and what I could guess was that the organisation he was asking me to collaborate with was undergoing certain questionable political influences which later were to cost me some unpleasantness.

However, I asked my friend for some time to think it over. My position in Kashmir was still relatively acceptable and I felt I was bound there by heavy responsibilities. I, therefore, returned to Srinagar quite pensive.

Soon after that Khwaja Abdul Aziz and the Tsakurs arrived. As they had large savings, they rented a beautiful house and moved in comfortably. Since they had decided to stay there and do business, I advised them to get into contact with Sonam Norbu, the well-informed and influential Ladakhi engineer. They preferred to try their luck in wood trade, which was flourishing thanks to the vast resources of forests in Kashmir. For this they wanted to buy a piece of land where a sawmill would be set up. I put them in contact with brokers specialising in real estate transactions, but in the meantime, they had already changed their minds and were running after other ideas…

Their business did not take a turn for the better after I had left Srinagar. They made still other various attempts at trade which ended up in repeated failure and they lost most of the capital brought out of Lhasa. This was the sad demonstration of their inability to adapt to a business world too different from old Tibet where it was enough for a merchant to be in the good graces of a few high aristocrats in order to cement his position.

As for my own business, it did not unfold in a much happier way. The opposition already noticeable after the formation of our co-operative grouping was reinforced and had found support with highly placed officials in the central administration in Delhi, who intervened in Srinagar. The man leading the intrigue was a former dairy and food supplier to the British army and the latter, in recognition of services rendered during the war, had been authorised to precede his name with the title 'Sir'. His manoeuvres resulted in the Kashmiri government deciding to impose his supervision over us.

An extraordinary session of the administrative council was convened in Leh. We went there by air and the meeting was held in our old family house. The majority of the administrators accepted the proposition of placing the Ladakh Pashmina and Wool Syndicate under government supervision, represented in the session by the government's judicial counsellor. Much embarrassed, they then came to me to apologise, swearing that they were under pressure that made it impossible for them to act differently.

It was apparently expected that I would be seen pursuing my work within the framework of the thus 'nationalised' enterprise but after having been director of an independent company I could not put up with now becoming a simple government agent. Fearful of the loss of my freedom, I therefore, refused. My attitude was certainly influenced by the proposition of Gyalo Tondup and by my desire to accept. Be that as it may, a new director was assigned in my place and I lost this last opportunity to perpetuate the trading tradition of the family.

~

I, therefore, informed Gyalo Tondup that I would accept his offer. He replied immediately that he was waiting for my family and me in Darjeeling where he was then residing. Soon after that we moved into a beautiful and comfortable house which he put at our disposal.

With my friend, his Chinese wife and their children, we felt almost like members of the same family and a strong intimacy grew amongst us. Our conversations obviously turned around Tibet. We were on the look-out for all the news coming out of Tibet for it goes without saying that before taking any action we first had to be informed.

As an Indian citizen I insisted that we remain perfectly loyal to the authorities under any circumstance and Gyalo Tondup did not have a different opinion. Unfortunately, it was the Indian administration itself which often seemed poorly disposed towards understanding our real position and attributed inadmissible intentions to my collaboration with the brother of the Dalai Lama. During my entire stay in Darjeeling I was to suffer from this suspicion.

It is true that a special circumstance arose which complicated the situation and increased the mistrust of the Indian authorities. My cousin Ataullah was still the consul of Pakistan in Shillong in Assam, a province periodically rocked by autonomy movements and revolts of tribes living in mountainous regions. Now the Indian government suspected Ataullah of having contacts with some of these movements, notably the Naga movement. He was supposed to have helped one of the leaders of this movement to go abroad. I never knew exactly what role he had really played in this affair or if he were truly mixed up in it. The fact remains that his Indian relatives had to undergo the unpleasant repercussions of the actions that were attributed to him and this was exactly my case. The Indian authorities could not ignore the close links of family and friendship that united us, Ataullah and me, and for the authorities this was sufficient reason for them to keep an eye on me.

If I managed to overcome these new difficulties I owe it once again to Marco Pallis who helped take advantage of them on the level of faith. In the ensuing correspondence that we exchanged, he made me understand how important it is to know how to relativise the setbacks undergone in this lower world.

From a material point of view our existence certainly was not lacking in comfort and pleasure. We lived in a milieu in which I frequently met interesting people. But it was hard for me to feel badly viewed by the authorities for the simple fact of being a Muslim and cousin of a Pakistani diplomat.

At first, after having sent for me to come, Gyalo Tondup did not give me any precise task and I had much leisure time. By contrast I kept many different police officials busy who spent a long time watching me but found nothing in particular to report about my movements. Evidently in the administration there were one or two influential persons who refused to admit that I was a real Indian despite my family background which went back to Kashmiri Pandits. They continued to consider me a more or less undesirable foreigner.

This did not prevent Gyalo Tondup and me from continuing to inform ourselves on the situation in Tibet. It seemed important to me to make it clear to my interlocutor, who perhaps didn't always see things clearly, that the fight going on in Tibet could not be compared to the one that India successfully led against the British power. In the case of India, it was a confrontation between adversaries, both with a sense of dignity and respect for human values. Despite everything that they can be reproached for—their stiffness, the heaviness of their domination and the injustices that they committed—the British did not usually go beyond the limits of honour and decency. On their side, most of the Indian nationalist leaders were people of a high moral level, beginning with Mahatma Gandhi. But the methods of fighting which had worked in confronting the British colonial power were doomed to failure in Tibet occupied by Chinese Communists. Non-violent resistance would always remain ineffective against such an implacable enemy and would never stop the Chinese from destroying and killing.

Faced with such a situation, one of the best things to do was to try to interest the international press in the fate of Tibet and gain sympathy for her. To do this, it was indispensable to begin by obtaining solid support in India, the only country capable of useful action for helping the Tibetans.

Now precisely during all the years following the Chinese occupation, the big disappointment of those who wanted to serve the cause of Tibet came from the Indian government. Pandit Nehru, still attached to the fraternisation policy between India and China called '*Hindi-Chini bhai bhai*', closed his eyes to the realities of Chinese Communism. At the same time he lacked any real understanding of the Tibetan cause. Nehru was too modernist and progressive to want to support such a 'feudal' regime. He believed or wanted to believe that the Chinese really brought reforms in the direction of progress to 'backward' Tibet.

It is a fact that Nehru had a fairly low opinion of Himalayan peoples and the traditions they remained faithful to. There was an example of this in 1949 when he visited Ladakh. He had gone there by plane and had attended the great celebration of the monastery of Hemis, the most famous in the valley. Whilst the monks were performing the ceremonies and ritual dances with all the solemnity and slowness required, one of my cousins who was near him heard him make this remark in an irritated voice:

'What a waste of time. I'd like to be able to draft all these monks into the army and make them work. What they're doing is no good to anyone and doesn't improve anyone's life.'

It is necessary to remember that the Tibetans themselves were not able to win the sympathy at the right time of those who were going to take power in India. In 1947, only a few months before the proclamation of independence, a conference of Asian relations was held in Delhi. Tibet was represented by a delegation headed by Sandu Photang, an aristocrat of the old school who still behaved a little as if the British empire were still in power. Showing more zeal towards the English than to the leaders of the Indian nationalist movement, the delegates had made a fairly poor impression on Nehru and even on Gandhi. One recalls an ironic remark about his simplicity and ugliness compared to the displays of the other Tibetans and the magnificence of their clothing.

Such memories must have contributed to maintaining with Nehru and his entourage the idea that Tibetan resistance to the Chinese occupation was above all, the act of aristocratic and clerical circles and not the people. The prime minister did not want to understand that all Tibetans, whatever their social class, assimilated the Chinese to foreign enemy oppressors of their religion, their *raison d'être*. He preferred to live in his dream, so well upheld by the sardar Panikkar, Indian ambassador to Peking, of uniting the two great nations of Asia, India and China, in a common march towards a new era of progress.

The cruel illusion, cracked above all, by the Himalayan war of 1962, was a blow from which Nehru's health did not recover until his death two years later. But long before this there were clear-thinking Indians who pointed out the dangers of the Chinese policy along the Tibetan border. Without the government of Delhi lifting a finger to oppose them, the Chinese had in effect penetrated into Aksai Chin, a mountainous desert theoretically a part of Ladakh and therefore India, and they had begun building a road to assure their communication with Sinkiang. Prime Minister Nehru, questioned in parliament about the presence of the Chinese in this region which in principle belonged to India, answered evasively, pointing out mainly that no human being lived permanently in the desert lands where not a blade of grass grew. He drew this remark from a member of the opposition, Pandit Kunzru:

'The fact of being bald is not sufficient reason for a man to have his head cut off!'

~

When I began my collaboration with Gyalo Tondup in 1958, this negative attitude on the part of the Indian government vis-à-vis Tibet made our position very unpleasant because a quasi-official disapproval resulted from our activity. I also soon realised that if I was poorly seen by the authorities, my friend was hardly any better viewed. I thought at first that the behaviour of certain officials who seemed to systematically doubt the sincerity of our intentions arose from the prejudices that upper caste Indians sometimes have towards Tibetans, Ladakhis and other Himalayans whom they consider a little like colonial peoples, but later, after I had left Darjeeling, another explanation of the cautious attitude on the part of the authorities was given to me; Gyalo Tondup was blamed for collaboration with the American secret service and for participating in arms smuggling destined for the Khampas and other Tibetan forces opposing the Chinese regime. He himself never told me anything of these secret aspects of his activities. I knew that mysterious emissaries often came to visit him and he had meetings with them that were very discreet. For my part I didn't see anything unusual about this and it seemed normal that he would maintain clandestine contacts with his brother the Dalai Lama as well as with other sources of information inside Tibet. In any case he followed what was going on across the frontier very closely and that is what enabled him to furnish me with most of the material I needed for the information-gathering tasks and the relations with the Indian and foreign press which he assigned to me some time after my arrival in Darjeeling.

Besides contacts with journalists, this work included writing brochures for publication mainly in Indian newspapers and for foreign embassies in New Delhi. These publications, entitled *The Voice of Tibet* or *Tibetan Courier*, contained information often dated from Shigatse which could be harmful, but usually corresponded to the real situation in Tibet where tension continued to increase. Thupten Ningje, the former director of education in Lhasa, and Wangdola, a married monk and former highly placed official in the Ministry of Interior, collaborated in this activity. We were supported by the famous Shakabpa who had dominated the Tibetan political scene during the years preceding the Chinese invasion. His house in Kalimpong was put at our disposal and I frequently stayed there. It was there on 2 January 1959, when we felt the storm ready to break out, that I participated in composing a letter addressed to Prime Minister Nehru. Gyalo Tondup went to Delhi and delivered it to him personally.

In addition to our difficulties with the Indian administration, the Tibetans staying in Kalimpong and Darjeeling, former residents or refugees in an ever growing number, created other problems for us. Amongst these Tibetans were the many aristocrats who had crossed the border to save their fortune and their skins. And since at the beginning at least other social classes were not represented amongst these new arrivals, the Indian authorities continued to consider that the resistance to the Chinese occupying force was not really from the people.

In any case certain of these refugee nobles were frankly objectionable. Talkative and indiscreet, they only thought about their own comfort and behaved with an egoism which seemed to make the Communist propaganda seem correct when it developed the theme of the oppression of the Tibetan people by the aristocratic class. These nobles seemed to have no sense of public welfare or of national solidarity. The spectacle of their petty disputes and their manoeuvres ever aimed at their personal interests whilst the very existence of their nation was threatened, confirmed my earlier impressions of the decadence of the Tibetan feudal system.

As almost always when a regime is overturned by a revolution, the Tibetan regime was more or less corrupt. But it was certainly not bad in itself. Anyway, I wouldn't think of criticising the feudal system as such. On the contrary, I think that the Tibetans were right to maintain an aristocracy and to remain faithful to the principle of hierarchy which corresponds to the deep laws of the universe. Now this regime, which for so long had assured what can be rightly called the happiness of the Tibetans, compared to what the Chinese Communists were bringing them, was in decline, as

I had plenty of occasions to witness. The traditional values and virtues were no longer respected by many who should have been their guarantors. On the eve of the fall, this was a regrettable aspect of Tibet that even her best friends could not deny.

Up until the uprising of March 1959 and the great upheavals that it provoked, crossing the border remained relatively easy and Gyalo Tondup frequently received the visit of travellers, some of whom had decided to leave Tibet for good and others who considered it their duty to return. Amongst these visitors, the most notable was undoubtedly the great Tsarong who appeared one fine day in Darjeeling accompanied by his younger son. I will never forget his meeting with my friend.

The old man, a former faithful servant of the Thirteenth Dalai Lama whom he had accompanied in exile and whose life he had even saved, remained ready to serve the Fourteenth with equal devotion. 'The Dalai Lama,' he said, 'personifies the now suffering Tibetan nation whose very existence is threatened.' Sensing the terrible events that were in store, Tsarong explained that preceding foreign invasions were only mild compared to that of the Chinese Communists with their sinister acts of 'democracy' and 'progress'. Never had times been so dark for Tibet.

Gyalo Tondup wanted to make Tsarong remain on Indian soil where friends of the Tibetan cause could benefit from his experience and his council. He wouldn't dream of it.

'My long life,' he said, 'has given me all that a man can hope for in this world. I now feel that my final day is near and I don't want it to come upon me in a foreign country whilst the Dalai Lama is in Lhasa. Whatever life I have left belongs to him.'

The little arrow maker who had become a national hero, who was showered with honours, who had many wives chosen from the greatest families and who had integrated himself into the traditional nobility whose virtues he practised better than many aristocrats of high birth, was wise enough to foresee how to maintain his position and influence throughout all the political shake-ups. Tsarong, therefore, returned to Tibet where he was to accomplish his destiny. Following the uprising of March 1959 and the escape of the Dalai Lama, he was thrown into prison at the same time as several other high Tibetan dignitaries. The day before the Chinese had decided to submit him to a *tamzing*, a public humiliation session, he was found dead in his cell. It was said he had committed suicide by swallowing ground-up jewellery.

CHAPTER 13

REPRESSION, DESACRALISATION, EVOCATION

At the beginning of 1959, we could see from Darjeeling that the situation in Lhasa and in several other regions of Tibet was becoming explosive. Gyalo Tondup received reports which stressed the increasing successes of the Khampa resistance army against the Chinese occupying forces and of the continuing active support given to the Khampas by the populace.

For my part, I saw many of my relatives arrive seeking refuge on Indian soil. My cousin Abdul Matin escorted them to Kalimpong and then returned to the Tibetan capital where he witnessed all the stages of the upheaval and the repression. He was later able to give me a detailed account.

In the Tibetan drama, two actors came on stage, one preparing to crush the other, and only India had the possibility of playing a firm third role, if not of protecting the victim, then at least of relieving his suffering. This is what I continually repeated to Gyalo Tondup in an attempt to point out to him the necessity of making new efforts with the Indian authorities. The situation was worsening and day after day events proved clearly enough that to speak of 'liberation' in relation to the Chinese occupation of Tibet was not only a disgraceful imposture, but also that the Tibetan people and not only the aristocracy, were opposed to the occupying forces whom they likened to tyrannical and oppressive foreigners. In effect, as my contacts with the press allowed me to perceive, the Tibetan cause had won much sympathy in Indian public opinion, and even in government circles, eyes began to open.

Although I insisted that we give priority to our relations with the Indian government, my friend hardly listened to me, having different ideas that he wanted to stick to and which seemed to me like dangerous illusions.

Like many Tibetan aristocrats, Gyalo Tondup was dazzled by the West. He persisted in placing hopes in the United States and Great Britain whence he thought decisive help could come. He was not naïve enough to bank on military intervention from these two great countries, but he thought they would be prepared to supply the Tibetan guerrillas in the interior with enough arms to keep the Chinese army at bay. When I pointed out to him that for this it would be necessary to get an authorisation from India to cross through her territory, a totally unreal possibility, or to transgress her air space, risking antagonising her even more, he only responded with a mysterious air, seeming to imply that I wasn't in on the big secrets.

In actual fact, armed parachute attacks and munition drops did take place in the regions of Tibet held by the Khampas who were leading guerrilla warfare against the Chinese. It seems the aeroplanes came mainly from Taiwan or sometimes from Pakistan, but their supplies to the resistance forces always remained too few and far between to exercise any real influence on the military situation. The effect of these supplies was mainly to encourage the Khampas and to foster an illusion of hope for them that more effective help would arrive. In this, these parachute drops were probably more harmful than useful, not to mention the suspicion which was reinforced and made known to us on the part of the Indian authorities who were obviously well informed after all.

It seems that the Khampas, who had no coherent idea about the world beyond the mountain chains bounding Tibet, seriously counted on more substantial help from the outside or even military intervention. And I believe that Gyalo Tondup, who kept up continual contact with resistance fighters in the interior, bears the responsibility for having entertained these illusions. Moreover, he himself undoubtedly was disillusioned as to the real power of the Khampa movement all the while underestimating the efficiency of the Chinese military machine.

On another very important subject, my friend observed great discretion and acted in secret. He was actively participating in the preparations for the escape of his brother, the Dalai Lama. I only realised this after the event had taken place.

During the months preceding the crisis of March 1959, he sometimes alluded to such an eventuality and he asked me how I would react if I saw the young sovereign seek refuge abroad to escape more serious threats which the Chinese could make towards his person. The question left me very perplexed and in principle I rather felt that the Dalai Lama should not leave Tibet because his sacred presence there maintained a protective virtue. Moreover, this presence could perhaps limit to some extent the disastrous effects of the upheavals which the growing tension between the occupying and resistance forces seemed to predict.

Gyalo Tondup responded that the Dalai Lama ran the risk of being arrested, taken to China or even killed, which would be felt by the Tibetans as a much greater sorrow than to see him escape abroad. The argument had substance but he did not take into account the immense risks that could result from a change of the status quo. There was no doubt in my mind that if the troubles became more serious, the Chinese repression would be merciless.

In the end the departure of the Dalai Lama did not provoke the crisis. It was the inverse that occurred. The spontaneous uprising of Lhasa sparked off the Chinese repression and this put the Dalai Lama's life in danger. After that, his escape out of the reach of the Chinese was the wish of the great majority of Tibetans.

Accounts of these fateful events have been made by various historians, Tibetanists and other authors and the principal stages of their unfolding arc well known. Contrary to what some have said or written, I am convinced that there was no deliberate provocation on the part of the Chinese who, on the contrary, with the support of Tibetan figures like Ngabo, tried to avoid a general confrontation up to the last moment. It was the Chinese on the other hand who felt provoked by the growing aggressiveness of the Khampas and this set into motion the fatal process of insurrection and repression.

For several months already the resistance army had considerably spread the zones of its power and the Chinese no longer dared venture into these areas. Their main bases were in the region of Tsethang, in Lokha, a province bordering Bhutan. From there, the Khampas stepped up their raids in the direction of Lhasa and the fame of their prowess was spreading. 'They are getting close,' people said. 'They're coming. They're very strong. They're going to chase out all the Chinese.' It was a veritable intoxication. People seriously began to believe that the Chinese weren't as powerful or formidable as they appeared and it would be possible to get rid of them if the whole town rose up.

In the first weeks of 1959, the Khampas actually infiltrated Lhasa and were becoming more and more aggressive there. They were armed with rifles, often of American origin, which they showed off with pride and uttered threats not only to the Chinese but also to any Tibetans who did not show enough respect for them. The inhabitants of the capital often felt themselves in double danger, at once from the trigger-happy Khampas and the Chinese whose reprisals were ever feared.

Lhasa began to simmer in February 1959 when the 'invitation' became known which was addressed to the Dalai Lama by the Chinese who were anxious for him to participate in the next session of the National Peoples' Congress in Peking. Opinions were divided amongst the members of his council. Ngabo obviously put the most emphasis on recommending him to accept. From the way things turned out in the end, it could be asked if after all, wasn't it he who was the most lucid.

Until then the Chinese had remained remarkably calm, seeking to avoid violent confrontations. But they felt the threat of trouble in Lhasa and were preparing themselves for it. Having at their disposal an efficient information service and good communication with their garrisons in the various provinces, they were aware of the magnitude of the insurrection and did not intend to let it go beyond certain proportions. Now in Lhasa, the limits of what they could tolerate had been reached.

It was another invitation to the Dalai Lama, this one calling upon him to attend a theatrical production at the quarters of the Chinese troops and this, strangely enough, set off the general uprising in the capital. It was known amongst the people that he had been asked to attend without his usual escort, which made people believe that the Chinese had set a trap to kidnap him. The troops around Norbulinka, the summer palace where he was residing, began to riot, some Chinese were injured, others killed, the occupying forces began to shoot, and the scuffle spread. The government had no more control over the events that followed their fatal course. The Chinese cataclysm which had broken loose precipitated the end of old Tibet.

When the news reached us in Darjeeling that the crisis had exploded in Lhasa, Gyalo Tondup immediately understood that the moment had finally come to carry out the escape plan for his brother that had been worked out a long time ago. The operation took place without a major incident and on 31 March 1959, the Dalai Lama reached the Indian border to the east of Bhutan from where he reached Bomdila, then Tezpur in Assam.

Gyalo Tondup did not even wait for confirmation of the news that his brother had arrived safe and sound on Indian soil to go to Delhi. He took me there with a group of Tibetan figures, amongst whom were several Khampa military leaders. The purpose of our trip was to be assured that the Dalai Lama would be received in good conditions and put up comfortably. On this point, our move was crowned with success and the authorities were well disposed towards receiving the young sovereign with dignity. His dramatic escape had aroused the emotions of Indian and international opinion.

However on another point, we were properly sent packing. At the Suisse Hotel where we were staying, a request was drawn up addressed to Prime Minister Nehru on the part of 'free' Tibet whom we claimed to represent. This document solicited the support of the government of India for the Tibetan cause under three main points:

- recognition of the resistance organisations
- an appeal to the UN in favour of an independent Tibet
- and an offer of mediation with China.

In collaborating in the drawing up of this request, I was totally conscious of its lack of realism and that is why I was not at all surprised that no one in government circles took it seriously.

Shortly afterwards, I returned to Darjeeling with the other members of the group. Gyalo Tondup in the meantime went to Assam to see his brother. It was said he was ill after his eventful crossing of the Himalayas. When he rejoined us a few days later, he was able to give us reassuring news of the Dalai Lama's health but told us he arrived practically without luggage and didn't even have a change of clothes. What a contrast to all the aristocrats who succeeded in getting so much precious cargo over the Indian side of the frontier where they also had come seeking safety.

The subsequent Chinese repression of the Lhasa uprising and the Dalai Lama's flight had set into motion a flood of refugees who broke through the Himalayan border. Receiving thousands of these unfortunate people and helping to relocate them presented innumerable problems. Many had been through terrible trials and had experienced the implacable brutality of the Chinese. Gyalo Tondup put me in charge of gathering their stories.

This activity led me to witness the anguish of an entire people handed over to barbarism in the name of 'progress'. The Chinese, who had observed remarkable restraint until the Lhasa uprising, suddenly broke loose, incalculably massacring and destroying. Refugees of every social class reported countless acts of violence and cruelty deliberately committed by the forces involved in the repression. These forces seemed to have it out for monks and religious institutions in particular. High-ranking officials of the former administration also described to me how the occupying forces had dissolved the legal Tibetan government to replace it with a puppet organisation. All these facts, the authenticity of which is confirmed by the unanimity of witnesses, underlined the enormity of the imposture which spoke of the 'liberation' of Tibet. To use a term borrowed from Guénon, I found myself in the presence of a monstrous crime and characteristic of the 'anti-tradition'.

It is not worth going into details here of the declarations made to me by refugees whom I went to meet in the areas near the border where several camps had been hurriedly set up to accommodate them. Holding back my emotion, I took many notes and translated the essential information into English. This then was the beginning of the documentation aimed at informing the world press and upholding the moves made in favour of Tibet at the international level, in particular the appeal that the Dalai Lama, against Nehru's advice, addressed to the United Nations in September 1959. It was known that it should have resulted in the vote by the General Assembly for a resolution recommending in vague terms the respect of the Rights of Man for the Tibetan people. Apart from this, no country of the so-called 'free' world made any concrete gesture towards Tibet the martyr.

We had expected to see the Dalai Lama settle in the region of Darjeeling and Kalimpong. But the leaders in Delhi decided that he would stay in the northwest of India. His first residence was therefore in Mussoorie, a high altitude station near Dehra Dun. Then after several months a more final place was put at his disposal in Dharamsala in the mountainous province of Himachal Pradesh.

At the beginning of June 1959, I was called upon to exercise a new function in the entourage of the Dalai Lama. I, therefore, left Darjeeling to stop off first in Delhi where I met Mr Shakabpa, the well-known Tibetan political man in whose company I made the rest of the trip to Mussoorie. We stayed in a hotel neighbouring His Holiness's residence. The latter then took part in a veritable family reunion: my friend Gyalo Tondup was there as well as Thubten Norbu, the eldest of all the brothers and sisters. At that time there was a disappointment in the little court because everyone thought the Dalai Lama would not delay meeting Pandit Nehru. But instead of this, the prime minister went to Nepal and delayed his interview with the exiled hierarch. I was not at all surprised at this lack of haste.

I was sent to Mussoorie to take up a position as translator for His Holiness. I had only begun my new function a short time before and was busy translating a text when Mr Shakabpa arrived in my room bearing surprising news: the Indian representative to the Dalai Lama had just informed him that his government was opposed to my presence amongst the collaborators of His Holiness and demanded my withdrawal. Although I was aware of the unfriendly inclinations of certain high-ranking government officials of Delhi, I didn't realise that I was so undesirable and I took the ostracism that was attributed to me very badly. As for the Dalai Lama, he was equally surprised and made this remark in light irony to his close collaborators who reported it to me:

'I wonder what the poor Wahid could have done to seem so feared by the government of India?'

It was futile to protest against this and there was nothing for me to do but leave the premises which I did, but much regretting not being able to work any longer in the immediate proximity of the Dalai Lama as he himself had desired. But this was not to end my work in the service of Tibet and Tibetan victims of the Chinese oppression. The flood of refugees did not let up at the main crossing points of the border and I once again started receiving them.

I, therefore, set about again gathering eye-witness accounts of the martyrdom that the Communists of Mao Tse-tung made Tibet and her people undergo. They reduced the people to a slavery which made the traditional and patriarchal serfdom seem like a kind and humane regime. I thus had a complete view of the action of the Chinese who, in this drama not only bear the responsibility for unpardonable atrocities and the stupid destruction of the treasures of civilisation, but also for putting an end to the last traditional theocracy in the world. This Communist regime, in the name of an ideology imparted from the West, was already incapable of bringing them happiness. The Tibetan regime was undoubtedly imperfect and often corrupt but it was still penetrated with the sacred and gave meaning to the life of every person.

Relocated in Darjeeling, I also worked with various aid programmes for the refugees and organised classes for children. I sometimes went to Delhi where information was put out aimed at supporting the Tibetan cause before international appeals and humanitarian organisations capable of giving aid to the refugees.

During this same period I collaborated with the former prime minister of His Holiness, Lukhangwa, who was staying in Darjeeling, in the translation of a manifesto destined to be sent out around the world in the name of the Tibetan people. I consider myself fortunate to have known this eminent man who incarnated the best of the former Tibetan leading class.

In 1961, I was called to Dharamsala to occupy the post of interpreter of the Tibetan Council for education which had just been formed under the patronage of the Dalai Lama. This time there was no objection on the part of the Indian administration and for two years I had the privilege of living and working in the close circles of His Holiness. The president of this organisation was a high-ranking lama, Kundiling Dzasa, whom I accompanied in the frequent meetings he had with the Indian authorities.

The activity of this Council was fruitful and ended with the opening of several schools in the areas where there were the most refugees like Dharamsala, Darjeeling, Mussoorie, Shimla and Chail. We collaborated with a representative of the Indian Ministry of Public Education who gave us useful assistance. It is true that since the beginning of 1962, the bitter experience which India tasted of Chinese aggression on her northern borders had made the Delhi leaders more understanding towards the Tibetans and their fight for freedom.

However, I also had to attend to the education of my own children. Now as they were growing up my family expenses were also increasing and that is why I began looking for more lucrative work. The Dalai Lama helped me by recommending me to the Aid Committee for Tibetan Refugees that had been formed shortly before at the initiative of Mr Ilya Tolstoy and Mr Thomas Lowell who were amongst the rare Americans to have visited Tibet long before the Chinese invasion. The organisation that they created was financed on an entirely private basis and had its headquarters in New York. I was employed by the agency they had opened in Delhi and which was in charge of practical tasks in favour of the refugees.

The jobs assigned to me gave me the opportunity for new and frequent contacts with people of all walks of life who had faced the dangers of an escape and others who had given their life and crossed the Himalayas, sometimes through the most hazardous crossings to escape the nightmare of the Chinese Communist regime. I noted that even the lay refugees were generally more inclined to deplore the destruction of monasteries and the persecution of monks than to complain of their own misfortunes. They thus confirmed that religion had always played a central place in the life of Tibet and the Communist Chinese action was equivalent to a desacralisation.

I carried on with this work for two years, travelling all over India, particularly in the regions near the northern border to meet Tibetans wherever they were staying, evaluate their needs and attempt to lighten their lot. The help thus given to the refugees was undoubtedly useful and benevolent but after some time I realised that the Indian government looked askance upon this committee financed by America, attributing political intentions to its humanitarian activities. In effect, the person who had the upper hand in the operations I participated in India seemed to have preoccupations not directly linked to the wellbeing of the refugees and therefore I was only half surprised to learn that he was suspected of being a CIA agent. In any case, his behaviour displeased the authorities who ordered the dissolution of the Indian branch of the committee.

Once again help came to me from His Holiness the Dalai Lama. I owe it to his intervention that I was to be employed at the library of the American congress in Delhi where I have worked ever since.

~

Thus ended my long journey, at least within geographical space, because on another plane I make every effort to continue my way. If I have undertaken to give an account of this journey, it is above all, with the intention of bearing witness to Tibet and her traditional values. It is also to try to explain that in this so-called 'backward' country, life was at least worth living and happiness was just as real as in the modern world dedicated to progress but where the sense of the sacred has disappeared.

After all, this is what distinguished Tibet from other countries where I have lived and travelled. One felt a presence there which escaped every analysis but which created an atmosphere of both recollectedness and exaltation. It was as if the physical altitude corresponded to a proximity of the heaven of those in bliss.

The fact of being born and having grown up in Ladakh

undoubtedly predisposed me to loving and understanding Tibet. The nature of my native country, its grandeur, its austerity, its high altitude, the grandiose beauty of her mountains, the dark blue of her skies, all of this was Tibet but even more immensely. Family circumstances obviously contributed to attaching me to Tibet. Our caravans had crossed her wide spaces so many times where my father is buried very close to Mount Kailash, sacred to Buddhists as well as Hindus. Here, despite the difference of religion, we never really felt like foreigners.

In fact, although some of my uncles adopted a perhaps less tolerant and more critical attitude towards other religious groups under the effect of the Islamic reform, more or less tinted by Wahhabism, one can nevertheless affirm that following the example of my grandfather Haji Muhammad Siddiq, the relations that we had as Muslims with Ladakhi and Tibetan Buddhists bore witness to what can be called a practising ecumenicalism. This manifested itself even on the level of our trade and what we, Muslim merchants, brought from Lhasa had a particular prestige for our Buddhist co-patriots, almost a sacred value, since it came from the sacred town. Moreover, on several occasions, we received special orders for Tibetan religious books from monasteries in Ladakh. It was thus that our caravans carried heavy cases containing the *Domangs*, *Kangyur Tengyur* or other classics of sacred lamaist literature for delivery to monks. Our Islam did not at all prevent us from deeply respecting their knowledge and piety.

My true spiritual centre is certainly Mecca towards which I have always turned to address my prayers to God. But, looking back, I see that my terrestrial existence has always been in a way centred on Tibet in whose tracks I have so often crossed. I have walked around the entire country on the exterior during the journeys which took me to China and Sinkiang. And for Tibet I laboured and toiled in India.

From my very first excursions into the interior of Tibet, I was deeply impressed by the ambience of recollectedness and spirituality even of small monasteries like Tadum, Soka Dzong or Phuntsokling to the west of Shigatse. Everywhere, even in poor villages like Marsar surrounded by deserts, the comportment of the people bore witness to their piety, to their attachment to the highest and invisible reality. This attitude of such authentic and spontaneous devotion seemed in perfect accordance with the austere sublimity of the countryside and its gigantic mountains with inaccessible peaks.

Already upon arrival in Shigatse, travellers were seized with admiration of the view of the famous Tashilungpo, the largest monastery in southern Tibet. On the outskirts of Lhasa, the feeling was even stronger and one couldn't help perceiving something celestial in the atmosphere. In front of the magnificent complex of Potala, the impression was imposed upon one that this majestic place was sacred. This was not only due to the beauty of this harmonious architecture in a grandiose natural setting, but clearly, impossible to describe or explain, there was a presence of the Spirit here. Lhasa was, and to a certain extent remains, a great spiritual centre which for Tibetan Buddhists, can be compared to what Mecca is for Muslims. Probably the most inexpiable crime of the Chinese Communists is having profaned it.

Certainly, my love for Tibetan spirituality was encouraged by the great privilege I had of being in the proximity of the one who was the personification of this spirituality: His Holiness the Fourteenth Dalai Lama, and also the privilege of linking me in friendship with the members of his family. I can never be grateful enough for the goodness and understanding that they have always showed towards me. My relationship with them was facilitated by a circumstance that is not uninteresting to bring out: Islam was familiar to them because of the fact that they came from Amdo, a region of the east populated by many Muslims and as I had very often noticed, they knew my religion relatively well, the doctrine and its practice, whereas generally even the most educated lamas were ignorant of everything about Islam.

However, their ignorance of Islam never prevented the Tibetan Buddhists from treating us, the Radhus, as if we were one of them. In fact, despite some differences of mentality that I have already pointed out, as Ladakhis, we belonged to the same nation as the Tibetans and shared the same cultural heritage. Our daily habits, dress and eating, were much the same and as for myself I always kept a predilection for *tsampa* and salted tea with butter. It is true that as a Muslim following the moral code of a Semitic origin, I distanced myself from certain aspects of Tibetan ethics like polyandry or tantric rites, but I could not really condemn them because I have always had the feeling that they had to be seen within the perspective of the Tibetans themselves whose entire lives were sacralised by the tradition.

These particularities aside, it always seemed to me that the Buddhist morality hardly differed from that of Islam. Buddhism recommends the same virtues, notably generosity, patience and above all, detachment. I have never learnt literary Tibetan and have remained incapable of reading the great classics but I know enough about them to grasp their spirit and to appreciate, for example, the life of Mila Repa, the celebrated ascetic who left such a strong mark on Tibetan Buddhism. As a Muslim, I consider him a very eminent spiritual master, entirely comparable to the great saints of Islam.

Although the virtues of simple people, their piety, humility, hospitality often deeply moved me, these same virtues were also present with the upper classes and one must recognise the patience and dignity which many Tibetan nobles manifested in misfortune. I remember how impressed I was with the attitude of Lungshar who, following the so-called 'republican' conspiracy, underwent with so much endurance a horrible punishment. His son Lhalu, former governor of Chamdo, also showed great courage when he was persecuted by the Communists. Submitted to a public humiliation session, he held his head high to his accusers with as much dignity as intelligence. His noble attitude, on the contrary brought out all the hateful lowliness of his oppressor. The refugees reported to me names of several other figures of the former regime who, facing their persecutors, practised the virtues of true nobility to the very end.

I also keep the precious memory of fleeting encounters in monasteries like Tashilungpo in Shigatse or those of Lhasa sometimes in the middle of the desert, with ascetics who seemed to be already residing more in heaven than on earth. They must have realised some degree of sanctity because a beatitude emanated from their face which was no longer a part of this lower world. These men, who were entirely devoted to the Spirit, probably represented the exact antithesis of the Communists and their materialist theories, but I am inclined to believe that these ascetics were situated at such a level that the persecution was unable to reach them.

This remark leads me to brief thoughts about the claimed 'mysteries' of Tibet which have so excited the imagination of certain Westerners and have even created an entire literature of fantasy. It was thus that a myth has evolved attributing to Tibetans and more especially to lamas, all sorts of occult powers, making them capable of voluntarily producing extraordinary phenomena or working wonders.

To try to see this more clearly, following Guénon, it is necessary to put things in their proper perspective starting by dissipating the confusion so often committed by modern people these days between two very different domains, the psychic and the spiritual. Tibet, which had remained aloof from the modern world, had undoubtedly kept alive certain forms of yoga and traditional sciences like magic, pertaining to the psychic realm, better than most countries had where they were lost somewhere. At least this is what one can safely assume because in daily life 'supranormal' phenomena played no role and Tibetans hardly seemed to be preoccupied by it. What was more important to them and what their piety aimed at above all was not of a psychic or phenomenal order but that of the Spirit and its immovable reality.

However, in principle, I do not deny the authenticity of certain phenomena which were inexplicable by the normal laws of nature and I myself happened to have been a witness to events which were beyond my comprehension. But I remain convinced that it is wrong to attribute the importance to these events that they have taken on in the eyes of some foreign authors who have speculated above and beyond all reason. And it is certainly not on this plane that it is possible to understand or evaluate what the spirituality of Tibet really was.

Even in the monasteries of Ladakh it was possible—and it undoubtedly still is—to witness extraordinary phenomena which the lamas obligingly made a spectacle of: they would cut off half of their tongues with a large knife, put a sword through their bodies or needles through their mouths or they would place an enormous stone on their stomachs and with one blow of a stick break it in half. We understood nothing of this but no one seemed to attach any more importance to it than they did to the tricks that enlivened Buddhist religious festivals.

Apart from the gift of healing which was relatively widespread, other powers were attributed to lamas, notably that of producing rain. Although I never saw such wonders, having heard credible accounts of them, I admit to this possibility.

On the other hand, I saw several times with my own eyes the extraordinary capacity some Tibetans had of developing body heat without exterior means. In Lhasa and other regions of Tibet, I saw lamas wearing only light clothing, sometimes even beggars in rags which only partly covered them, barefoot and bare-headed, endure the most intense cold of winter that would oblige us, ordinary people, to muffle ourselves up in thick fur. Taken by surprise at first, I asked questions to try to understand and I usually got this answer: 'They practise special mantras.' No one seemed to pay special attention to this because it was a relatively common thing, so much so that even I was not too surprised by it in the end.

However, this phenomenon had intrigued me so much that during one of my stays in Kalimpong I questioned Gyendum Chombel about this subject, the wise lama who was part of our circle of friends. He answered something like this:

'It's only a question of relatively ordinary yoga exercises. People with a gift of slightly deepened knowledge don't see anything particularly remarkable about this and it is surprising that Westerners make so much of this order. It is best not to worry about it but if you are asked questions about this subject, just laugh and then remain silent.'

Such facts and the exaggerated importance given to them by some authors have probably contributed to creating the strange 'myth of Tibet' which seems to be propagated in the Western public amateurs of pseudo-mystic occultism and has put many writers with a fecund imagination on great form.

To really understand what Tibet was before the Chinese invasion, it seems to me imperative to dispense with all the ideas about the power of magic and occult powers that have been abusively associated with the country. In reality Tibetans were a well-balanced people with common sense, happy, spontaneous, quick-witted, fun-loving. Hypocrisy was on the whole unknown to them. They found pleasure in this present life but knowing how to accept the inevitable evils of it, remained conscious of the precariousness of this lower world and of a more lasting reality of another world preferable to this one.

Certainly, Tibetans also had their faults, the most flagrant one being their physical uncleanliness—often excusable in their mountainous deserts—also superstition, and in the upper classes, the taste for power and intrigue. It is also true that many were very poor without, however, reaching a degrading poverty. They had many of the characteristics of what modern people call 'backwardness' but nevertheless in the almost unanimous opinion of foreign travellers who had the opportunity to visit Tibet, they were a happy people. The Chinese Communists killed this happiness and this is the saddest remark I can make at the end of this account.

At the time my journey began and I left the highlands of my childhood for the first time, the Himalayan people which we were, still led a natural peaceful life. It was undoubtedly rough and austere but also harmonious and tinted with beauty. Perched as we were on the 'roof of the world' we constantly had to confront the challenge of an overpowering nature which forced us to work hard to survive. One had to be hard oneself and as we weren't better than other peoples, also having our human weakness and our bad instincts, our existence as Himalayans was far from paradisiacal. And now, however, those who evoke times gone by speak of those days almost as a lost paradise.

I believe that in effect with the end of the era of the caravans, irreplaceable human values of Central Asia also disappeared. All of us, Ladakhis, Tibetans, Khampas, Amdos, nomads of Changthang, lived in accordance with our destiny. Travelling along the tracks which crossed the immensity of the Himalayas, we never dreamed of rebelling against our destiny. We conformed to it. We identified ourselves with it. This acceptance carried with it a spiritual attitude of worship and contemplation of the supreme reality whose majesty and perfection was felt by unspoilt nature.

The fundamental harmony of this existence was also expressed in the attitude of caravaneers towards their animals whom they treated with exemplary kindness. They never insulted them. At each stop, animals were taken care of first, men came second. A saying comes back to mind which was often heard in the times of the caravans: 'If descending a slope you don't walk alongside your mount, you are not a man, but if when riding, the animal doesn't carry you on its back, it is not a mount animal.'

We would walk for the weeks and months that the shortest of our journeys lasted, and never did curiosity or greed accelerate the slow pace of the caravans. Everyone went to meet that which was destined for him. In the valleys and the plateaus of Tibet or Sinkiang, on the slopes of the passes crossing the Himalayas, the Karakoram or the Kouen Love, the caravaneer pursued his way without haste, without worry, always submitted to the Supreme Power whose majesty appeared wherever he turned.

We prayed in the deserts of Central Asia, we suffered there and died there too. We knew that all of this was in the normal order of things. There could be no question for us to try to overcome it. On the contrary, we aspired to conform to it, to become one with all that surrounded us and made up our life, with men, with what we did and what we saw, the gigantic mountains, the glaciers, the plateaux. By crossing these spaces at a slow pace, the caravans were integrated into this reality which suggested another, higher one. And in such an existence where everything was true and conformed to the divine order, man found his spiritual sustenance naturally. Far from civilised multiplicity, he spontaneously concentrated on the essential, on the One, and the desert became a retreat, a *khalwa*, as the mystics of Islam say where the remembrance of God imposes itself like a necessity more imperious than drinking and eating and also as the greatest happiness.

On foot or on his mount, the Buddhist caravaneer often adapted the movement of his prayer wheel or the repetition of the mantra *Om mani padme hum* to the gait of his pace. In the immense 'lotus' which the mountains and valleys around him represented, he sensed the 'jewel', the truth which alone was liberating from the fatigue and suffering of his earthly journey.

Our lives as caravaneers, usually lived at high altitudes far from the futility of the 'civilised' world, remained in its simplicity, its purity, its slowness, a trace of the sacred and totally foreign to the profane modernity of our time. This life was, therefore, condemned to disappear and to mourn it would be futile. The only possibility which remains for us is to symbolically relive it by accomplishing an inward journey which, with divine grace, can lead us to other heights.

EPILOGUE

If my thoughts are still capable of being termed as sensible and my struggle for spiritual rectification is still alive, then I would say that the diary with the 'black cover' written in 1942 contains the beginning of an outpouring of fervour for faith and understanding. Upon my departure with the Lopchak caravan, I ventured articulating my haphazard thoughts into that diary. It was a search for an ambience conformable to my inclinations in the wake of an unpredictable avalanche of modernism.

With the help of my noble and revered Western friends, I was introduced to the writings of René Guénon in those critical days of World War II. His works gave my soul a vision and a new understanding. The spiritual journey took a long time and today, re-reading those lines, it has refreshed my fervour. It is providential that I am able to regain my stamina by venturing these few lines as an epilogue to my four decades of sleeping on that travelogue.

I must say that this steep journey plunged me into a struggle between the carnal soul and the spiritual objective. This book being originally published in French, it was difficult to gauge fully where my expressions lay. Today I am extremely grateful to the translator, Jane Casewit, for her untiring efforts to make known to me the contents in French. At the same time I must not fail to express my heartfelt thanks to Roger du Pasquier for rendering so accurately my disorganised writings. It is all *tawfiq*—a grace from Allah—on me poor in spirit.

My youthful days were spent in the thick of Gandhian nationalism and the turmoil in the subcontinent of India with unprecedented disputes over the unfortunate partition. I met many of the Indian officers and politicians as well as those from Pakistan. The world showed diverting spirituality into mundanity and I found myself in an atmosphere more and more devoid of human virtues. From an ambience imbued with Tibetan, Ladakhi and Kashmiri culture one had to face a world in the midst of intense Western impact. But, as God would have it, my noble benefactors from the Western world warned me of the oncoming onslaught. Wisdom dawned from the West and I was cautioned to move with thoughts imbued from those of the wise men in the West who knew the pitfalls. My children were also influenced by the higher spiritual values and also received words to express my thanks to those of my friends who advised me. As a spiritual benefactor I feel it would be improper to mention their august names.

I am also providentially indebted to some outstanding Tibetan personalities whom I had the privilege of meeting whilst passing through the Trans-Himalayan region and also whilst in pursuit of the family trade in Lhasa as well as in China in those days. I would begin with Rimpoche Gyendum Chombel, an Amdo reincarnate lama. A middle-aged man when I met him, he was extremely humble but with a dignity and inspiring spiritual vision. He belonged to those virtuous spiritual beings that go beyond moral descriptions. He unassumingly has influenced many of the youths of the Tibetan nobility as well as Tibetan intellectuals. His knowledge of Islam kept me amazed for years. Once he told me very casually, 'Your Prophet (Muhammad SAW) is rarely understood by the world,' and 'Faith-Belief needs a sword.' He smiled and added, 'I am ready to hold the sword.'

He suffered from many political intrigues although he was never involved in any of them. His words were misused and he was made a scapegoat by many of the political figures, through no fault of his own. He died in Lhasa in the late forties and upon his death told many of his friends not to try to escape death. It is easy if you grasp the Absolute.

My introduction to Rimpoche Gyendum Chombel led me to meet his teacher in the Lhasa monastery, Gyehse Sherab Gyatso. I later met him in 1947 in Nanking as an important officer of the Kuomintang regime. He wielded great influence amongst the pro-Kuomintang Tibetans in China. Many of these Kuomintang officers in the late forties were pleading for Tibetan independence. One said, 'Generalissimo Chang Kai-Shek intends to see Tibet independent when Outer Mongolia becomes independent.' Others said, 'It's the weakness of Tibet that makes China claim Tibet.' In his famous historical writings, Gyendum Chombel proved Tibet's historical stand as an independent country and many of the young Tibetan nobility rallied round him.

I was introduced to Rimpoche Gyendum Chombel in absentia in Lhasa by my noble and kind friend Thupten Jolden Tethong. It was at his palatial mansion that we used to talk about great saints, writers and historians of Tibet and I would fail in my gratitude towards the Tethong family if I neglected to mention how much I learnt about the spiritual aspects of the Tibetan tradition at his feet. Traditional nobility have an atmosphere of peace and calmness in their homes that cannot escape a visitor. Actually these noble families were all in the thick of politics and its usual susceptibilities but the cultural air and the noble behaviour make one immune to these worldly habits. One finds oneself in an environment conducive to acquiring salutary habits. I am deeply grateful for the impact which Tibetan culture had upon me.

Through the Tethongs I also got to know an outstanding incarnate lama of Phontsokling during my stay in Kalimpong. I had the privilege of learning a lot through his sermons and lectures in Bodh Gaya and Benares in the forties. Those were of tremendous spiritual import and helped sustain my own spiritual pursuits.